"In an era of escalating competitive pressure, companies must be innovative and proactive in keeping an increasingly female workforce vibrant and productive. Some companies are getting it. Thanks to Hewlett for showcasing these companies and putting a spotlight on corporate leaders who have the courage and the savvy to make the necessary changes for women not only to survive, but to bring themselves fully to the leadership table."

—**Ella L. J. Edmondson Bell**, associate professor of business administration, Tuck School of Business, Dartmouth College

"*Off-Ramps and On-Ramps* provides a compelling model for rethinking career development for the twenty-first century. Illustrated with vivid business case studies, this book is an essential guide for how to manage talent so that employees and employers can succeed."

—**Ellen Galinsky**, President and cofounder, Families and Work Institute

"How can both women and men find satisfying and rewarding careers that are not necessarily continuous and cumulative? And how can companies and organizations keep talented employees in whom they have heavily invested? This carefully researched book provides innovative, practical, win-win answers to both questions."

—**Myra H. Strober**, labor economist; professor of education, School of Education; and professor, Graduate School of Business, Stanford University

"Sylvia Hewlett's analysis of how women need to work, and how that impacts the current corporate model, creates a blueprint for the workplace of tomorrow. Given the coming talent shortages, all companies need to build more on-ramps."

—**Richard Robinson**, CEO, President, and Chairman, Scholastic Inc.

"On both sides of the Atlantic, women pay a huge price when they take an off-ramp. Our research shows that in Britain, it can take a woman twenty years to regain her previous footing. Hewlett demonstrates the link between on-ramps and the bottom line, and shows what employers must do if they are to remain competitive. Written with clarity and conviction, this book lays out the next generation of private-sector policy."

—**Jenny Watson**, Chair, Equal Opportunities Commission, United Kingdom

Off-Ramps
and On-Ramps

Off-Ramps
and On-Ramps

Keeping Talented Women
on the Road to Success

Sylvia Ann Hewlett

Harvard Business School Press
Boston, Massachusetts

Library of Congress Cataloging-in-Publication Data

Hewlett, Sylvia Ann, 1946-
  Off-ramps and on-ramps : keeping talented women on the road to success / Sylvia Ann Hewlett.
     p. cm.
  Includes bibliographical references.
  ISBN-13: 978-1-4221-0102-5 (hardcover : alk. paper)
  ISBN-10: 1-4221-0102-9
  1. Women in the professions—United States. 2. Women—Employment—United States. 3. Corporations—United States—Case studies. 4. Working mothers—United States. 5. Work and family—United States. I. Title. II. Title: Keeping talented women on the road to success.
  HD6054.2.U6H49 2007
  658.3'12082—dc22

                                                           2006038271

*Dedicated to the
leaders of the Hidden Brain Drain Task Force,
a band of heroes:*

*DeAnne Aguirre
Deborah Elam
Anne Erni
Patricia Fili-Krushel
JoAnn Heffernan Heisen
Antoinette La Belle
Carolyn Buck Luce
Horacio Rozanski
Cornel West
Billie Williamson
Melinda Wolfe*

And to my mother who laid the path for me and my daughters.

CONTENTS

FOREWORD

June 2006 was a watershed moment—and for me quite magical. On the nineteenth and twentieth of that month, "change agent" teams from the thirty-four global companies that constitute the Hidden Brain Drain Task Force assembled in New York for our first annual Hidden Brain Drain Summit—to drive action on the ground. Two and a half years after its formation, the task force was ready to share cutting-edge research and spearhead a second generation of policy and practice designed to keep talented women on the road to success.

The summit succeeded beyond our wildest dreams—accelerating change, spurring new action. The reaction of Rachel Lee (vice president of human resources at American Express) was typical. In her words: "This summit provided true, leading-edge thinking—a rarity today. It has given me ideas, data, stories, a new language, a valuable network—and a boost of energy and confidence to deliver something richer for women."[1]

Lee's enthusiasm is already bearing fruit. As the lead on an initiative called Embrace, she and her team have created an "internal consulting pool" for the OPEN small business division at American Express, which offers high-performing individuals—men and women—a way to scale back their working hours in order to attend to child care, elder care, or other personal priorities. If you are accepted into the pool, all kinds of flexibility can become possible—a four-day week, a ten-month year, or work hours arranged around school schedules. Through this program the company is committing to "chunking out" high-value work in different ways to accommodate part-time project work that can be undertaken from home. Participants must work a minimum of twenty-one hours a week—to ensure that they can retain benefits—and the arrangement must be for a minimum of six months. Lee thinks there will be a "sweet spot" of two to three years.

Amex hopes to keep the pool fresh—the concept is for people to rotate in and out. The company sees this program as being highly selective, attracting high-caliber talent both from within Amex (primarily from OPEN) and outside (former employees looking to return, individuals from other companies looking for an on-ramp).

When asked why this initiative is being launched at OPEN, Lee explained, "It's a burning issue for this division—and a microcosm of the challenges elsewhere. OPEN is a fast-growing business with aggressive growth plans. This creates huge pressure to do a better job attracting and retaining top talent. The majority of OPEN's employees are women, and what's more, many are in the child-bearing years—a trigger zone for off-ramping decisions. Right now many women do not return from maternity leave because they feel they cannot achieve the balance they want in their lives. The internal consulting pool is meant to change that in short order."[2]

But let's back up. Why is there this need for a second generation of policy? Why is it that after decades of creating opportunities for women and proactively nurturing diversity, companies are still struggling with the challenge of retaining and advancing women? An editorial in the *Wall Street Journal* reminded us that "at big established companies, women in recent years have made little progress breaking into senior ranks."[3] The fact is, the first generation of policies and practice took us only partway there. In the 1970s, 1980s, and 1990s, the challenge was thought to be about providing equal access—and then allowing enough time to go by so that the pipeline could fill. The reasoning was simple: if you eliminated barriers and created a truly level playing field so that men and women competed on equal terms, then, over time, as successive cohorts of well-qualified female professionals filled the pipeline, women would eventually be fairly represented in top jobs. This has not happened.

At the nub of the problem is the fact that women are not male clones, they are not merely "men in skirts," to use Shirley Conran's inimitable language. A large percentage of highly qualified professional women have different needs and wants and find it extremely difficult to replicate the white male competitive model. They tend to have serious responsibilities on the home front (to children, to elderly parents), and they have somewhat different professional aspirations. Their ambitions are constructed and fueled in multidimensional ways. Women seek meaning and connection in their work lives and are less focused on money and power than their male peers.

We therefore need a second round of policy that moves beyond access and opportunity and creates alternative pathways to power and alternative work models better suited to the talents, ambitions, and life rhythms of women. We need to develop work environments where women can both take charge and take care. That's where the task force comes in.

In February 2004, Sylvia Ann Hewlett (Center for Work-Life Policy and Columbia University), Cornel West (Princeton University), and I founded the Hidden Brain Drain Task Force. The idea was to persuade progressive corporations to become stakeholders in an effort to fully realize female talent over the life span of their careers. The mission of the task force is to identify, develop, and promote a second generation of corporate policies and practices that support women's ambition, work, *and* life needs.

It's hard to believe that the task force was founded less than three years ago. Since then, we've grown and prospered. We started with just six companies—a small band of true believers. The task force now comprises thirty-four global corporations, representing 2.5 million employees, operating in 152 countries around the world, and is led by co-chairs from an impressive roster of companies—Booz Allen Hamilton, Ernst & Young, General Electric, Goldman Sachs, Johnson & Johnson, Lehman Brothers, and Time Warner—who help shape the arc of our research and spearhead action on the ground. Task force member companies have a market capitalization of $3 trillion and are a force to be reckoned with. Together, we have the capability of messing with the model and we're beginning to do so. All eighteen examples of innovative best practices featured in part II of this book are taken from task force companies, many of them a validation and/ or direct result of the research we have done together. As a group, we have created rich data sets and developed powerful new language around policies and practices that better accommodate women's nonlinear careers.

A word on the beneficiaries of this second generation of policy. Over the last two and a half years, the task force—understanding the need to have a global perspective—has established a tradition of launching its research studies in London as well as in New York. At a 2005 research launch held at the House of Commons in London, various private-sector leaders spoke about the European baby bust and the urgent need to restructure work so that older workers can stay in their jobs longer—to fill out the talent pool and to lighten the pension burden. At this event, Patricia Fili-Krushel, executive vice president of administration at Time Warner, task force co-chair, and the closing speaker, came up with a powerful image that has since loomed large in task force conversations: "These women who leave or languish, are, in effect, the canaries in the coal mine, the first and most conspicuous casualties of an out-dated, dysfunctional career model." Fili-Krushel then went on to enumerate some of the other casualties: "58-year-old baby boomers who don't want to retire but are no longer willing to put in 70-hour weeks; and 28-year-old Gen X and Y men who want to be better, more involved fathers than their dads were, and need flexible work."[4]

In short, there is a whole queue of people—important constituencies all—who also want to mess with the male competitive model. Thirty-two- and thirty-seven-year-old working mothers are merely the early warning system, telling of impending shortages and losses and heralding a potential disaster we've still got time to prevent. But only if we pay attention to it now.

—Carolyn Buck Luce
Chair, Hidden Brain Drain Task Force
New York City, September 2006

ACKNOWLEDGMENTS

In many ways this book represents a coming together of my private and public life. It therefore gives me particular pleasure to acknowledge the extensive help I have received from family, friends, and colleagues.

My greatest debt is to my husband, Richard Weinert, and to our children Shira, Lisa, David, Adam, and Emma, whose generous love has buoyed my spirits—and given me the resilience to grapple with problematic off-ramps and on-ramps in my own career.

I am deeply grateful to Peggy Shiller, longtime friend and colleague, for the extraordinary energy, effort, and wise judgment she has contributed to this book. And a special word of thanks goes to Carolyn Buck Luce, close friend and co-conspirator, whose leadership of the Hidden Brain Drain Task Force has been transformative.

I also owe a debt of gratitude to Tom Stewart at the *Harvard Business Review*, whose insights and perspective were immensely valuable to the shaping of this research; to Melinda Merino (Harvard Business School Press), whose strategic vision has been powerful in positioning this book; and to Evelyn Roth, whose editorial skills contributed enormously to the sharpening of the final draft. Thanks also to Julia Kirby, Eric McNulty, Brian Surette, Cathy Olofson, Siobahn Ford, Cathryn Cranston, and Hollis Heimbouch of the *Harvard Business Review* and Harvard Business

School Press. I am also appreciative of the generous support of my literary agent, Molly Friedrich.

I am extremely grateful to the co-chairs of the Hidden Brain Drain Task Force: DeAnne Aguirre, Deborah Elam, Anne Erni, Patricia Fili-Krushél, JoAnn Heffernan Heisen, Antoinette La Belle, Horacio Rozanski, Cornel West, Billie Williamson, and Melinda Wolfe for their courageous leadership and willingness to be the band of true believers that spearheaded this enormously important work.

I am indebted to the members of the task force for their ideas and collaborative energy that helped us distill the case studies: Elaine Aarons, Noni Allwood, Ann Beynon, Angie Casciato, Kathleen Donovan, Ana Duarte-McCarthy, Harriet Edelman, Stephanie Ferguson, Amy George, Timothy Goodell, Paul Graves, Laurie Hodder Greeno, Janet Hanson, Rosalind Hudnell, Barbara Jeremiah, Susan Johnson, Fran Laserson, Tara Murphy, Patricia Nazemetz, Rhodora Palomar-Fresnedi, Lisa Quiroz, Cyndi Selke, Sabrina Spitaletta, Lynn Utter, Nerys Wadham, Muriel Watkins, and Meryl Zausner.

I would like to thank the sponsors of the survey research that underpins this book: American Express, BP plc, Ernst & Young, Goldman Sachs, Lehman Brothers, ProLogis, and UBS for their support. I would also like to thank Kathleen Christenson of the Alfred P. Sloan Foundation and Susan Gewirtz of the Annie E. Casey Foundation for grants that supported case study and toolkit research.

I am indebted to Steve Richardson of American Express, Emily Deakins of BP, Billie Williamson of Ernst & Young, Melinda Wolfe of Goldman Sachs, Anne Erni and Antoinette La Belle of Lehman Brothers, Dessa Bokides of ProLogis, and Mona Lau of UBS for their vision, commitment, and generous counsel. We are grateful to Dana Markow of Harris Interactive, who expertly guided the survey research and was an invaluable resource throughout the studies.

There are many "experts" in our midst who have lent advice and counsel. In particular, I would like to acknowledge: Cynthia Augustine, Lisa Belkin, Ella L. Bell, Jyoti Blew, Ellen Bloom, Ann Bohara, Carol Borghesi, Madeleine

Bunting, Barbara Byrne, Marcelo Cardoso, Jennifer Ceslak, Naomi Chavez, Kenneth Chenault, Helen Chernikoff, Forrest Church, Debbie Cohen, Francine Darragh, Mike Dormer, Brooks Dougherty, Melissa Eisenstat, Carol Evans, Anna Fels, Andrea Flynn, Kaye Foster-Cheek, Bet Franzone, Lucy Friedman, Maryella Gockel, Joe Gregory, Deborah Epstein Henry, Deborah Holmes, Marion Hochberg-Smith, Susan Horst, Melanie Hughes, Edith Hunt, Jane Hyun, Jeremy Isaacs, Aynesh Johnson, Barbara Jones, Amy Jumbelic, Lisa Kennedy, Catherine R. Kinney, Sakiko Kon, Nancy Lane, Ilene Lang, Rachel Lee, Rayna Leiter, Patricia Lennon, Mimish L'Esperance, Laura Liswood, Daniel Loveley, Beth McCormick, Kevin McDermott, Rhonda Joy McLean, Mary "Mish" Michaud, Jami Miller, Marc Monseau, Jennifer Moreland, Bridget O'Connor, George O'Meara, Catherine Orenstein, Alan Pace, Richard Parsons, Pauline Perry, Susan Peters, Joanne Petrossian, Laura Quintana, Rick Rieder, David G. Richardson, Jeanne Rosario, Sam Rubino, Jonelle Salter, Danielle Samalin, Richard Schack, Anwar Shaikh, Tina Sharkey, Leslie Silverman, Alex Southwell, Ruth Spellman, Ilona Steffen-Cope, Maja Thomas, Linda Tischler, Molly Tschang, Andrea Turner, Laura D'Andrea Tyson, Vera Vitels, Caroline Waters, Christina Way, Angela Williams, Joan Williams, Peggy Wolf, Heidi Yang, and the women and men who participated in our interviews and focus groups.

I am extremely grateful to the staff of the Center for Work-Life Policy—Linda Bernstein, Shelley Haynes, Sandy Southwell, and Karen Sumberg—for their unstinting support over the last three years. I am also grateful to my colleagues at Columbia University who have contributed ideas and enriched and expanded the scope of my research. In particular, I would like to thank Lisa Anderson, Dean of the School of International and Public Affairs, who has had the courage to lend institutional weight to the policies and practices contained in this book.

Part One

The Challenge

The first part of this book "maps" career pathways and explores career drivers. The focus is on contrasts and differences between highly qualified men and women.

Forty years after the women's revolution transformed female opportunities, women's work lives remain very different from men's. Fully 60 percent of highly qualified women have nonlinear careers. They take off-ramps and scenic routes and have a hard time conjuring up continuous, cumulative, lockstep employment—which is a necessary condition for success within the confines of the white male competitive model. The end result: too many talented women either leave their careers or languish on the sidelines.

Employers miss out too. For reasons that range from a tightening job market to retiring baby boomers, a "war for talent" is heating up. Companies can ill afford to lose experienced, well-qualified women—they are not easily or cheaply replaced. A recent study by the Washington-based Corporate Executive Board, which features a survey of four thousand hiring managers, reports that because of heavy demand, the quality of candidates has declined 10 percent since 2004.[1] Perhaps most worrying: a third of respondents say that they are hiring less than satisfactory candidates "just to fill a position."

The tugs and pulls of family life explain part of the divergence between male and female career paths, but other kinds of distinctions need to be weighed too. Women's ambitions, it turns out, are different from men's. While money is a prime motivator for men, it is much less important for women. Several other factors—including high-quality colleagues, recognition by bosses, and flexible work options—trump compensation as reasons women go to work.

Understanding that women have a different "value proposition" from men is critical information for companies attempting to retain female talent. The fact is, many talented women need to clear a higher bar. Some have a choice as to whether they go to work or not, and many struggle with serious opportunity costs. As we shall see, highly qualified women tend to see a tight—and guilt-ridden—connection between work commitments and family well-being. Given this mind-set it's hardly surprising that women need more than "just money" if they are to stay in their careers.

These challenges are getting more urgent by the minute. Chapter 3 describes how high-level jobs are becoming more intense and more burdensome—and leaving women behind in new ways. Our increasingly extreme work model is yet another reason to reexamine career paths and career drivers.

A word of caution. In describing differences between male and female aspirations, I do not mean to imply that women are necessarily less committed. Attachment to career reverberates like a drumbeat throughout this book. Highly qualified women love their work. It sits at the core of their identities, providing status, standing, meaning, and purpose. Properly nourished and appreciated, high-achieving women can and do contribute as substantially as their male peers.

1

Why Mess with the Male Competitive Model?

In the winter of 2005–2006 Lehman Brothers, the global investment banking and financial services firm, launched an initiative called Encore—a program designed to provide individuals who have quit jobs in finance with a second shot at career and ambition. The program was designed specifically with women in mind. The launch events, first in New York City in November, then in London the following February, featured an update on recent developments in the sector, help in crafting a midcareer narrative, and, most importantly, a broad range of actual job opportunities.

The value of a program such as Encore to off-ramped women—women who'd left demanding careers in order to take care of equally demanding personal obligations, such as young children or ailing parents—is clear enough, and the women who signed up for the launch events were extremely appreciative. "I can't believe a Wall Street firm is reaching out," said one grateful attendee. "It's incredibly difficult to find an on-ramp once you've been at home for a while. I should know because I've spent the last seven months sending my résumé into the void." But what's in it for Lehman? In his welcome address at the London launch,

Jeremy Isaacs, CEO, Europe and Asia, began to answer that question. "We absolutely need to attract the best talent from the broadest pool," he said. "It's all about competitive advantage. Most of us on the leading edge of investment banking are really good at what we do—we all have creative products and market depth. The thing that differentiates us is how good we are at constructing the best people model and being optimal at the margin.

"This is how I see the problem," Isaacs continued,

> The old career model doesn't work. It's a model that was originally conceived by white males, with white males in mind. And so it's not surprising that across industry it has tended to work best for white men—a segment of the talent pool that is shrinking. For too many talented women this model doesn't work, which is why many companies find it difficult to attract and retain female talent, just when the need for the broadest talent pool is greater than ever.

> At Lehman, we don't subscribe to these old models. We want the broad sweep of talent and we want to bring out the best in this talent. We're intent on learning how to be truly inclusive. How do we retain women with serious family responsibilities? How do we re-attach women who have stepped out for a period of time? *Encore* is a big part of the answer. This program enables us to reconnect—and reengage with qualified, committed women.

> We're beginning to think through what women need to make them feel comfortable. A mobile office? A crèche [day care center] in the building? A three-day-a-week job? These items are all on my list. I would absolutely take three days a week of someone who is truly talented. My questions are: "What do you need to make this work? How can we help you?"

> We're not there yet. I'm fully aware of the fact that we continue to get a lot of "regrettable leaves," that we fail to retain a lot of talent. But personally I have a huge appetite for the work involved in getting this right.[1]

Isaacs's speech drew stunned silence—followed by thunderous applause. His audience, forty-nine on-ramping women who had gathered at Lehman's Canary Wharf headquarters for Encore's European launch, could not have been more enthusiastic. Throwing British reserve to the wind, they rose to their feet and gave Isaacs a standing ovation. Sitting on the dais was Anne Erni, a managing director and Lehman's chief diversity officer and the person who had spearheaded the Encore initiative. Erni had a delighted smile on her face, thoroughly understanding the significance of this moment. Having male leaders so totally on board made a great deal of difference in her ability to drive this program at Lehman.

New and radical initiatives by firms such as Lehman Brothers are at the heart of this book. Revolutionary change is brewing. As Jeremy Isaacs intimated, there's a new willingness on the part of cutting-edge firms to "walk the talk" and change the rules of the career game to better realize female talent. This signals a seismic shift in corporate culture. But why now?

This shift is being driven by two factors. First, business leaders are newly aware of just how many talented women are being forced off the career track. New data—much of which I have helped develop—shows that two-thirds of highly qualified women either leave the workforce or languish on the sidelines. Second, demographic and other structural shifts are giving an urgent edge to this challenge of better utilizing women. Baby busts and global expansion mean that companies these days are heavily reliant on female talent. As Isaacs pointed out, it's a question of competitive strength and economic survival.

How stalled or sidelined are talented women? Clearly, there has been a great deal of forward progression in efforts to advance women in the workplace. Over the last forty years we've witnessed a sea change in the opportunities available to women. The differences are all around us. Whether one is talking Wall Street or the White House, most management teams now contain conspicuous and powerful female talent. Think of secretary of state Condoleezza Rice, eBay's CEO and president Meg Whitman, publishing entrepreneur Martha Stewart.

But is the face of power really changing? Across occupation and sector, are talented women bringing their hard-won credentials and work experience to bear and taking their fair share of top jobs? The answer is still a resounding no.

Two figures say it all: men constitute 98 percent of CEOs at *Fortune* 500 companies.[2] Men also constitute 92 percent of top earners at these companies. Indeed, fully 75 percent of *Fortune* 500 companies report no women as top earners.[3] Rice and Whitman notwithstanding, women are still having a hard time making it to the top.[4] Despite the fact that women these days are highly credentialed (49 percent of law school graduates and 36 percent of business school graduates are female), they are not being promoted or advanced at a rate commensurate with their weight in the talent pool.[5] Most women become stalled or sidelined during the early or midpoint stretches of the career highway. Few make it into the fast lane or get to participate in the end game.[6]

Why is this happening? Who or what is to blame? The premise of this book is that the problem is not the women—they are increasingly qualified and ever more committed—the problem is the career model. Judith's story begins to tell us why.

BATTLING THE CORPORATE CULTURE

In 2003 Judith looked like a rare success story. A senior executive at a Texas-based telecommunications company, this highly accomplished African American woman had both carved out an impressive track record in corporate America and done a fine job on the family front. She was justifiably proud of her long-standing marriage and three well-adjusted children.[7]

But unbeknownst to her colleagues, Judith's life had become unsustainable. She was about to off-ramp—pushed out by the rigidities of a corporate culture caught in a time warp.

Looking back at her twenty years of working at a telecommunications firm, Judith sees her company's corporate culture as being more in tune with 1964 than 2004. In her words:

The face time requirements were real and rigid. Core hours were 7:30 a.m. to 7:30 p.m. God help you if you weren't present and available between those times. It wasn't unusual for an e-mail to go out at 5:30 p.m. announcing a meeting at 7:00 p.m.—which could then drag on to 8:30 p.m. I never fully believed that these evening meetings were necessary. Very little was covered that could not have been dealt with by e-mail—or in person the next morning. I always thought of these meetings as some kind of test—you needed to prove by your physical presence that you were single-mindedly devoted to your job. Women, of course, tend to fail this test. Not too many women with family responsibilities are able to spend evenings at the office, day in and day out.

Judith had a very clear memory of the incident that made her realize what she was up against.

My boss—the CFO of the company—called a Saturday meeting. The pressures were real and urgent. We were working on an earnings announcement slated for the following Monday. On Friday afternoon some key numbers changed, and it quickly became apparent that we weren't ready and the team needed to work through the weekend. I had no problem with this—the reasons were compelling enough. What was unclear, however, was whether we needed to be in the office. This was hard for me. I had three children and no weekend child care. I asked my boss if I could work from my home office. "Absolutely not," he said. "We've got to get in here and kick some tires—this is a collective, in-person effort." I swung into action, conjuring up Saturday babysitting for my two youngest children and developing a plan to take my eleven-year-old into the office with me—suitably equipped with homework assignments and a video.

So what happened?

We all converged at the office at 9:00 a.m. The CFO wasn't there. He called in at 9:45 a.m. and again at 10:30 a.m. No apology. He merely told us he was "running late." We tried to get started, but it was hard without his input. He didn't actually show up until 1:00 p.m. and then only stayed a short while. Before he left, he made a point of telling me how "surprised" he was to find my daughter quietly doing her homework in an empty conference room. His voice was thick with disapproval. Clearly, he found her presence in the office inappropriate. I was cut to the quick. She had been beautifully behaved all morning, bothering no one. Why couldn't he be more understanding?

My retrospective on the day? We all would have done a better job working from home, exchanging drafts via fax and e-mail, consulting by phone, and relying on limited direction and input from our boss—which was all he was prepared to give anyway. This coming-into-the-office-on-Saturday deal was just one of those tests.

My boss, the CFO, could have been sent down from central casting. He was a conventional man with a nonworking wife and a traditional division of labor on the home front. His idea of coping with family demands was to off-load them onto his spouse. He had no idea what it was like to find—on short notice—weekend babysitting for three children. Don't get me wrong. I don't think he was a bad person—or even particularly hostile toward me. Indeed, he saw himself as some kind of mentor, taking me out for the occasional coffee and handing down kindly, avuncular advice. He just didn't have a clue as to the realities of my life.

In June 2003 Judith's frustrations came to a head. The corporation was streamlining some of its operations and offering attractive severance packages to senior executives. Judith took one—with alacrity.

I saw this as a rare opportunity to take a sabbatical. I was exhausted, worn out from twenty years of juggling twelve- to fourteen-hour workdays and three children, and burned out from the cumulative strain of "battling the corporate culture." I was hungry to recoup and reconnect with the rest of my life, most particularly my children, who were entering their teenage years. From a purely personal vantage point, the fact that the company was downsizing was a godsend—it afforded me a lifesaving break.

For a year, I took full advantage of my freedom. I hung out with my kids, got to know their friends much better, and finally figured out what kind of music they liked. I also had time to do some hands-on volunteer work in the community—a first for me. But after twelve months I was ready to get back to work. I felt recharged and was beginning to miss the substance of my work— not to mention the stimulation and challenge of professional life. Also, as a family, we were beginning to feel the financial pinch. We needed my income.

So in June 2004 I hit the job market. I was determined and organized—mobilizing my network and meeting with the top executive recruiters (Korn/Ferry, Spencer Stuart, etc.). I went on a ton of interviews and received at least some positive feedback. Indeed, one job went down to the wire. I was short-listed, and over a three-month period I went through fifty hours of interviews and even met with the CEO. Everyone seemed to love me. It was down to two candidates. In the end, the other candidate got the job.

So where am I? The hard fact is: it's twenty months later and I'm still unemployed. Getting a job, finding that on-ramp, is turning out to be much more difficult than I had anticipated. I've asked myself time and time again, "Where's the problem? Why am I hitting a wall?"

This is what I've come up with: recruiters and employers are hugely suspicious of the fact that I've taken some time out, that I voluntarily left my last job. What does it mean when I say I was "burnt out" in June 2003? How come I gave myself a sabbatical? Have I lost my drive, my ambition? Can I be counted on in the future?

There are other issues that set me apart. This time around I'm looking for a job that doesn't require much travel (no more than twice a month) and provides a measure of flexibility, and I'm willing to downshift if necessary. In other words, if attaining these goals means taking a job with a smaller paycheck than I otherwise could expect, that's fine with me. All of which tends to somehow reinforce the perception that I've lost my edge. Potential employers don't understand how anyone would opt for a pay cut. They simply can't grasp that an ambitious professional would not want to make as much money as possible; they seem unwilling to understand that other goals could be more important.

Despite these needs on the flexibility and travel front, the gap in my résumé remains my key problem. This is the thing recruiters and employers keep coming back to. I find it so frustrating. How can a twenty-month employment break cancel out a twenty-year track record? It makes no sense. I can't believe that people really think I've lost my skill set. I guess it's just one of those tests. A continuous employment history demonstrates that you're fully committed—that you're one of the boys.

Judith's story is sobering, to say the least. If a high-performing female with two decades of work experience can't find an on-ramp, who can? Judith's failure to find a job is particularly hard to understand since she's seriously experienced in a sector—telecommunications—that professes to be desperately seeking female and minority talent. The stigma attached to taking "time out" seems to trump even the most sought-after credentials.

Judith's story is loaded with meaning for women. But what are some of the "takeaways" for companies?

To begin with, CEOs should beware of managers who fail to appreciate that female executives don't have "wives" at home to take care of family business.[8] As we will see in part II, this attitude is commonplace in middle management.[9] Indeed, middle managers are often referred to as the "permafrost" by women frustrated by the thoughtlessness of their immediate bosses. Ernst & Young's People Point program and Cisco's initiative on microinequities (see chapter 10 for both) are among the programs described in part II that go some distance toward melting this permafrost.

In addition, companies need to get into the business of offering serious forms of flexibility.[10] A smart employer might have offered Judith a reduced-hour load for a year or two—enough time for her to catch up with her teenagers and replenish her energies. Had her company thought ahead, they would have realized that this gesture of support would have locked in her commitment—and her energies—over the long haul.

Whether or not a woman off-ramps has a whole lot to do with whether an employer can conjure up imaginative support—and flexibility—in the workplace.

INCHING TOWARD A SCENIC ROUTE

Jonelle Salter, an offshore installation manager (OIM) for BP (formerly known as British Petroleum), is inching toward a scenic route, and while BP isn't exactly planting rose bushes for her to stop and smell, the company is offering arrangements attractive enough to ensure that this thirty-two-year-old Afro-Caribbean woman engineer won't off-ramp.

Salter has proved her worth to BP. She's done a tour of duty as an OIM on an oil platform in the North Sea off the coast of Aberdeen and on a gas platform in her native Trinidad—where she married and had a child. As the head person on an oil platform Salter has been responsible for the health and safety of eighty-plus workers trained to deal with physical extremes and the remote possibility of life-threatening emergencies: gas leaks, chemical spills on the platform, helicopter crashes, you name it. To prepare for her position Salter went through a year and a half of physically punishing, highly realistic simulations. "Think of subzero temperatures, ice coating all surfaces, making everything slick, gale force winds—and then a wall of fire, breaking pipes, oil gushing," she says. "It's easy to get rattled and make mistakes of judgment in these situations."[11] As an OIM in the North Sea Salter was on a four-week rotation: two weeks offshore, two weeks onshore. But her offshore rotations were fraught with loneliness because she was cut off from friends and family. Later, rotations were hard on her marriage. "I got irritable and brittle the Monday before leaving—I always seemed to pick a fight with my husband. It's the tension of knowing you are about to leave for a while." After her maternity leave BP created an onshore OIM position for her; more of a human resources role than a conventional OIM position, it was a job better suited for someone with a small child.

Looking into the future Salter sees herself climbing the ladder at BP. She credits her mentor—Gro Kielland, a Norwegian woman, married with a son, now a managing director for BP Norway—for her ongoing ambition. Salter says, "When I talk to Gro, I feel there's nothing I can't do."

Moreover, Salter notes that BP also offers a "9/80" schedule option that is extremely attractive to parents: this option allows an employee to shoehorn a full-time schedule into nine days over the course of two weeks and then take the tenth day off.

Jennifer Ceslak's experience at Johnson & Johnson is an example of how another company is increasingly offering flexible and reduced-hour options to valued employees.[12] Ceslak, a thirty-nine-year-old mother of three, had crafted a fast-track career as a sales director in the firm's consumer products division.

In a July 2004 focus group Ceslak shared some issues that were beginning to trouble her. She had noticed a personality change in herself and didn't like who she was becoming. She felt she was increasingly shrill and brittle because she just couldn't get her work done in the hours she had available. Colleagues would follow her out to her car or stop her on the way to the bathroom, asking questions, taking notes. Everyone—including her children—needed a bigger piece than she was able to give.

It took Ceslak a while to pluck up the courage to ask for some changes—she was, as she characterized herself, this "burning treadmill woman," and was potentially risking her job. But finally she took a deep breath, walked into her boss's office, and asked for a reduced-hour schedule. To her great surprise and relief, he said yes. Indeed, he was completely supportive. He helped her craft a thirty-hour-a-week job on the people management side—and kept her on his management team. Ceslak loves her new schedule. She's back in her comfort zone, feeling that she's doing a good job both at home and at work. Her boss obviously shares this opinion since he has offered her an opportunity to ramp up. She's just said no to his offer of a promotion. It was tempting but would have meant going back to a five-day week, something Ceslak is not quite ready for; but she's sure she will be, a little way down the road.

THE MALE COMPETITIVE MODEL

Unfortunately, Ceslak's and Salter's experiences are still something of a rarity in the corporate sector. Judith's tale of woe is a lot more familiar. But let's back up for a moment and look more carefully at why Judith was forced off track. What is it about the conventional career model that makes it so very challenging for women?

What I call the "white male career model" (or even more simply the "male competitive model") evolved to fit the life rhythms of middle-class white males in the 1950s and 1960s—decades when access to well-paying jobs was primarily limited to this privileged group. The success of this model relied on a traditional division of labor between men and women, where men were the breadwinners and women were full-time wives, mothers, and homemakers—and the model was characterized by the following features:[13]

- A strong preference for cumulative, lockstep careers and a continuous, linear employment history.

- A huge emphasis on full-time employment and on face time work—being physically present in the office ten-plus hours a day.

- An expectation that the steepest gradient of a career occurs in the decade of one's thirties. In other words, that is the time when an ambitious professional either "catches a wave" or doesn't. There are no second chances.

- An assumption that professionals are motivated primarily by money.

While this career model suited the needs of Jack Welch and his peers, it's exceedingly problematic for women. Not that some women didn't and don't bend their lives to fit into the constraints of this male competitive model. A minority of them do. But a majority either can't or don't choose to.[14]

The ways in which the white male model excludes or marginalizes women are obvious. A strong preference for a continuous employment history penalizes women who need to take time out. The fact is, the dynamics of the model simply don't mesh with the imperatives of women's lives. Take the preferred shape of the career path. For many women, thirty-three or thirty-seven can be precisely the wrong ages to "catch a wave." At these ages, childbearing and child-rearing demands are at their peak and can be enormously time-consuming. Establishing a framework where careers need to take off in one's thirties ensures that work and life clash and collide in the worst possible way for women.

The survey data showcased in this book demonstrates that the white male model derails large numbers of talented women. For example, fully two-thirds of highly qualified women have discontinuous or nonlinear careers. Thirty-seven percent take an off-ramp at some point in their careers, voluntarily quitting their jobs for a short period of time. Another 30-plus percent take what I call a "scenic route" (a reduced-hour job, a flexible work arrangement, a telecommuting option). The vast majority of these women see their decision to step back as temporary—an expedient measure designed to deal with a period of overload in their lives. But, as Judith found out, something conceived as temporary can quickly become semipermanent. The data shows that for many women, finding an on-ramp is exceedingly difficult—no matter how qualified or committed they might be. Employers simply don't trust those who take time out.

Which brings us to the $64,000 question: if the white male model is detrimental to women—and wasteful of their qualifications and experience—why does it continue to dominate? Women, after all, are a large part of the current and potential talent pool. More than half of *all* professional and graduate degrees are now awarded to women.[15] Even more sobering: the future pool of professional talent is disproportionately female. According to the U.S. Department of Education, the number of women with graduate and professional degrees is projected to grow by 16 percent over the next decade, while the number of men with these degrees is projected to grow by a mere 1.3 percent.[16]

So why the resistance? Why does a model that fits the needs of white men—who make up a shrinking proportion of the talent pool—continue to hold sway?

Here's my theory: accommodating discontinuity or nonlinearity in career paths can be deeply disturbing to business leaders because it spells the end of an era. Developing serious forms of flexibility that allow women who take an off-ramp (or a scenic route) to on-ramp without major penalty and become newly ambitious at a later point in their lives is profoundly threatening because it means messing with a model that has stood corporations in good stead for many decades.

It also means that men lose a last piece of competitive advantage over women. Think of how much has been already taken away! Today, men no longer have an educational edge (Yale College and Columbia Law School are no longer male monopolies), and young, highly qualified women are snapping at their heels in most professional occupations. So what men continue to rely on to propel them to the top is a significant advantage on the hours-spent-at-work front—particularly in the key decade of their thirties. Men can pony up a sixty-hour workweek year in, year out, without any real problem, primarily because they are relatively unencumbered by family responsibilities (picking up a mere 25 percent of housework and child care). This ability to conjure up a smooth, cumulative, and uninterrupted career trajectory is a huge advantage under the present rules of engagement. It enables men to "shake off" most women—or at least the large group that take off-ramps and scenic routes. If you are a man, it's hard not to appreciate these facts—albeit on a subliminal or subconscious level. I am not arguing that there is any kind of male conspiracy at work here; rather, it's just that a preestablished model offers men an advantage they'd be foolish to pass up.

In May 2006, for part of its annual New York symposium, The Conference Board organized a panel session called "White Males, White Models and Diversity." This session—which featured senior executives from General Electric, Boehringer-Ingelheim, Ernst & Young, and Porter Novelli, as well as myself—was enormously popular, drawing a large number of female and minority executives. The conversation centered on the "invisibility of privilege" and the difficulties of fully engaging white males in the diversity discussion. Greg Waldron, partner and chief talent officer at Porter Novelli, the global public relations firm, and the only white man on the panel, kicked off the session by talking about how the processes that confer privilege are often invisible to the privileged. In his words, "White men have the luxury of not needing to think about race or gender every minute of every day, and are therefore able to pretend that these differences aren't there."[17] Waldron urged the audience to read Peggy McIntosh's celebrated essay "White Privilege: Unpacking the Invisible Knapsack," which describes some of the benefits that come to people simply because they are white or straight or middle class or male.[18] If a white man were to unpack this invisible knapsack, he would find all kinds of good stuff: maps, passports, codebooks, visas, tools, and blank checks.

Waldron's remarks triggered impassioned discussion. But by the end of the session the group was in agreement: there is a substantial package of unearned assets that white males can count on cashing in each day, but to which most white men are oblivious. Among the most important of these unearned assets is a career model that fits like a glove.

The "invisibility" of the problem is profoundly discouraging. It's hard to fix something that's so difficult to see—particularly by male leaders. So what are the chances any of us can really mess with the white male career model and create alternative pathways to power?

A GROWING TALENT VOID

Our main chance lies in an increasingly powerful business case.[19] As Jeremy Isaacs outlined in his February 2006 speech introducing Lehman Brothers' Encore program to his U.K. audience, cyclical and structural factors are aligned in new and alarming ways and are beginning to force action. Consider the following trends.

The job market is heating up. After a several-year jobless recovery in the earliest years of the twenty-first century, the high-echelon labor market is noticeably tightening.[20] Fourteen percent more college graduates were hired in 2005–2006 compared with 2004–2005. According to the National Association of Colleges and Employers (NACE), nine out of ten employers say competition for college hires has increased, and a large percentage plan on raising starting salaries. Business school graduates are also in heavy demand. Corporate recruiters are planning to hire 18 percent more MBAs in 2005–2006 than in 2004–2005, and salaries are on the upswing.[21] According to the Graduate Management Admission Council, when you include benefits and bonuses, total compensation is up 23 percent over 2004–2005.[22] One out of two newly minted MBAs is getting a signing bonus.[23]

The booming search firm sector provides a barometer of just how hard it has become to find talent. After a two-year slump in the wake of the attacks on the World Trade Center, the headhunting industry began to grow again in 2003 and 2004. In 2005 and 2006, this sector expanded with the four largest companies racking up double-digit growth.[24]

The demographic trends driving this tightening labor market cut deep. As baby boomers age and members of the smaller baby bust generation hit their most productive years, the supply of thirty-five- to forty-four-year-old workers is at a low ebb. Indeed, the size of this prime age group will drop by 7 percent between 2002 and 2012.[25] Other demographic trends now converging with this one only exacerbate the challenge. According to AARP, over the next ten years, as boomers move into their sixties at least 21 million will retire—and those remaining on the job are likely to demand flexible part-time work.[26]

In the past, immigrants have often acted as a "safety valve" in the U.S. labor market—filling in shortfalls and eliminating bottlenecks. They can no longer be counted on to serve this function. Hiring foreign nationals or recruiting from abroad is fast becoming a pipe dream for talent-hungry U.S.-based employers. As a result of post-9/11 security concerns, Congress has dramatically cut the number of green cards and temporary visas available to noncitizens seeking to work in the United States. But even if visas were in ample supply they wouldn't solve the problem since the supply of highly educated immigrants is drying up. Because of economic expansion around the world, particularly in China and India, foreign nationals are increasingly drawn to job opportunities in their own countries. Take the Indian case: rapid economic growth on the subcontinent is leading to a "reverse brain drain," possibly drawing back to their native country as many as 20 million Indian citizens currently residing in the United States and the United Kingdom. "Overseas Indians" are beginning to move home, lured by high salaries and exciting job opportunities.[27]

So, in the absence of immigrant labor, who will fill the talent void? Women are the best—and most obvious—candidates.

To begin with, they've got the intellectual goods. As was mentioned earlier and confirmed by the findings of the National Center for Education Statistics, women now earn 59 percent of the bachelor's degrees, 60 percent of the master's degrees, and slightly more than half of first professional degrees in the United States. Indeed, the achievement gap between men and women is widening around the world.[28]

In addition, they've got spare capacity—under the current rules of engagement women are dramatically underutilized. In a recent speech chairman of the Federal Reserve Board Ben S. Bernanke pointed to this underutilization of female talent and noted that it translated into a slower rate of growth.[29] As we will see in chapter 2, highly qualified women who take time out experience considerable difficulty reconnecting with their careers. Fifty percent of those seeking on-ramps and mainstream jobs fail to find them. The net result: a great deal of talent is "lost on reentry." It stands to reason that if career models were less rigid, if women were permitted to both flex their schedules and flex their careers, a much higher percentage would choose to stay in or return to the labor market. The potential, in terms of expanding the talent pool, is huge. We are, after all, talking about decades of enhanced productive activity. Women these days have a life expectancy of eighty-one and an expectation of working deep into their sixties.

The cyclical and structural factors outlined earlier mean that the stage is now set. Competitive strength increasingly rides on a company's ability to retain and reattach female talent.

I'm convinced that we are at a watershed moment, that employers are finally ready to act. I don't pin my hopes solely on abstract analysis but on something much more substantial and concrete: the recent track record of the Hidden Brain Drain Task Force, which I founded in collaboration with Carolyn Buck Luce of Ernst & Young, and Cornel West of Princeton University. The idea behind this private-sector task force, which was started in early 2004, was to persuade progressive corporations to become stakeholders in a research effort that would examine how to better utilize female talent over the life span.

Though we started with just six companies, the task force has grown to comprise thirty-four companies, including Alcoa, American Express, BP, Citigroup, Intel, Microsoft, ProLogis, Unilever, and White & Case. Over the last three years it has garnered considerable clout and is beginning to "mess" with the male competitive model. All eighteen examples of innovative second-generational practice featured in part II are taken from task force companies, and at least some of these models are a direct result of research we have done together.

This would seem to be living proof that a sizable group of global companies newly "get" the urgency of the job at hand. They understand that the full realization of female talent is no longer a discretionary frill—but at the very core of a company's competitive strength. In the words of Mike Dormer, worldwide chairman, medical devices, Johnson & Johnson, "If you look at our entry-level managers these days, we've had a great influx of women. We've got to ensure we remain serious about our entire global talent pipeline."[30] I find these words particularly significant because they were spoken by a male leader. It's not just the standout women leaders spearheading the work of the Hidden Brain Drain Task Force who feel the urgency of the challenge; it's also their male colleagues. In an address to the task force in October 2005, Ken Chenault, chairman and CEO of American Express, put it well when he said, "There's no choice but to be inclusive if you are to win in the marketplace."[31]

A word on the research, and the data sets, that underlie this book. Early in 2004, the Hidden Brain Drain Task Force targeted women's career paths as a prime area on which to focus its research energies. Among task force members there was considerable enthusiasm for "mapping" the career trajectories of well-qualified women—it was seen as an important first step in rethinking or reengineering career models. The consensus of the group was that women's nonlinear career paths were imperfectly understood. Despite a plethora of magazine stories and television programs on dropout women, no one seemed to know the basic facts: How many talented women were opting out? How many years were they staying out? How many wanted to get back in? And what policies and practices might help them get back in?

In the summer of 2004, three Task Force member companies (Ernst & Young, Goldman Sachs, and Lehman Brothers) sponsored a national survey designed to answer these and other questions. The survey, which was fielded by Harris Interactive, comprised a representative sample of 2,443 highly qualified women and 653 highly qualified men in the twenty-eight- to fifty-five-year-old age group.[32]

Just over a year later the Hidden Brain Drain Task Force chose to undertake further survey research in this area, prompted by the idea that jobs—particularly top jobs—were becoming more extreme. The notion proved to be true. Fed by globalization and canny communications technology, workweeks are lengthening and work pressures are ratcheting up in myriad ways. The danger is, unless we are able to restructure and reengineer extreme jobs, off-ramps will become more prevalent, and women will be left behind in greater numbers. In November 2005, four member companies (American Express, BP, ProLogis, and UBS) sponsored two surveys designed to map extreme jobs. Again, these surveys were fielded by Harris Interactive and comprised a sample of 1,564 highly paid men and women in a U.S. survey and 975 respondents in a global companies survey.[33]

Over the June 2004 to June 2006 period, this quantitative research—which allows us to map both careers and jobs—has been supplemented by twenty-five focus groups. Nineteen of these were conducted with groups of executives who work for large global companies (some task force members, some not). Five were conducted with groups of off-ramped women not currently employed. And one focus group was conducted with a group of men married to off-ramped women. These focus groups were designed to illuminate a much more intimate reality—the feelings and frustrations of the women and men dealing with the phenomena laid out in the survey research.

Highlights from the quantitative research, which can be found in chapters 2 and 3, were first published in the *Harvard Business Review* in March 2005 and December 2006 in articles titled "Off-Ramps and On-Ramps: Keeping Talented Women on the Road to Success" and "Extreme Jobs: The Dangerous Allure of the 70-Hour Workweek," respectively. The detailed data and the qualitative findings—released in this book for the first time—provide important new dimensions. They allow us to paint a much more dynamic picture of women's life paths and job challenges than has been available to date. And they allow us to see how work and life increasingly clash and collide. The fact is, as jobs become more intense and work pressures ratchet up, it is becoming ever more difficult for women with family responsibilities to manage their lives. It's as though they are dealing with a moving target—jobs that are becoming more extreme by the day.

Even more important, they allow us to move beyond analysis and fashion a springboard for action. The treasure trove of data accumulated in the survey research has allowed task force companies to both improve existing policies and practices and experiment with a host of new initiatives, which are showcased in chapters 5 through 10.

A final note on the target audience for this book: individual women will want to read this book—particularly wives, mothers, and daughters who are seriously committed to their careers yet need to deal with important responsibilities on the home front. The voices of such women thread through this book and lend it passion and credibility.

Educators—particularly educators in the business school space—will also want to read this book. Dartmouth's Tuck School has just started a Back in Business program for on-ramping women—shaped, in part, by the *Harvard Business Review* "Off-Ramps and On-Ramps" article. The Harvard Business School has developed New Path for on-ramping alumnae. And Wharton is slated to launch Career Comeback in March 2007.

However, my central targets are business leaders—those who head up large leading-edge companies and those who are piloting midsize but growing companies. Though the models of best practice that dominate part II were developed by a subset of progressive companies, they provide effective road maps for new action that other large companies can surely emulate. And though some programs may be too difficult for smaller companies to adopt, many of the initiatives described in part II can—in some form—be implemented by midsize companies as well.

I've been asked whether these targets mean that I run the risk of preaching to the choir. Large progressive companies already have a slew of policies and practices in this area, so why aren't I reaching out to more challenging constituencies—laggard or recalcitrant companies, for example, or very small companies?

The fact is, no company—no matter how progressive—has cracked this particular nut. Even companies that are considered to be part of the gold standard on gender issues and regularly turn up on *Working Mother* magazine's list of "100 Best Companies for Working Mothers" or *Fortune* magazine's list of "100 Best Companies to Work For" understand they are both leaders and learners when it comes to realizing female talent over the long haul.

I want to end this introductory chapter on a personal note. The themes of this book—the discontinuities in women's work lives, the prevalence of off-ramps and on-ramps, and the importance of second chances—echo through the generations. Looking back at my mother's life, I now appreciate it in new ways.

You see, my mother found herself a lifesaving on-ramp at the age of fifty-six. As a young woman she trained as a teacher, but from ages twenty-six through fifty-six she was a traditional housewife. For thirty years, she plowed her considerable energies into her family, raising six daughters in a home without a washing machine, a refrigerator—or household help. Where she found the time to also tutor her girls so they all won scholarships to university, I'll never know. Then, in her mid-fifties, the unthinkable happened. Her eldest daughter died—a heart-sickening, senseless accident. Unhinged by grief, my parents drifted apart. My mother had no space for anything but her overwhelming pain and sorrow. How grievously she mourned—for her best-beloved firstborn child and for her wrecked family.

She existed this way for eighteen months; then, one day, she somehow found the grit to pick herself up. She learned to drive and got herself a job. She was totally clear-eyed as to why she was doing this. "I need to resurrect my identity," she told me. "It's the only way to survive."

Learning to drive was a huge deal—but absolutely essential if she were to hold down a job. I took her out for innumerable practice runs. Her courage and her resolve were palpable. A tiny woman, she needed to sit on a cushion in order to see over the bonnet of the car. But she didn't allow this to get in her way. I remember the determined set of her jaw as she peered anxiously over the steering wheel, the tension in her white-knuckled fists as she tentatively shifted gears, and the smile of pure delight when she finally brought off a respectable three-point turn.

How did she find a job after being out of the workforce for so many years? Well, we lived in a small, close-knit community. Several members of the local municipal council were aware of my sister's death and bent over backward to give my mother some sort of a second chance. I don't think for a minute they expected her to turn a very part-time teaching job into something that would eventually become full-time or to get rave reviews from her students and stellar O- and A-level results. As is the wont with male leaders, they were skeptical of the motivation and ability of women who take time out.

As I look back on my mother's experience, what occurs to me now is how very splendid the results were—for her, for her students, but certainly for her employer. That win-win-win situation is precisely what we will be talking about in this book.

2

Women's Nonlinear Careers

Lisa Kennedy's career path at Ernst & Young exemplifies the ways in which imaginative forms of flexibility help companies retain top talent—and go some distance toward transforming corporate culture. Kennedy was given a flexible work arrangement that allowed her to have a reduced schedule, but ultimately she still felt the need to off-ramp. After two years she on-ramped, and for the next three years worked again on a reduced schedule. Last year she made partner—still working on a part-time schedule.

Kennedy started at Ernst & Young right out of college, and after approximately ten years of acquiring skills, experience, and contacts, she gave birth to her first child and decided she needed to ramp down her work commitments. Her local managers knew they would lose a valued employee if they didn't offer a customized approach to Kennedy's situation, so after her seven-month maternity leave ended, she was invited to return to work on a reduced schedule: three days a week except for the busy season, when she'd work a full-time schedule. To facilitate the plan, Ernst & Young reduced her client load. That, she says, was the key factor in allowing her continue to do her job well and manage her family responsibilities.

Two years later Kennedy gave birth to her second child. After another seven-month maternity leave she decided to resign—though it was a tough decision. "I had a two-and-a-half-year-old and an infant. I couldn't imagine getting both kids dressed, taking them to day care, handling my commute, and still having the energy to do my job the way I wanted. Though it was an incredibly difficult decision, I decided to quit." What made her decision so difficult, Lisa notes, was that she had literally forged her identity at Ernst & Young. It was a big part of her adult persona. Letting go of that was frightening. Ultimately, it came down to priorities. In her words, "With a baby and a toddler I didn't think I could do both work and family well, and my kids came first."[1]

Kennedy kept in touch with various people at Ernst & Young through periodic e-mails and phone calls, and during her time at home she would occasionally complete a project for a former client. After about two years Lisa started to realize that she just wasn't wired for staying home full-time over the long term. Around the same time a partner from Ernst & Young called and asked Lisa to fill in while a colleague was on maternity leave. It was a perfect on-ramp. A part-time job for a limited period would enable her to test the arrangement. "It was difficult at first. I felt tremendous guilt. My two-year-old would throw tantrums about going to day care, and it wasn't as though I was going back to work because I needed to earn a living. I was doing it for myself. I rationalized that ultimately it would make me a more fulfilled person and a better mom."

That part-time limited arrangement gradually expanded. For a while, Kennedy worked a 50 percent schedule, then 60 percent, then 70 percent, and finally 80 percent, a schedule she has kept to this day. As Kennedy ramped up, Ernst & Young's flexible work arrangement programs came on stream. By the time she was at a four-fifths workload, flexible work arrangements were in full swing throughout the company and at all levels. Over the last few years, flexibility—for both senior and junior associates—has become pervasive at Ernst & Young. Kennedy says that a key to the success of her arrangement is that there's flexibility on both sides—hers and the firm's. Though she's on a reduced schedule Kennedy is never rigid about not working on a particular day—if she needs to attend a client meeting or meet a deadline, she's on the case. The commitment to flexibility is equally strong on the firm's side. In Kennedy's words, "It's now part of the firm's culture."

When asked why Ernst & Young has done so much on the flexibility front Kennedy says, "Ernst & Young recognizes that their biggest asset is their people. Someone who's accumulated skills, experience, and contacts over the course of ten years can't really be replaced by an outside hire. Flexible work arrangements ensure that fewer people will leave, but if they do leave, more will ultimately return. I never thought I would be one of them, but here I am. This would not have happened without all kinds of flexibility."

Last year, three years after she on-ramped, Kennedy made partner. She was, and still is, working less than full-time. She says she never felt her arrangement would affect her chances for partnership. When asked whether she experiences any stigma associated with her schedule she says, "I don't think it would even occur to people to think I'm not deserving of my partnership. I have a formal flexible work arrangement, but everyone here is entitled to flexibility in some form or another."

I wish I could say that Kennedy's story is standard stuff. The problem set she faced certainly is. The tugs and pulls of family (whether toddlers, teenagers, or elderly parents) continue to interrupt professional women's work lives. But the employment outcome is much less familiar. Few bosses, and even fewer companies, reach out to valued employees with these kinds of imaginative policy. All too often, a woman in Kennedy's situation would simply be forced to quit.

OPTING OUT: TREND OR HYPE?

Quitting has been in the news quite a bit lately. Two years ago a noisy debate erupted on both sides of the Atlantic over what Lisa Belkin of the *New York Times* called "the opt-out revolution." For a number of months after her article describing how large numbers of highly qualified women were dropping out of mainstream careers appeared, it was difficult to turn on the television without encountering various "talking heads" scare-mongering about the disturbing trend. Even the wild success of *Desperate Housewives* was attributed to a supposed glut of dropout women—bored silly and looking for trouble on Wisteria Lane.

In the mainstream press there was a great deal of speculation as to what might be behind this trend. Left-wing commentators tended to blame public policy (shortfalls in child care and flexible work options), while more-conservative pundits simply blamed the victims. In their view women had a variety of problems ranging from a failure of ambition to an unwillingness to work long hours. Larry Summers, then president of Harvard University, in an astonishing speech went so far as to accuse women of genetic inferiority when it came to success in scientific fields.

Despite the heat of this debate, it's yielded little in the way of new insights or solutions, at least in part because of the absence of hard data. No one seemed to know the basic facts: How many talented women are opting out? How many years do they stay out? How many want to get back in? And what policies and practices might help them get back onto the career highway?

In 2004 the Hidden Brain Drain Task Force targeted this subject area and sponsored a national survey designed to map the trajectory of women's work lives. The survey, fielded by Harris Interactive, comprised a nationally representative sample of highly qualified women and men defined as those with a graduate or professional degree or a high-honors undergraduate degree.[2] The survey research was supplemented by focus groups conducted within task force companies and companies on the outside (mostly "sister" companies in similar sectors). These focus groups serve to illuminate a much more intimate reality—the feelings and frustrations of the women on the front lines. The resulting study (highlights of which were published in "Off-Ramps and On-Ramps" in the March 2005 issue of the *Harvard Business Review*) paints a much more comprehensive and nuanced portrait of women's careers than had been available to date. Here are the key findings.

ARE PROFESSIONAL WOMEN OPTING OUT?

The answer is a resounding no. Certainly, a sizable number take some time out. The survey data showed that 37 percent of highly qualified women voluntarily leave their careers for a period of time (see figure 2-1). But the amount of time spent outside the workforce is surprisingly short—on average 2.2 years. Across sector and occupation, the length of time spent off-ramped varies, ranging from 1.5 years in the banking/finance sector to 3 years in the legal profession. Just a little way down the road the vast majority of off-rampers (93 percent) are trying to get back onto the career highway. Hype and scaremongering notwithstanding, contemporary women are deeply committed to their careers.[3]

Off-ramps are conspicuous and tend to create waves—we are, after all, talking about highly skilled women quitting. But there are other ways in which women veer off the professional fast track. Some choose what I call a scenic route. They don't step out entirely; rather, they step back a bit—

FIGURE 2-1

How many women off-ramp?

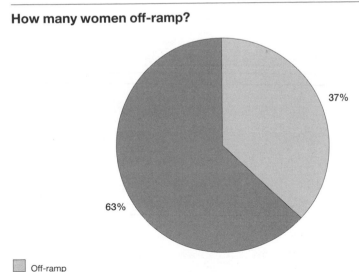

37%

63%

☐ Off-ramp
■ Never off-ramp

taking a part-time job, a flexible work arrangement, or a telecommuting option, or turning down a promotion, deciding that they cannot take on additional responsibility. For a period of time these women deliberately choose a less ambitious career path. This way they are able to look at the scenery, smell the roses—and fulfill serious responsibilities in the rest of their lives.

Our survey showed that 16 percent of highly qualified women currently work part-time. Part-time employment is more prevalent in the legal and medical professions—where 23 percent and 20 percent of female professionals, respectively, work less than full-time—than in the business sector, where only 8 percent of women work part-time. Another common work-life strategy is telecommuting: 8 percent of highly qualified women work exclusively from home, and 25 percent work partly from home.

Scenic routes seem to be as prevalent as off-ramps. Looking back at their careers, fully 36 percent of highly qualified women say they have worked part-time for some period of time as part of a strategy to balance work and personal life. In addition, 25 percent say they have reduced the number of work hours within a full-time job, and 16 percent say they have declined a promotion (see figure 2-2). What's more, a significant proportion (38 percent) say they have deliberately chosen a position with fewer responsibilities and lower compensation than they were qualified for, in order to fulfill responsibilities at home.[4] (This resonates with Judith's story in chapter 1.)

In focus groups women talked about learning how to "stay below the radar" at work. They were intent on doing a great job in the positions they held but did not want to ratchet up. One reason for remaining below the radar was avoiding the risk of being offered a promotion. Participants feared that declining a promotion would reflect badly on their level of commitment. In the words of one woman, "I just don't think my boss would understand that saying no has nothing to do with my level of ambition. I love this company. It's just that I can't ratchet up until my daughter reaches first grade."

FIGURE 2-2

How many women take a "scenic route"?

By sector

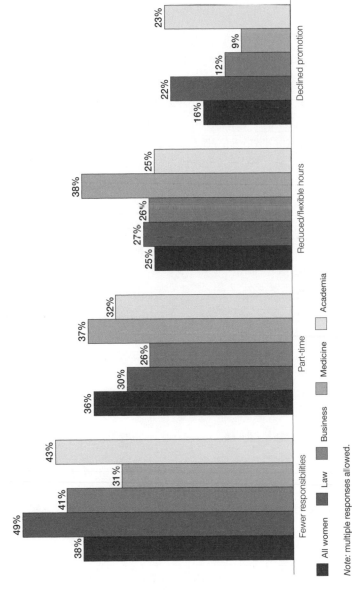

Note: multiple responses allowed.

THE PREVALENCE OF STIGMA

Another powerful theme that cropped up during our focus group discussions was the pervasiveness of stigma around alternative work arrangements. Across a range of sectors—in law firms, media companies, and investment banks—we found that women (and men) perceive many work-life policies (telecommuting, job sharing, part-time or flexible jobs, etc.) as essentially "off-limits" at their company, even if they are offered as official corporate policy (see figure 2-3). One new mother described flexible work arrangements as "toxic." At her fast-paced tech company—which has an exemplary set of work-life policies—flexible work arrangements are so illegitimate, so toxic, that women routinely quit rather than apply for policies that ostensibly are on the books. Paid parenting leave seems to be a little less stigmatized than other work-life policies, at least since the passage of the 1993 Family and Medical Leave Act (FMLA). Parenting leave has become established public policy, and this seems to have conferred a measure of legitimacy—at least for women. Interestingly, a higher percentage of men perceive paid parenting leave as stigmatizing at their companies.

WHY DO WOMEN LEAVE?

There's no simple, one-size-fits-all explanation for why women take time out. For most, career interruptions are the result of a complex interaction between "pull factors" (centered within the family) and "push factors" (centered at work).

Going into this research, I thought the tugs and pulls around children would dominate. And to an extent I was right. For 45 percent of the women in this survey, a child-care challenge—specifically the need to devote more time to a baby or an older child—was the issue that triggered the off-ramping decision (see figure 2-4). But there are other powerful pull factors in play here. For example, 24 percent of women in the survey reported that an elder-care crisis was the trigger issue—the consideration

FIGURE 2-3

The prevalence of stigma

Percentage of respondents who experience stigma whose company provides option

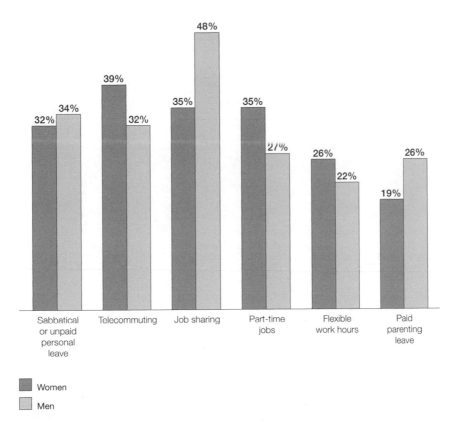

Women

Men

Note: multiple responses allowed.

that ultimately forced them out. The pull of elder-care responsibilities is particularly strong in the business sector and for women in the forty-one-to-fifty-five age group, a demographic referred to as the *sandwich genera-tion*, positioned as they are between growing children and aging parents. One in three women in that age bracket reported having left the work-force for a period of time in order to care for a family member who was not a child.

FIGURE 2-4

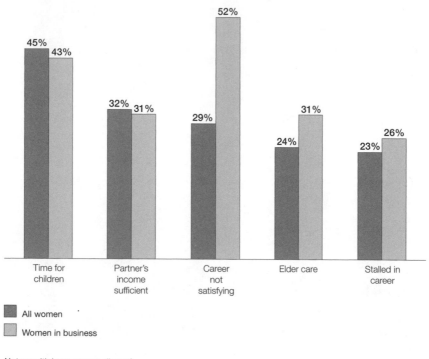

Why do women leave? Family responsibilities top the list

All women

Women in business

Note: multiple responses allowed.

Linda Bernstein is a case in point. Bernstein, a successful magazine editor, found she had to quit her job when the responsibilities associated with caring for her elderly mother became all-consuming. "I had no idea how weak my mother had become. Even though he was very ill himself, my father was covering for her," Bernstein remembers.[5] After her father's death, Bernstein realized her mother could not live on her own and moved her from Florida to an assisted living residence near Bernstein's home in New York. The new schedule was harder than she'd anticipated. Bernstein found that her mother needed her for several hours daily—to hold her hand and ward off loneliness and to take her to countless doctor's appointments. Layered on top of twelve-hour workdays and responsibilities to her own children, Bernstein's new load pushed her to the breaking point.

Bernstein describes the moment she decided to quit her job: "I was turning forty-eight, getting my annual physical, and I fell asleep sitting up while the nurse was taking my blood pressure. When my physician remarked on this, I started sobbing—something I had been doing a lot. He told me I was heading for a physical collapse. I just decided my job was expendable; my mother wasn't." Her decision was fraught with financial risk since her oldest child was about to begin college, and she worried about the effect the loss of her substantial income would have on family finances, not just then but into the future. She was, after all, almost fifty, and colleagues warned her that she might have trouble reentering the magazine world since she was "aging out." But Bernstein quit anyhow; she felt she had no choice.

The problem with conventional work-life policies is that they tend to target young children. For many years, the best benefits in large corporations—and the best programs—have gone to employees with small children.

Increasingly, this doesn't work for highly qualified women. Almost half (44 percent) of the professional women we surveyed are childless.[6] But if these women don't have two-year-olds, they do have serious elder-care responsibilities. And it is not just parents we're talking about. The survey data shows that nearly one in five professional women regularly care for a parent, grandparent, aunt, or uncle. If you are not derailed by a two-year-old at age thirty, you may be derailed by an eighty-year-old at age fifty!

As the first of 78 million baby boomers turn sixty this year and their parents live past eighty-five, it's becoming apparent that elder-care needs are distinct from child-care needs—and from the benefits companies traditionally provide for dependent children. Elderly parents' needs are often unpredictable and crisis driven—a trip to the emergency room for a broken hip, help sorting out the dozens of prescription plans for Medicare Part D before a looming deadline, a fender bender that signals it's time for an aging parent to give up his or her driver's license, or the myriad and acute needs of a parent with Alzheimer's. The average length of time devoted to elder care is four years, but a daughter may care for an aging mother or grandmother for ten to twenty years or more.[7] It's also true that ailing parents may live hundreds—or thousands—of miles away. A 2006 *New York Times* article makes the point that the growing number of working women who care for frail, elderly parents are embarking on a "daughter track" equivalent to the much more familiar mommy track. Both tracks drive women out of their careers.[8] These trends are even more exaggerated for African American women professionals who deal with a particularly challenging set of responsibilities. Many cope with a triple burden of care: nuclear family, extended family, and needy people in their communities.[9] This cumulative load generates significant time demands. On average, African American women involved in this type of care spend more hours per week on elder and extended family care than do white women (12.4 hours, compared with 9.5 hours for white women).[10] African American women are also more likely to be caring for children who are not their own and don't live with them—acting as a surrogate parent for a niece or nephew or godchild.

We shouldn't forget that lurking behind these pull factors—all of which ultimately revolve around family care—is a traditional division of labor between men and women that remains entrenched and pervasive. Even when women are highly qualified and highly paid, they routinely pick up the lion's share of domestic responsibilities—typically 75 percent of the housework and child care.[11] Indeed, in a 2001 survey conducted by the Center for Work-Life Policy, fully 40 percent of highly qualified women with spouses felt that their husbands created more work around the house than they performed.[12] So much for the dream of a 50/50 split!

Alongside these pull factors are a series of push factors, features of the job or workplace that make women head for the door. Twenty-nine percent of women report taking an off-ramp primarily because their jobs were not satisfying or meaningful. The data shows that feeling underutilized or underappreciated is a more significant problem than overwork. Not being consulted or not getting a sought-after (and deserved) plum assignment is much more difficult to contend with than dealing with additional responsibilities. Only 6 percent of women off-ramped because the work itself was too demanding. It's interesting to note that in the business sector, a variety of push factors have more weight than pull factors. Fifty-two percent of women in business off-ramped at least in part because their career was not satisfying (versus 29 percent of women overall), while time for children was a less important factor (43 percent) (see figures 2-5 and 2-6). The contrast is even more dramatic in law, where 59 percent said their careers were not satisfying, compared with 26 percent who wanted more time for children. These figures indicate that certain work cultures—especially large corporations and law firms—have done a particularly poor job developing a supportive environment for talented women.

Of course, neat distinctions between pull and push factors tend to break down in the hurly-burly of daily life. In the real world most women deal with an interaction of pull and push factors—one often serving to intensify the other—creating a cascading effect. For example, women are much more likely to respond to the pull of family when they feel hemmed in by a glass ceiling. In the words of one off-ramped television producer, "My two-year-old suddenly appeared more needy, and yes, more appealing, during the spring I was passed over for promotion. Objectively speaking I don't think anything changed, but I was newly looking for a reason to take some time off, and I wanted to believe that my child needed me at home full-time."

In a strange way this interactivity between pull and push is good news for companies. It means that nothing is written in concrete. A new child or a mother-in-law recently diagnosed with Alzheimer's does not necessarily signal that a woman will quit. Whether or not a woman off-ramps also has a whole lot to do with whether an employer can conjure up support—and opportunities—in the workplace.

We need to remember that, whether pulled or pushed, only a relatively privileged group of women, those married to high-earning men, have the option of not working. Indeed, for a subset of women in the survey, the fact that they had a high-earning spouse was in and of itself an important trigger. Fully 32 percent of the women surveyed cited the fact that their spouses' income "was sufficient for our family to live on" as a reason behind their decision to leave the workforce (see figure 2-4).

FIGURE 2-5

Pull factors

By sector

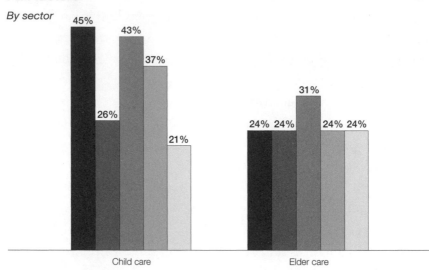

Child care   Elder care

Note: multiple responses allowed.

FIGURE 2-6

Push factors

By sector

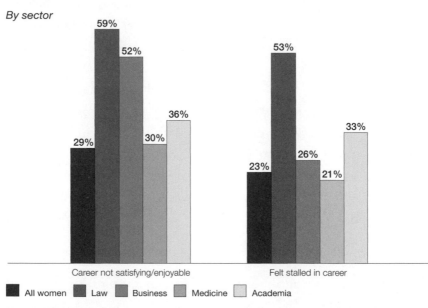

Career not satisfying/enjoyable   Felt stalled in career

■ All women   ■ Law   ■ Business   ■ Medicine   □ Academia

Note: multiple responses allowed.

Off-ramping is not limited to women. Our survey data also shows that fully 24 percent of highly qualified men voluntarily leave their jobs for a period of time, but they do it for a different set of reasons. Child care is much less significant: only 12 percent of men cite this as their trigger factor, compared with 45 percent of women (see figure 2-7). Men cite switching careers (29 percent) and obtaining additional training (25 percent) as the most important reasons for taking time out. For highly qualified men off-ramping seems to be about strategic repositioning in their careers. That's a far cry from the family-centered concerns of their female peers.

In addition to their own distinct off-ramping experiences, men, as husbands and fathers, factor into and condition their wives' decision to quit a job. Our survey uncovers a broad range of attitudes toward a wife's decision to off-ramp.

More than half of all husbands (60 percent) claim they are enthusiastically supportive, but 55 percent also say they are either envious or angry. Money matters loom large. Almost a quarter of the male respondents in the survey (22 percent) say they are worried about the financial implications of their wife's decision to quit. In one focus group I held,

FIGURE 2-7

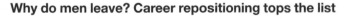

Why do men leave? Career repositioning tops the list

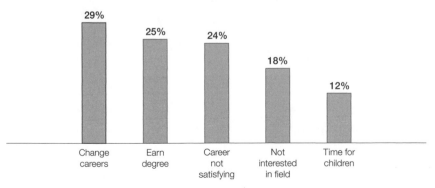

Change careers	Earn degree	Career not satisfying	Not interested in field	Time for children
29%	25%	24%	18%	12%

Note: multiple responses allowed.

which pulled together husbands of women who had quit, the conversation centered on overload and burden. A surprisingly high percentage of the men in the room felt resentful of the extra wage-earning load dumped on their shoulders, and were concerned that they might not be able to make up the shortfall in family income. Some regarded their wife's quitting work as not being part of the original deal. One focus group participant described his feelings this way: "I feel the rug has been pulled . . . I thought I was marrying a high-earning professional, not a stay-at-home wife."

WHY DO WOMEN WANT BACK IN?

Desperate Housewives notwithstanding, talented women who blithely throw their careers to the wind are the exception rather than the rule. As mentioned earlier, the overwhelming majority of highly qualified women currently off-ramped (93 percent) want to return to their careers.

Many of these women have financial reasons for wanting to get back to work. Nearly half (46 percent) cite "wanting to have their own independent source of income" as an important motivating factor. Women who participated in our focus groups talked about their discomfort with "dependence." However good their marriages, many disliked needing to ask for money. Not being able to splurge on some small extravagance or make their own philanthropic choices without clearing it with their husbands did not sit well with them either. It's also true that a significant proportion of women seeking on-ramps are facing troubling shortfalls in family income: 38 percent cite "household income no longer sufficient for family needs" and 24 percent cite "partner's income no longer sufficient for family needs." Given what has happened to the cost of housing (up 55 percent over the past five years), the cost of a college education (up 40 percent over the past decade), and the cost of health insurance (up 87 percent since 2000), it's easy to see why many professionals find it hard to manage a family budget on just one income.[13]

But financial pressures do not tell the whole story. Many of these women also found deep pleasure in their chosen careers and want to reconnect with something they love. Forty-three percent cite the "enjoyment and satisfaction" they derive from their careers as an important reason to return—among teachers this figure rises to 54 percent, and among doctors it rises to 70 percent (see figures 2-8 and 2-9). A further 16 percent want to "regain power and status in their profession." In our focus groups women talked eloquently about how work gives shape and structure to their lives, boosts confidence and self-esteem, and confers status and standing in their communities. As one former executive put it, "Cocktail party chitchat is so much easier if you can claim to be a professional, even a lapsed professional. Besides which, my children insist on it. My fifteen-year-old daughter doesn't want to be caught dead with a mom who is 'just' a housewife." For many off-rampers, their professional identity remains their primary identity, despite the fact that they are currently taking time out. This makes a great deal of sense given the length of women's working lives—which

FIGURE 2-8

Why do women on-ramp?

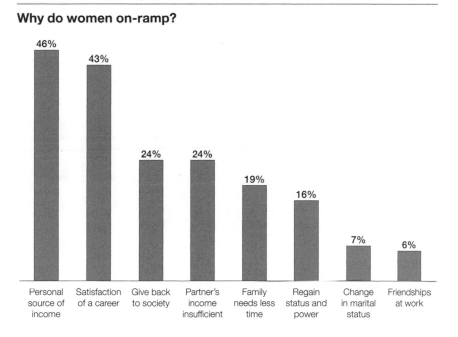

Note: multiple responses allowed.

FIGURE 2-9

Why do women on-ramp

By sector

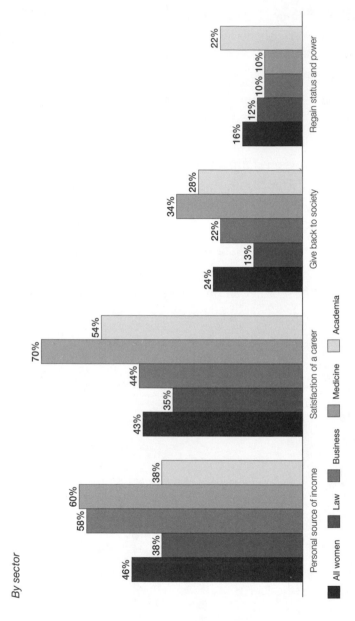

Note: multiple responses allowed.

currently spans thirty-five to forty years. For many off-rampers time out represents a mere blip on the radar screen.

Perhaps the most unexpected reason women give for returning to work centers on altruism. Twenty-four percent of women currently looking for on-ramps are motivated by "a desire to give something back to society" and are seeking jobs that allow them to contribute in some way. In focus groups off-ramped women talked about how their time at home had changed their aspirations. Whether they'd gotten involved in protecting the wetlands, supporting the local library, rebuilding a playground, or being a "big sister" to a disadvantaged child, they all felt newly connected to the importance of what one woman called "the work of care."

LOST ON REENTRY

Though the overwhelming majority of off-ramped women have every intention of returning to the workforce, few understand how difficult doing so will be. While 93 percent of the women surveyed want to rejoin the ranks of the employed, only 74 percent manage to do so. And among these, only 40 percent return to full-time, mainstream jobs. Twenty-four percent end up taking part-time jobs, and another 9 percent become self-employed (see figure 2-10).

The implications are clear: off-ramps may be around every curve in the road, but once a woman has taken one, opportunities to reenter a career are few and far between—and exceedingly difficult to find. Like Judith—whose story was detailed in chapter 1—a great many talented women find the on-ramping struggle a humiliating experience—baffling, unfair, and replete with rejection.

When "Off-Ramps and On-Ramps" appeared in the *Harvard Business Review* in March 2005, it provoked a flood of letters, e-mails, and phone calls. The response was remarkably emotional. Many women saw their own life stories reflected in our data. Many were still smarting from having been cast aside in the wake of an off-ramp, and their pain was

FIGURE 2-10

Employment status of women who succeed in on-ramping

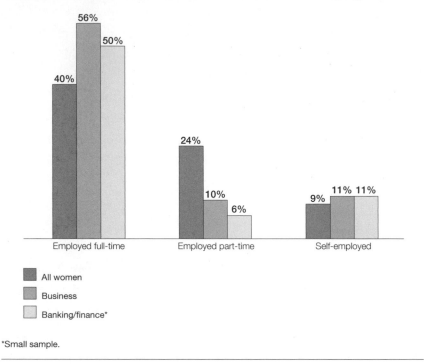

*Small sample.

sharp and raw. Judi Pitsiokos was one of many women who shared her story:

> I am a graduate of a top-ten law school who worked in the securities department of an AMLAW firm for six years before taking an off-ramp. After several years at home raising my children, I tried to gear up and reenter the workforce. Ten years later, I'm still trying to weasel my way back into a decent job. The best I've been able to come up with is working on my own, doing real estate closings, going to landlord-tenant court, and so on. I am bored and angry—with myself and with the law firms who won't even look at my résumé. When I've had heart-to-heart talks with partners at major firms or legal recruiters, they say, "Why would

we hire you when we can get a young kid right out of school?"
(Since I've been out of the mainstream for so long, I am looking
for a job at the bottom rung.) *Why?* I tell them, "Because I'm very
smart, very well educated, have a track record, am done with
child-care responsibilities and ready to work long hours." They
laugh. Literally.

I wonder what is wrong with a society that cuts smart women
adrift when they take time off to raise children. The dollars lost to
the economy must be astronomical.[14]

THE PENALTIES OF TIME OUT

As our data has revealed, women off-ramp for surprisingly short periods
of time—on average, 2.2 years. However, even these relatively short
career interruptions engender heavy financial penalties. Our data shows
that, on average, women lose 18 percent of their earning power when
they take an off-ramp (see figure 2-11). In the banking/finance sector,
penalties are especially draconian. In these fields, women's earning power
dips 28 percent when they take time out. As one might expect, the longer
the period of time that's spent out, the more severe the penalty becomes.
Women lose a staggering 37 percent of their earning power when they
spend three or more years out of the workforce.

Our findings in this area of financial penalties attached to time out
jibe with the scholarly research. Columbia University economist Jane
Waldfogel has analyzed the pattern of female earnings over their life
span. When women enter the workforce in their early and mid-twenties,
they earn nearly as much as men. For a few years, they continue to almost
keep pace with men in terms of wages. At ages twenty-five to twenty-
nine, women earn 87 percent of the male wage. However, when women
hit their prime child-raising years (ages thirty to forty), many off-ramp
for a short period of time—with disastrous consequences on the financial front. Largely because of these career interruptions, by the time they
reach the forty-to-forty-four age group, women earn a mere 71 percent

FIGURE 2-11

The high cost of time out

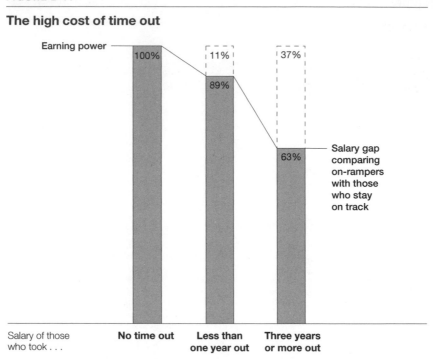

Earning power

| | No time out | Less than one year out | Three years or more out |

100%

11%

89%

37%

63%

Salary gap comparing on-rampers with those who stay on track

Salary of those who took . . .

of the male wage.[15] All of which underscores the importance of producing a continuous, cumulative employment history in the decade of one's
thirties. The words of MIT economist Lester Thurow underscore this
reality: "The 30s are the prime years for establishing a successful career.
These are the years when hard work has the maximum payoff. Women
who leave the job market during those years may find that they never
catch up."[16] One final point on the price attached to time out. Penalties
are not limited to individuals. Companies also must deal with significant
consequences when valued employees off-ramp. The financial costs associated with high rates of turnover are examined in some detail in chapter 4, but one particularly dramatic finding is worth flagging right here:
only 5 percent of highly qualified women attempting to on-ramp want
to go back to the company they once worked for. Indeed, in business,

FIGURE 2-12

Financial penalties

By sector

Earnings differences, comparing on-rampers to those who stayed on track, expressed as a percentage

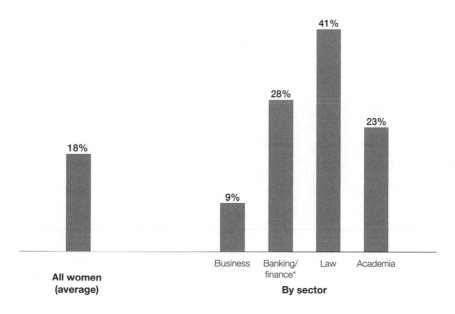

*Small sample.

banking, and finance, none of the women surveyed (0 percent) want to return to their previous employer. In retrospect, the vast majority of off-ramped women feel that they were not supported in those last months or weeks on the job—that their request for a flexible work arrangement or a more meaty assignment was deflected or turned down. Some were made to feel that "they were letting the side down" when they struggled with their decision to quit. The fact that these bad feelings linger should be a wake-up call for companies. If employers expect to tap into this labor pool of women returning after a time out, they need to understand that the "terms of disengagement" matter.

DOWNSIZING AMBITION

It turns out that reduced earning power is not the only penalty attached to taking time out. Women also end up downsizing their ambitions, losing sight of their aspirations, and losing faith in their dreams. One newly on-ramped woman described her changed attitude by saying, "It took me three years to find this much-less-good job, and during that time, I had to accept that I had lost traction in my career. It was a bitter pill. I felt the unfairness of it. I had been out for only twenty months. But it was a fact nonetheless. So I've redefined what I can expect for myself." Another woman, who participated in the same focus group, described her old self—before an off-ramp—as this "soaring, thrusting person." That person doesn't exist anymore. In her words, "reality bites." Off-ramps and on-ramps make the career highway extremely slippery.

Our survey data shows that highly qualified women are significantly less ambitious than their male peers. Almost half of the men (48 percent) surveyed consider themselves very ambitious, as compared with one-third of women (35 percent). In the business sector the gap is even wider—63 percent of men describe themselves as very ambitious, compared with 45 percent of women. However, our data also shows that at young ages, there isn't much of a gap between men and women in terms of ambition. But there is a distinct drop-off in female ambition as women head through their thirties. Young, highly qualified women are more likely than older women to see themselves as extremely or very ambitious (39 percent versus 31 percent). In the business sector, for example, 53 percent of younger women describe themselves as being very ambitious, while only 37 percent of older women are comfortable with this label (see figure 2-13).

In her book *Necessary Dreams*, published in 2004, psychiatrist Anna Fels argued convincingly that ambition stands on two legs—mastery and recognition.[17] To hold on to their dreams women must attain the necessary credentials and experience, but they must also have their achievements and potential recognized in the larger world. The latter is often

FIGURE 2-13

Fall-off in female ambition

Percentage of women describing themselves as "extremely/very ambitious"

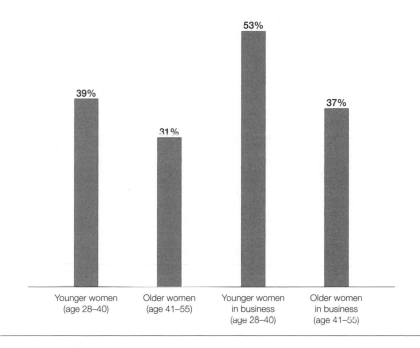

missing in female careers. Particularly in the wake of an off-ramp, employers and bosses tend to be skeptical about a woman's worth. A downsizing cycle emerges: a woman's confidence and ambition stalls; she is perceived as less committed; she no longer gets the good jobs or the plum assignments; and this serves to lower her ambition yet further (see figure 2-14).

Other research in the field reveals complex ways in which ambition is a gendered issue. A 2003 study by the Families and Work Institute (FWI) found that men aspire to higher positions than women—19 percent of male executives would like to have the top job (CEO or managing partner), compared with 9 percent of women.[18] The FWI study also confirmed the fact that women are more likely than men to downsize their

FIGURE 2-14

The downsizing cycle

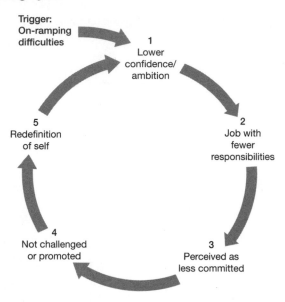

ambition as they move through their thirties—34 percent of women become less ambitious, as compared with 21 percent of men.[19]

Of particular interest is a 2004 study by ISR (International Survey Research), a global HR research and consulting firm, which reveals that men and women are driven by very different factors. When asked what motivates them at work, male executives highlight power and money, while female executives highlight connection and quality. The two top drivers for men are career advancement (20 percent) and financial rewards (10 percent), while the two top drivers for women are relationships at work (14 percent) and delivering a quality product/service to customers/clients (10 percent). In this study, career advancement and financial rewards did not even make it into the top four picks by women.[20] As we will see in chapter 3, our survey data on extreme jobs tends to confirm the fact that men and women respond to different incentives. For example, 41 percent of young men in high-impact jobs see compensation as a top motivator; this compares with 26 percent of young women.

WHAT DO WOMEN REALLY WANT?

The survey data allows us to develop a complex vision of what women actually want. At the top of the wish list are a series of career goals that speak to the quality of the work experience itself.[21] Talented women very much want to associate with people they respect (82 percent); to "be themselves" at work (79 percent); to collaborate with others and work as part of a team (61 percent); and to "give back" to society through the work that they do, both inside their organization and outside in the larger world (see figure 2-15). They also value recognition from their company or organization (51 percent). In general, women tend to emphasize value sets rather than compensation or benefits. Access to flexible work schedules, the only employment benefit to make it onto the wish list of the majority of the women in the survey, is a priority for 64 percent of the

FIGURE 2-15

What do women want? Connection, flexibility, and recognition more important than money

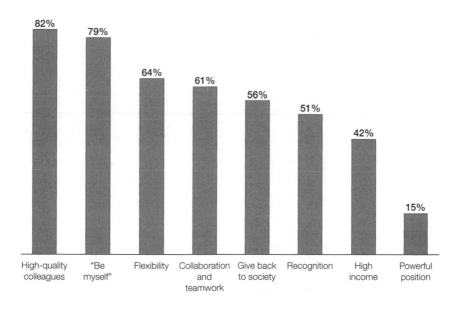

Note: women in the workforce; multiple responses allowed.

women in the survey. Only 42 percent cite a high salary, and just 15 percent cite a powerful position as an important career goal.

Women's priorities thus constitute a sharp departure from the conventional white male model and become yet another powerful reason why success within this model is so elusive for women.

A final word on altruism. As is evident from figure 2-15, a majority of highly qualified women find giving back to society a powerful motivator.

Jennifer Moreland, a senior executive at Johnson & Johnson Healthcare Systems, is a case in point. Moreland, who is of Jamaican descent, had been with her company for almost thirty years when a series of devastating hurricanes struck the Caribbean in August 2004. She had long been thinking of a way she could "give back" to her homeland and the timing seemed right for her to join the relief effort: her only child—a daughter—had been "launched," as she put it; and she was newly able to put family responsibilities on the back burner. But when she went to management to tell them that she wanted to be part of the recovery effort she felt it was a huge risk: she imagined that she might have to leave her job, or, at best, take an unpaid leave of absence. Within Johnson & Johnson, as part of shared responsibility for career development each employee works with management to assess such opportunities. For volunteer opportunities management also considers the risk to the safety of each employee. As it turned out, her timing was perfect: Johnson & Johnson had just created a hurricane fund and Moreland's boss saw a pivotal role for her. So Moreland spent six months based in Jamaica dispensing grants in the Caribbean region and otherwise driving the relief effort. She described it as "one of the most fulfilling experiences of my life—and one which cemented my loyalty to this company." Moreland's biggest surprise was that "far from forcing me out, playing a role in the relief effort actually gave my career new traction at Johnson & Johnson—I will always be grateful."[22]

Upon returning, she was invited to make a presentation to senior management at company headquarters, which afforded great visibility for her but also great visibility for her "cause." It was also good for the company. Moreland had, after all, been able to align her desire to "do good" with her company's philanthropic interests in the Caribbean. The initiative she helped drive both burnished the company's image in the region and won new loyalty among local employees and customers. In sum, it was a huge win-win. In February 2006, Moreland received an award from her affinity group at Johnson & Johnson. In her words, "It was in recognition for what I did—and what the corporation did."

In focus groups women talked eloquently about the importance of giving back—to various communities. For some, their interest lay in their corporation or in their professional associations. Heading up a women's network, acting as a mentor to young women, getting involved with "girl" power, and nurturing young talent were typical pursuits. For others, their passions lay in the wider community—fund-raising for a charter school, volunteering in a meals-on-wheels program for elderly shut-ins, tutoring in the inner city. Focus group participants talked wistfully about how neat it would be if employers were to recognize this philanthropic work.

Stephanie is a young highflier with a bright future at her consumer products firm. A recently promoted brand manager, she could be contributing even more, however, if she felt comfortable sharing more of who she is with her colleagues. What does Stephanie keep to herself? The fact that she runs an award-winning Girl Scout troop in a local homeless shelter. She has been doing this for years, bringing warmth and strength to girls from destitute families. "These kids are not going to Harvard; they don't have a place to live; they don't know how many times they're going to eat today; and they need to take care of siblings not much younger than they are," she explains. But she's teaching these girls real skills that may help them build better futures.

In the process of organizing the troop Stephanie is serving as an unofficial goodwill ambassador for her firm. But her work with the troop demands that she leave work at 5:30 p.m. a few times a month. This doesn't bother her, but it does seem to bother her boss, despite the fact that she arrives at 7:00 a.m. on those days. Stephanie is acutely concerned about being thought of as less than fully committed to her job. So she refrains from talking about her Girl Scout program at work—even though the initiative earned her a Future Leaders Today award and a ceremony at the White House.[23]

In the few instances where bosses are supportive and celebratory of altruistic or philanthropic activity (such as in Moreland's experience at Johnson & Johnson), the dividend to the company in terms of increased loyalty and engagement is big. Talented women are hugely appreciative of support on this front.

In terms of the big picture, what is the significance of the data presented thus far? Thirty-five years after the women's revolution transformed female opportunities women's work lives remain very different from men's. Grouping together women who take off-ramps with those who take scenic routes, we find that a majority have nonlinear careers. A great many women just need to step out or step to the side for a period of time. Looking back at their work lives almost 60 percent of the highly qualified women in this survey describe their careers as nonlinear: they had not been able to "follow the arc" of a traditionally successful career in their sector.[24] An off-ramp or a scenic route had knocked them off course.

Obviously, what all this amounts to is that large numbers of talented women fail to fit the conventional career model. Emulating that male competitive model is simply a huge stretch for a great many women. Some obviously do manage to do it. Among them are women who sacrifice family life—childlessness is a problematic issue for high-level corporate women—and at least some superwomen who somehow or other "do it all."[25] But women who are successful within the confines of the male career model are a minority, and this book is not about them. It is about the other 60 percent, the ones who struggle with off-ramps and on-ramps and have a difficult time claiming or sustaining ambition.

For three and a half decades policy wonks and business leaders have waited for women to get with the program. The challenge was thought to be about providing access and opportunity and then allowing enough time to go by so that the pipeline could fill. The reasoning was simple: if you created a truly level playing field so that men and women had equal access to employment opportunities, then, over time, as successive cohorts of well-qualified female professionals filled the pipeline, women would eventually be fairly represented at the top. As we've already seen, this is not happening. Over the years, there has been so much leakage from the pipeline that progress has effectively stalled. While the proportion of partners at law firms who are women has climbed slightly over the last five years, the number of women CEOs at *Fortune* 500 companies has fallen slightly over the same time period. If progress moves along at this lugubrious pace it will be a hundred years before we have significant numbers of women in top jobs.

My advice—to policy wonks and business leaders alike—is to quit waiting. The pipeline as currently constructed won't work, because it requires shoehorning women into the male competitive model—and most of them just don't fit. What we need now is the development of second-generation policies that provide alternative pathways for women with nonlinear work lives. As we will see from the next chapter, this challenge has become particularly urgent with the rise of extreme jobs. The goalposts, it seems, are shifting in ways that threaten women's progress in heretofore unimagined ways.

3

Extreme Jobs, Extreme Demands

The setting was tranquil enough: an elegant London conference room with celadon carpets, a ming tree, and a misty, romantic view of the River Thames. In sharp contrast, the lives on display at this focus group were hardly serene—or bucolic. Nine corporate executives (seven men, two women) in the thirty-five- to forty-five-year-old age range were present, all clearly "high potential," all wrestling with oversized jobs and gargantuan expectations.[1]

Take Ravi:

> I work over a range of time zones, but my main responsibilities are in London and Boston. My "team" is located in both places. That does a number on my evenings. It's not unusual for it to be midnight and I'm just starting a conference call with my U.S.-based colleagues.
>
> These last six months, with China coming on stream, my days are starting earlier and ending later. I find myself fielding e-mails at 5:30 and 6:00 in the morning. The last thing my wife needs to deal with is me on my BlackBerry before breakfast when I didn't

show up until 11:00 the night before. It's an issue between us. I'm now unavailable at both ends of the day.

Then there's Shane:

At least you're doing something productive when you're talking to your guys in Boston or China. What sends me nuts here at corporate is the tone at the top. It's all about jumping through hoops. Here's what my senior manager likes to do: late on a Friday—it could be 9:00 p.m. or 11:00 p.m., depending on where he is in the world—he sends a two- or three-paragraph e-mail asking me to work on some project. To be honest, these e-mails don't make a lot of sense. They're generally full of half-formed ideas and contradictory instructions. But one message is clear. I'm supposed to spend a good chunk of the weekend doing my darnedest to figure out what he wants or needs. And it's not just me who gets to spend my weekend this way, it's the support staff too.

So what happens Monday morning? I walk in with all kinds of feedback (facts, figures, analysis, opinion, you name it), and nine times out of ten it's all irrelevant. I failed to get the assignment quite right.

Does it matter? Not much. It turns out that this exercise is not about what it purports to be about. It's not about substance, it's a test. It's his way of measuring commitment—seeing how high I will jump.

Gwen chimes in:

You guys seem to have complicated challenges. For me, it all comes down to one question—can I grab the 6:30 p.m. to 8:30 p.m. time slot for my kids? I don't mind going back to work from 9:00 p.m. to 11:00 p.m., but if I can get that earlier window on a regular basis, I'm in good shape. I have three children, and it's hugely important to me that I'm home a few evenings a week in time to put them to bed. I travel one night a week, on average. I head up a supply chain for the company, and two days a week I have to be somewhere in Europe. The other evenings are precious and I try to protect them. This week I'm beside myself. It's only Thursday and already two evenings have been shot by business dinners. With our increased global reach, there always seems to be an important customer in town needing to be wined and dined, needing attention.

Ravi's addendum:

I just want to set the record straight in one regard. I'm obviously dealing with a lot of pressure—and I know I sound stressed out—but I love this job. Riding this wave of expansion in Asia— being part of the reason a country "takes off"—is enormously exciting. Most days, I feel it's a privilege to do what I do. Add in the fact I'm paid a ton of money to do this job—and you've got a pretty alluring package.

Those are just three voices from one of our many focus groups, but enough to afford a glimpse into the escalating tensions, pressures, and rewards of professional life these days. Driven by globalization and facilitated by savvy—and continually improving—communication technology, work pressures are ratcheting up, and jobs, particularly high-level, well-paying jobs, are becoming more and more extreme. As noted by leadership guru Rosabeth Moss Kanter, corporations are increasingly "greedy" institutions and workaholism has become pervasive.[2]

In the fall of 2005, the Hidden Brain Drain Task Force identified the growth of extreme jobs as a new and urgent challenge facing talented women. American Express, BP, ProLogis, and UBS came on board to fund a research project on this topic, and over a nine-month period (October 2005–June 2006), the task force fielded two surveys and conducted a series of focus groups to investigate the impact of the emerging extreme work model on women's advancement. What was the trend we suspected we'd find? As work hours and performance pressures ratchet up, women (particularly those with significant caregiving responsibilities) are being left behind in new ways. If an older generation of working mothers had diffi-culty coping with fifty-hour workweeks, surely their younger peers are having an even more difficult time managing sixty-plus-hour workweeks along with a slew of additional performance pressures.

Before we look at our findings though, it's important to clarify the components of an extreme job.

OUTSIZE DEMANDS, OUTSIZE RESPONSIBILITIES

I coined the term *extreme job* four years ago after an interview with a sen-ior banker at a London-based investment bank. Marilyn was enthralled by extreme sports—skydiving, snowboarding, triathlon, bungee jumping, surfing, mountaineering, and the like—anything that provided a rush of adrenalin and a frisson of danger. She urged me to read Jon Krakauer's *Into Thin Air* (a book that describes the doomed efforts of a group of amateur mountain climbers who attempted to scale Mount Everest in 1996) to gain a better understanding of why people push themselves to the limits of their physical endurance. Marilyn identified with extreme sports—she felt they spoke to her life as an investment banker. In fact, she admitted, her job and her avocation shared some of the same characteristics. First there were the extraordinary time demands and performance stressors. Seventy-hour workweeks, grueling travel requirements, and relentless bottom-line pres-sures meant that she was constantly being pushed to the limits of her capacity—both physically and intellectually. Second was the allure of her job. Much like extreme sports, investment banking was exhilarating and seductive, Marilyn told me. "It gives me this adrenalin rush. Like a drug, it's irresistible and addictive."[3]

As Marilyn made clear, an extreme job is characterized by a set of out-size demands. Individuals who hold extreme jobs expend huge amounts of talent, time, energy, skill, and commitment on their jobs. These jobs are as noteworthy for their challenge and intensity as they are for sheer hours spent at work. To get at the complexity of extreme jobs we identified ten key characteristics—or performance pressures—in our early focus group research. These characteristics were then layered on top of workweek and income data. Respondents are considered to have extreme jobs if they are well paid, work sixty hours or more per week, *and* have *at least* five of the following extreme job characteristics:

- Unpredictable flow of work

- Fast-paced work under tight deadlines

- Inordinate scope of responsibility that amounts to more than one job

- Work-related events outside regular work hours

- Availability to clients 24/7

- Responsibility for profit and loss

- Responsibility for mentoring and recruiting

- Large amount of travel

- Large number of direct reports

- Physical presence at workplace at least ten hours a day

With this complex definition our data tells us that a great many high-level, high-impact jobs these days are "extreme."[4] In our national data survey we find that fully 21 percent of high-echelon workers have extreme jobs. In our global companies survey this figure rises to 45 percent (see figure 3-1). These jobs are no longer limited to Wall Street and the City. Extreme jobs are spreading and are now all over the economy, in large manufacturing companies as well as in medicine and the law; in consulting, accounting, and the media as well as in financial services. They are prevalent on a global scale and are held by fifty-five-year-olds as well as thirty-five-year olds. Extreme jobs are not a young person's game or a short-term sprint anymore. Rather, they characterize the beginning, middle, and tail end of many careers.[5]

FIGURE 3-1

Who has an extreme job?

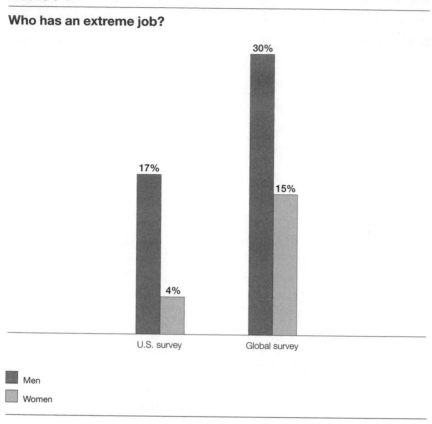

Men

Women

For our analysis one fact is particularly important: extreme workers are predominantly male. Rather few highly qualified women hold extreme jobs. Only 4 percent of women in our national sample of high-level, high-earning workers hold extreme jobs—a figure that rises to 15 percent in our global companies survey. Within the universe of those that hold extreme jobs, 20 percent are women.

What are the hot-button issues? Which characteristics of extreme jobs generate the most stress and strain for high-echelon workers? And why are these stressors "gendered"—why do they have a differential impact and tend to deal out women? In focus groups and interviews, extreme workers talked graphically about the gargantuan demands of work these days. In particular, they emphasized the long workweeks, the always-on 24/7 culture, and the intense performance pressures.

EXTENDED WORKWEEKS

First, there are the time pressures of extreme jobs. According to our data 56 percent of extreme workers are on the job 70 hours a week or more, 25 percent are on the job more than 80 hours a week and 9 percent are on the job a mind-numbing 100-plus hours a week. Fully 42 percent of people with extreme jobs say they are working an average of 16.6 hours more than five years ago—a stunning finding.

What these hours mean in terms of overload is sobering. Add in a modest 1-hour commute, and a 70-hour workweek translates into leaving the house at 7:00 a.m. and getting home at 8:00 p.m. seven days a week. Such a schedule leaves little time—and little energy—for anything else.[6] Sudhir, twenty-three, works as a financial analyst at a major commercial bank in New York. He refers to summer—when he works 90 hours a week, including weekends—as his "light" season. The rest of the year he works upward of 120 hours per week—leaving only 48 hours for sleeping, eating, entertaining, and (he smiles) bathing. Sudhir stays late at the office even when he has nothing specific to do. The face-time culture is one of the hazards of his job—but in Sudhir's eyes, well worth it: this twenty-three-year-old working his first job takes home $120,000 a year and is among the top 6 percent of earners in America.[7]

The impact of long workweeks is exacerbated by a paucity of vacation time. Forty-two percent of those with extreme jobs take ten or fewer vacation days per year. And 55 percent regularly cancel vacations because of work pressure.

In one focus group that took place at a Los Angeles–based media company, a forty-eight-year-old executive talked about an amazing recent experience he'd had. For the first time in his fourteen-year career, he'd taken two consecutive weeks of vacation. "It was a revelation," he said. "I had no idea I even had it in me to enter into this other zone where I was able to focus on my nine-year-old son, and I mean *really* focus. By the second week I was listening to meandering stories of a tiff he'd had with a best friend and his description of what had happened in the last episode of his favorite TV show, without urging him to get to the point or wrap it up. And we spent hours playing Ping-Pong—a game he loves but I generally have no patience for." The other focus group participants listened intently, clearly trying to wrap their minds around what a two-week vacation would feel like. The fact is, no one else in the room had ever taken that much time off—at least not in one chunk.[8]

Rather than being part of a three-to-five-year sprint, long workweeks now seem to persist over the arc of an individual career. It used to be that young professionals would prove themselves by working long hours, but once they had made the cut and moved up the ranks they would be rewarded with more manageable schedules and gentler workdays. But our data shows that long workweeks no longer recede with age: professionals between the ages of thirty-five and forty-five are working longer hours than professionals age twenty-five to thirty-four.

Betty, a fifth-year, newly married associate at a blue-chip law firm, is dismayed by what she sees ahead of her: partners working insanely long hours. Betty regularly bills seventy hours a week—which means she actually puts in closer to eighty to eighty-five hours. Her arduous schedule is becoming problematic—not only because she is thinking of having children but because she sees no prospect of relief. "You work so hard for the brass ring," she says, explaining what really bothers her, "but getting the brass ring just means you have to work harder. The junior partners at our firm work more hours than the associates. You can no longer look forward to easing up as you go up."[9]

Long workweeks—and little vacation—are no longer about breaking into the business; they *are* the business.

ALWAYS CONNECTED

Overload has, of course, been facilitated by modern communication technology and an always-on 24/7 business culture. The advent of the Internet and its associated hardware (BlackBerrys, Treos, cell phones) has lengthened the working day and blurred the lines between time on the job and off. These "weapons of mass communication" have shifted expectations and behavior. Response time has been reduced from days or weeks to minutes, allowing a 24/7 flow of decision making across sectors, functions, and time zones. We see the result all around us: professionals glued to their cell phones or BlackBerrys, no matter the day, time, location, or occasion.[10] In focus groups men and women told anecdotes about how they scrambled to keep up. They pull all-nighters or defy jet-lag to attend a meeting in Singapore and immediately return to make a presentation in New York, or they wake up in the middle of the night to participate in global conference calls.[11]

In our survey 67 percent of people with extreme jobs say that being available for clients all day, every day—in other words, around the clock—is a critical part of being successful at their job.[12] Sudhir describes the pressures to stay connected:

> Senior people in my industry are very cutthroat and have this belief that everything must be done immediately—at that very instant—even when you're in a meeting; waiting an hour to respond to an e-mail is just not acceptable. Well, I believe that at the end of the day, this is a financial advisory service. I'm not an ER doctor. Advice can wait. But the senior guys don't think that way, and in order to get the performance review—and the great bonus—you have to shift your mind-set and think like them. Being on call, every minute, 24/7, is part of the deal. Working weekends is part of the deal. Whatever the client needs or wants is the culture here.

UNPREDICTABLE, ESCALATING PRESSURES

One of the most demanding elements of the always-on 24/7 culture is managing an unpredictable flow of work. In focus groups, executives talked about being constantly sideswiped by deadlines they had not predicted or planned for. One Dallas-based accountant described how, over the previous weekend, her boss had tracked her down at a five-year-old's birthday party and insisted she join a ninety-minute conference call because something had blown up with a client. A colleague at the same focus group immediately chimed in, explaining how he'd lost all credibility with his wheelchair-bound, elderly father because he'd canceled so many promised weekend visits recently because of work demands.

Finally, extreme jobs often entail intense—and escalating—performance pressures. Again, global competition and modern communication technology are largely, though not solely, to blame. These drivers have contributed to and facilitated a shrinking and flattening of hierarchy—companies and organizations are leaner, and responsibilities are spread across fewer shoulders. Today's executives often find themselves with dramatically increased and far-flung responsibilities—and very little in the way of support staff to help grease the wheels.

Eighty-two percent of extreme professionals say they must work at a fast pace under tight deadlines simply to do their job. And 66 percent say they don't have sufficient staffing to manage their work; 71 percent have no dedicated administrative assistant—37 percent don't even have a shared assistant. All of this contributes to a workload that can spiral out of control—professionals find they ride a razor's edge that veers between exhilaration and exhaustion.

Alex is a federal prosecutor focusing on securities fraud. He works long hours, typically arrives home at 11:00 p.m., and routinely skips meals. Instead of dinner, he will have a power bar at his desk—or a peanut butter and jelly sandwich when he gets home late at night. He hardly ever makes it home before his two young children are in bed, although he does make a point of taking his oldest to preschool in the morning. He laments that he has made his kids more of a priority than his wife—their time together as a couple is really squeezed—and the occasional "date" seems difficult to manage. On a recent outing with his wife—to a jazz club—Alex found himself falling asleep after just one drink. It's not hard to imagine why: he averages a seventy-five-hour workweek—but when he's on trial or preparing for trial the average can rise to ninety-five hours. "I'm just exhausted a lot of the time," Alex says.[13]

Nevertheless, he derives enormous satisfaction from his work. A Princeton graduate who majored in urban policy at the Woodrow Wilson School of Public and International Affairs, he has always yearned to give back to the city in which he grew up. He believes his work as a federal prosecutor is enormously worthwhile and he is honored to serve the public in that role. He does, after all, have a hand in enforcing important laws, seeing that justice is served, and helping protect shareholders and employees.

But there's one real problem with Alex's great job—its size, he says "makes it undoable. It sometimes seems like we're painfully understaffed," Alex explains. "We're a government agency, and there are severe budget constraints. I always seem to be juggling too many really important cases, asking for an extension here, an adjournment there—and working evenings and weekends. This 'forever playing catch-up' is not my preferred way of working but it's the only way to keep my head above water in this job. Over the last five years I've built some great relationships with our FBI agents who often bring me compelling cases—but I can only handle a small proportion of them. It's disappointing and frustrating, but I just can't drive myself any harder."

BADGE OF HONOR

Given the increasingly extreme—and brutal—work model that our data describes, one might imagine that we would have uncovered a great many bitter or burned-out or dissatisfied professionals. Quite the opposite is true. The extreme work model is enormously alluring. Far from resenting the

grind, a great many extreme workers adore their jobs. They love the intellectual challenge and the thrill of achieving something big. And they are
turned on by their oversize compensation packages, their brilliant colleagues, and the recognition and respect these jobs engender. If extreme
jobs have outsize demands they also have outsize rewards. Far from seeing
themselves as workaholic drones extreme workers wear their commitments
like a badge of honor. There is very little sense of victimization. Two-thirds
say that the pressure and the pace are "self-inflicted"—a function of a type
A personality. All in all 66 percent of extreme professionals say they love
their jobs—and this figure rises to 76 percent in the global companies survey. Nearly 60 percent call their jobs very satisfying—ranking them as 8 or
higher on a satisfaction scale of 1 to 10, with 10 being extremely satisfying.
Money is an important motivator—especially for men; compensation
ranks third for men and fifth for women (see figure 3-2). Only 28 percent

FIGURE 3-2

Why extreme workers love their jobs

U.S. survey

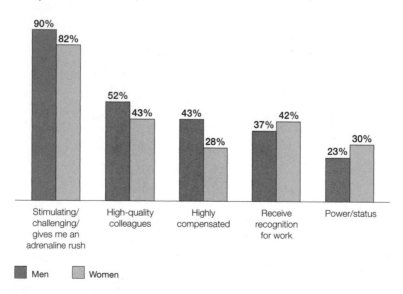

Men   Women

Note: multiple responses allowed.

of women holding extreme jobs see compensation as a prime motivator, compared with 43 percent of men. For women four other factors weigh more heavily: stimulation, high-quality colleagues, recognition, and status.

As can be seen from figure 3-3, women are somewhat less likely than men to be completely in love with their extreme jobs. This owes something to the fact that women get fewer payoffs than men from the extreme work model.

GOOD FOR MEN, LESS SO FOR WOMEN

A man in an extreme job is on track to win the triple crown. As psychiatrist Anna Fels points out in her book *Necessary Dreams*, success at work

FIGURE 3-3

Men and women love their extreme jobs

U.S. survey

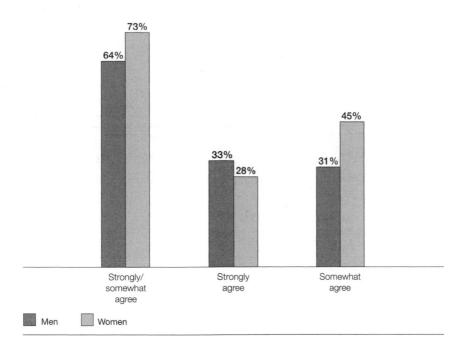

	Men	Women

for men often translates into success in the marriage market and success on the family front. For the male of the species these three things are aligned.[14] A man with an extreme job—and an eye-catching compensation package—is seen as extremely eligible. Universally regarded as good husband and father material, he very often gets the girl and the kids. These three dimensions of success are not nearly as aligned for women. Instead, for women, success in an extreme job might well threaten potential mates and get in the way of marriage. These hazards were underscored in a much-talked-about August 2006 opinion piece by Mike Noer in *Forbes* magazine, which argued that men should think twice before marrying a high-earning career woman because "she is more likely to grow dissatisfied" with her man.[15] It seems as though Noer himself is threatened by successful women!

In a similar vein, success in an extreme job may well preempt children for women. A sixty-plus-hour workweek and a variety of other performance pressures are tough things to combine with motherhood in a world where women continue to be the primary caregivers. It's interesting to note that in the global companies survey 20 percent of women who hold extreme jobs have househusbands. Like Carly Fiorina (whose husband took early retirement), they marry men who are prepared to offer real support at home.

Dessa Bokides, the CFO of ProLogis, has four almost teenage sons—and a stay-at-home husband, Will. He left his career ten years ago to take primary responsibility for their home and children. At the time Bokides had a demanding career on Wall Street and the family was stretched thin. Bokides remembers the moment well: "I had this enormous feeling of relief when Will decided to stay home. Finally I could count on my children being taken care of—not just in terms of their physical care but also in terms of their values and behavior. Having Will at home made it possible for me to do my job."[16]

Bokides's situation is unusual. The survey data shows that men in extreme jobs are much more likely than women in extreme jobs to have the support of an at-home spouse (25 percent versus 12 percent). It's also true that older men are more likely than younger men to have this kind of support (28 percent versus 21 percent).

TOLL ON PERSONAL LIVES

Regardless of gender extreme jobs take a heavy toll on personal lives. Our data shows that the extreme work model is wreaking havoc in private lives—and undermining health and well-being. Much of this fallout has particular significance for women.

Housework and home care seem to be the first things to go. Seventy-seven percent of women and 66 percent of men feel they can't maintain their homes (see figure 3-4). One executive who participated in a London-based focus group told us that he had lived in his South Kensington flat for two years but still had no real furniture. A mattress and a sleeping bag were the sum total of his furnishings. His schedule was such that he hadn't been able to make a commitment to be home to take a delivery.

Health comes next. More than two-thirds of professionals we surveyed don't get enough sleep, half don't get enough exercise, and a significant number overeat, consume too much alcohol, or rely on medications to relieve insomnia or anxiety (see figure 3-5).[17] The deficit on the exercise front seems to be most acute for women. In focus groups women with extreme jobs—to a much greater extent than their male counterparts—were conscious of the toll these jobs were taking on their bodies.

At one focus group that took place on Wall Street, senior women from the financial sector shared their concerns over weight gain, sleep deficits, and infertility. One thirty-four-year-old investment banker talked about her brutal travel schedule and how she felt it was impacting her fertility. "I'm pretty much commuting to London these days," she told me. "Sometimes when I fly overnight, deal with back-to-back meetings, then fly home the same day, I'm so deeply exhausted, I wonder what I am doing to myself. My blood pressure's up and my menstrual cycle is out of whack. Am I depleting my egg supply? This really worries me. I tell you, I'd jump ship for any employer who offered to freeze my eggs."[18]

FIGURE 3-4

Fallout on home and intimate life

U.S. survey

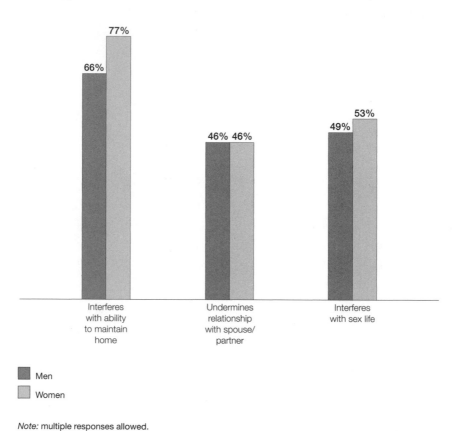

Men

Women

Note: multiple responses allowed.

Moms with extreme jobs tend to do better than dads—in terms of coming through for their children. Women with extreme work schedules really fight to find time for their kids, prioritizing them over exercise, for example.[19] Men do less well on this front—and pay a price they might not immediately appreciate.

At a focus group at a media company in Los Angeles, John, a forty-five-year-old father of two teenagers, decided to hand out some advice. "My biggest regret is that for years I've missed dinner with my kids," he said,

FIGURE 3-5

Fallout on health

U.S. survey

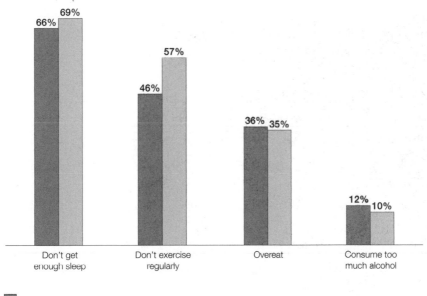

Men

Women

Note: multiple responses allowed.

looking around at ten colleagues, some of whom were younger men. "If I'm honest, for at least ten, fifteen years, I've gotten home in time for dinner barely once a month. It's only now, when my kids are too old to want it, that I realize what I've missed." The room was silent, and John let out an embarrassed laugh. The emotion was a little raw for a noontime meeting. "So listen up," he finally said. "Those of you with young kids need to figure out your priorities—now. Thirteen-year-olds, even when they're good kids, don't choose to hang around their parents that much."[20]

Spouses and partners also suffer from this work model. Extreme workers dramatically underinvest in intimate relationships. Some of the data is quite startling. For example, at the end of a twelve-plus-hour working day, nearly half (45 percent) of all extreme workers in our global companies survey are too tired to say anything at all to their spouse or partner—they are literally "rendered speechless." Intimate life is similarly blindsided. Thirty-four percent of extreme workers in our global companies survey are too tired to have sex on a regular basis. Fully half say that their job interferes with a satisfying sex life—and this rises to 55 percent in our global survey. Focus group conversations were sprinkled with half-joking references to four people in bed these days: oneself, one's partner, and two BlackBerrys. In the words of one recently divorced thirty-two-year-old: "Before we went to bed my ex would put his BlackBerry on vibrate and hide it under the pillow. It used to go off every half hour or so. I felt he was more turned on by his BlackBerry than by me."[21]

In her book *The Time Bind*, sociology professor Arlie Hochschild gets inside the skin of some dual-career couples and describes how home life can become seriously depleted when both husbands and wives work at long-hour jobs.[22] She also shows how the situation is cumulative—becoming ever more exaggerated over time. As households and families are starved of time they become progressively less appealing, and both men and women begin to avoid going home. It's easy to see how returning to a house or an apartment with an empty refrigerator and a neglected teenager might be an unappealing prospect at the end of a long working day. So why not look in on that networking event or put that presentation through one more draft instead? Hochschild shows that for many professionals "home" and "work" have reversed roles: home is where you expect to find stress—and guilt; while work has become the "haven in a heartless world"—the place where you get strokes and respect, a place where success is more predictable.

Singles who work extreme jobs don't necessarily have it any easier. In focus groups women voiced their frustration with dating—given the constraints of their jobs making any kind of social arrangement was well nigh impossible. The beginning stages of a relationship, when you need to pay attention, need to come through, were seen as particularly difficult. Sharon, a thirty-four-year-old investment banker with an eighty-hour workweek and a bunch of exceedingly demanding clients told of her most recent disaster:

> Last night I had a first date with a guy I was really interested in. I was held up by a conference call that dragged on for three hours. So my "date" drove around the block for an hour. Then he parked in a lot, waited another hour, and tried again. At 9:30 p.m. he gave up—just went to eat dinner by himself. I doubt I'll hear from him again. One thing I've started doing is arranging dinners with more than one person. Then if I can't show no one is left in the lurch. [Sharon laughed ruefully.] But this doesn't solve my dating problem—the thing is, you can't have someone dating for you . . . if I could have some kind of backup out there it would be great.[23]

IS THE EXTREME WORK MODEL SUSTAINABLE?

So, are we heading for a cliff? The data is sobering. Both men and women find it difficult to stay with their extreme jobs; 48 percent of men and 57 percent of women don't want to continue working at this pace and with this intensity for more than a year (see figure 3-6). And only 24 percent (27 percent of men, 13 percent of women) expect to be working at this pace in five years. In our global companies survey these figures rise appreciably. In this data set fully 80 percent of women in extreme jobs don't want to work that hard for more than year.

Sustainability is perhaps the key challenge in this world of extreme jobs. In focus groups extreme workers talked about feeling as if they were teetering on the edge. On the one hand they continued to be exhilarated by the tremendous challenges of their jobs. On the other hand they were seriously exhausted and increasingly aware of negative spillover in their private lives. They talked about how they couldn't keep up the pace much longer; of how they had one foot out the door. But while men threaten to leave (yet often stay put), women actually do quit.

FIGURE 3-6

Flight risk and sustainability

Extreme workers planning to work at this pace for one year or less

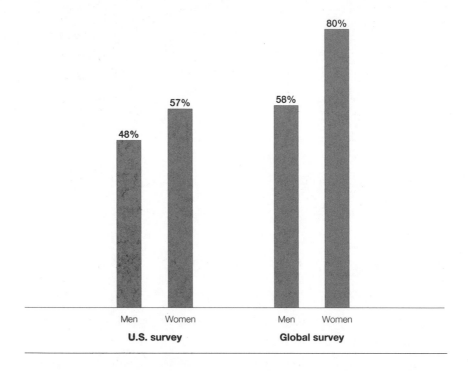

In explaining why women are willing to walk out on their extreme jobs two factors are particularly important. To begin with, women want relief from their extreme jobs more urgently than men (as mentioned earlier, 57 percent of women versus 48 percent of men don't want to work this hard for more than twelve months). This desire to opt out (or ramp down) is often related to what is going on with their children. More so than men women are closely tuned in to—and often deeply pained by—negative fallout on their children. The data shows that a large percentage of women connect their extreme job to a range of troubling problems they face with their children. Whether a child is eating too much junk food or under-achieving at school, many working moms with extreme jobs feel directly responsible. The data in figure 3-7 offers up a veritable "portrait of guilt."

FIGURE 3-7

Portrait of guilt

Percentage of extreme workers believing their jobs impact children

Global survey

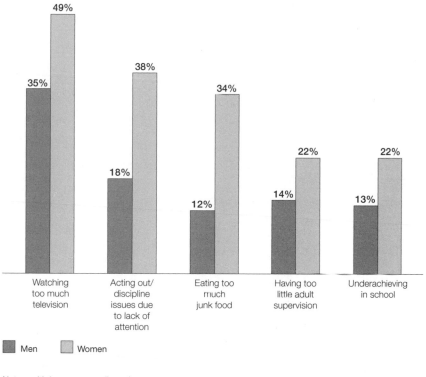

Men   Women

Note: multiple responses allowed.

Maternal anxiety begins to explain why high-powered women are more likely to quit their extreme jobs than are high-powered men.

Women also have more choices than men—a sizable number continue to have options on the work-life front. Data from the national survey tells us that 24 percent of women in extreme jobs have husbands earning more than them, while only 2 percent of men in extreme jobs have wives who outearn them. Quitting an extreme job is easier—and a whole lot less risky—when you have a partner who earns more than you do.

The data also tells us that Gen X and Gen Y "want out" more than baby boomers. In the twenty-five- to thirty-four-year-old age group more than a third (36 percent) of extreme workers say they are likely to quit their job over the next two years. In the forty-five-to-sixty age group this figure drops to 19 percent.

Does all this mean that women are being left behind in new ways?

Our data has already confirmed that extreme workers are predominantly male. The data displayed in quadrant charts A and B (see figures 3-8 and 3-9) show that women are reluctant to take on the long workweeks associated with extreme jobs—only 6 percent of women in our national sample hold jobs with sixty-plus-hour workweeks compared with 29 percent of men. In our global companies survey 18 percent of women hold

FIGURE 3-8

Quadrant chart A: more hours, fewer women

U.S. survey

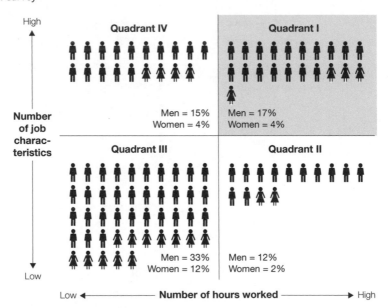

Each figure represents 1% of the total population of high earners.
High number of hours = 60+/week
High number of job characteristics = 5+
Quadrant I represents extreme jobholders.

jobs with sixty-plus-hour workweeks, compared with 36 percent of men. Women are particularly reluctant to take on long-hour jobs if they do not also carry significant responsibilities. Quadrant II in charts A and B are the least favored quadrants for women to be in—only 2 percent of women in our national sample and 3 percent of women in our global companies sample elect jobs that have sixty-plus-hour workweeks but little in the way of other extreme job characteristics (fast pace, tight deadlines, 24/7 client demands, etc.). Men are somewhat more tolerant of long hours/little responsibility jobs. Perhaps women are more discriminating—less tolerant of low-impact work—and more likely to walk away from jobs that involve unproductive face time, because they are more aware of the "opportunity costs" involved in being at work in the first

FIGURE 3-9

Quadrant chart B: more hours, fewer women

Global survey

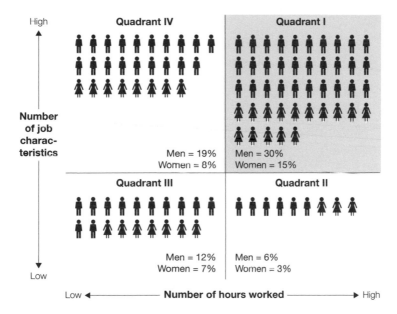

Each figure represents 1% of the total population of high earners.
High number of hours = 60+/week
High number of job characteristics = 5+
Quadrant I represents extreme jobholders.

place. Remember our poignant portrait of guilt? Women who trace a direct link between their extreme job and their child underachieving at school may well have a high bar when it comes to assessing the value of their work.

In a focus group held at Canary Wharf in London a woman lawyer put it succinctly:

> When I walk out the door in the morning leaving my two-year-old with the nanny, there's usually a bit of a scene. Tommy clings, pouts, and whips up the guilt. Now, I know it's not serious—most of the time he likes his nanny. But it sure makes me think about why I go to work—and why I put in a ten-hour day. It's as though every day I make the following calculation: do the satisfactions I derive from my job (efficacy, recognition—a sense of stretching my mind) justify leaving Tommy? Some days it's close run. One thing I do know. It couldn't be just the money. I need a whole lot of things to be happening for me at work.[24]

The data generated by our global companies survey contains some rich additional insights on women in extreme jobs. For starters, women seem to be better represented in extreme jobs in large global companies than they are across a range of sectors and occupations in our national sample (32 percent versus 20 percent). Women are also better represented in extreme jobs in North America than they are in Europe and Asia (40 percent versus 23 percent)

REFORMULATING EXTREME JOB PARAMETERS

Heidi Yang, a Hong Kong investment banker in her mid-thirties, illustrates the "edge" some global companies are developing as an employer of choice for young talented women.

Yang is definitely considered a high-potential manager, and she's on the fast track. During her three and a half years in the investment division of

UBS in Hong Kong she's been promoted twice and now runs a team of twenty-five. When I first interviewed Yang in November 2005 she was pregnant with her first child and trying to figure out how to cope with the immediate future. She described her firm's parenting leave policy as impressive: she was eligible for fifteen weeks of paid leave in all—which is five weeks more than the Hong Kong statutory ten-week paid maternity leave. She could also add onto the leave any vacation days she had accumulated. In Yang's view, UBS had every reason to be proud of this policy—it was as generous as any "on the street." Yang also pointed to two other policies at UBS that had caught her eye: a flexible work option that targets parents, and a short-term, global assignments program that is ideal for working moms. She felt both programs would be useful to her down the road.

Yang's main worry was that these policies weren't "for real." In her words: "I'm fearful that if I take a long maternity leave I won't be taken seriously ever again. Will taking these options undermine my career? Will they deal me out of the next promotion?"[25]

A lot was riding on Yang's ability to balance her extreme job with motherhood from her employer's point of view as well as her own. UBS—along with most other firms in the financial sector—is attempting to do a much better job of retaining female talent. Yang therefore saw herself as "this huge role model. I sometimes feel that the retention of junior female talent rests on my shoulders."

The good news is that Yang's fears were not realized. In a follow-up interview in July 2006 Yang told of taking seventeen weeks of maternity leave, which, in her words, "is extremely long by investment banking standards," and then going back to work and finding UBS to be surprisingly supportive. "There's been a real change at this firm," she says. "The culture is shifting. They're allowing me to work flexibly—as long as I come through for my clients I can work wherever I want. There's none of this face time stuff. My bosses seem to understand the importance of keeping women."[26]

Kudos to UBS—and other global companies that are beginning to figure out what's needed in terms of both programs and culture change if they want to retain key female talent. The stakes are high. Our survey data shows that young talented women are particularly well represented in jobs that have moderate hours (forty to sixty hours a week) but high performance requirements (fast pace, tight deadlines, 24/7 client demands, etc.). Our global companies survey shows that fully 39 percent of individuals in these jobs are female (see figure 3-10). This data suggests that women are not afraid of the pressure or the responsibilities of extreme jobs—they just can't pony up the hours. This fact creates an opportunity for employers. If high-caliber work were "chunked out" differently, if flexible work arrangements were more readily available, companies would have a better shot at tapping into this pool and thus better realize the talents of women who are willing to commit to hard work, pressure, and responsibility but cannot take on the long hours.

When asked to consider the structural forces that propel the extreme work model, women and men in our survey identified two drivers. First, they pointed to organizational culture. Seventy-four percent of respondents felt that extreme jobs emerge from the value sets and managerial style of a company—or business unit (see figure 3-11). We encountered an example of this at the beginning of this chapter, in our London focus group. When Shane spent his weekend jumping through hoops, he was responding to what he called "tone at the top" in his corporate culture.

FIGURE 3-10

Targeting high-potential women: young talent, age 25–44

Global survey

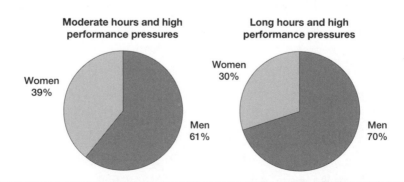

Second, respondents cited competitive factors emanating from our increasingly "flat" global economy.[27]

Both employers and employees can derive a measure of comfort from this data. If our respondents are correct and extreme jobs are driven more by cultural factors than by economic pressures, it becomes easier to "re-engineer" these jobs and create a different and more sustainable work-life model for people who hold them. This would be particularly beneficial to women.

FIGURE 3-11

Drivers of extreme jobs

U.S. survey

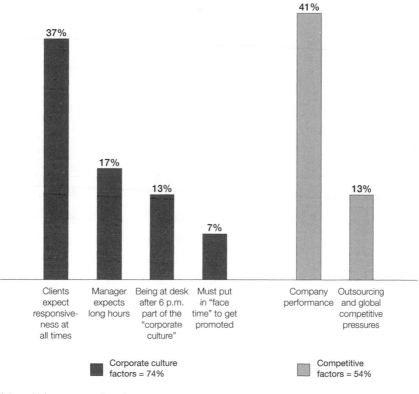

Corporate culture factors = 74%

Competitive factors = 54%

Note: multiple responses allowed.

A word on how we categorized the various drivers of extremity. In one of our focus groups a heated discussion erupted as to whether the driver "clients expect responsiveness at all times" belonged in the cultural or the economic category. After an impassioned debate, a consensus emerged: precisely how a business handled responsiveness to clients or customers owed more to tone at the top than any objective business imperative. Executives who had worked in different regional offices of the same multinational firm argued persuasively that expectations on the responsiveness front varied considerably from one regional office to another, and had more to do with managerial style than the corporate bottom line. In some regional offices the value set was crystal clear: *the client was king.* Whatever the client wanted was done—no matter that the demands placed upon the employee team might be totally unreasonable, including pulling all-nighters or working through the weekend. In these environments, responsiveness was described as "knee-jerk" or "blind."

In other regional offices the tone at the top was quite different. Here the value set allowed a degree of "push-back." If a deadline had a little give— and was not tightly linked to the success of a project or a deal—it was OK to negotiate with the client to create a more reasonable time frame. Executives who participated in this focus group were at pains to point out that the flexibility that resulted from this push-back was often minimal—a deadline could be pushed from 9:00 Monday morning to noon—but even those few hours could make a huge difference in terms of salvaging a five-year-old's birthday party or a weekend visit to dad. One thing these executives were sure of: insisting that the client was king did not necessarily produce great bottom-line results. Some of the more profitable regional offices allowed a considerable degree of push-back. Flexibility did, after all, enhance the ability of the firm to retain valued employees—and what clients disliked most were high turnover rates among the professionals they relied on.

Which brings us to possible solutions. Our survey data tells us that flexible work arrangements are at the heart of the challenge—especially for women. The wish list emanating from extreme workers shows that three out of six of their top picks center on flexibility. For example, 71 percent of women currently working in an extreme job would like a flexible schedule within the framework of a full-time job, 52 percent would like a flexible part-time job, and 61 percent would like "time out" after periods of intensive work (see figure 3-12). Many men also want flexibility—49 percent want paid leave after periods of intensive work—as do 61 percent of women—and 45 percent of men want to work flexibly within a full-time job. Generation X and Y in particular (men as well as women) find these options extremely appealing.[28] The data shows that for young men ages twenty-five to forty-four, the ability to work flexibly tops their list of solutions.

Extreme workers are also hungry for other kinds of help from their employers. Exercise facilities, stress reduction classes, restrictions on weekend

FIGURE 3-12

Extreme workers hungry for help

U.S. survey

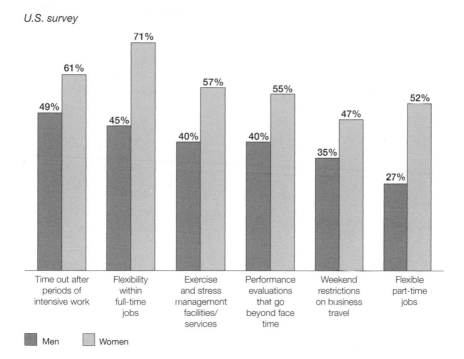

Men   Women

Note: multiple responses allowed.

business travel, and redesigning performance evaluations to de-emphasize face time are all in heavy demand—particularly by women.

In our focus groups the yearning for flexibility came through loud and clear.[29] And frankly, some of the most sought-after accommodations seem modest in scope. At the beginning of this chapter, in our London focus group, Gwen spoke eloquently about the importance of being able to spend the 6:30 p.m. to 8:30 p.m. time slot at home. She didn't mind putting in another two hours late at night but a degree of flexibility in those early evening hours was extremely valuable to her. This was a common refrain among all our survey respondents. One woman in another focus group said she would relocate thousands of miles if an employer would guarantee she could be home for her children's bedtime.

Unfortunately, many professionals with extreme jobs find it difficult to achieve this kind of flexibility. In many corporate cultures, the early evening hours are particularly demanding. According to one focus group participant who regularly arrived at her office at 6:00 a.m. so that she could put in an eleven-hour day and still be home for dinner: "Employees who are around and available between 6:00 p.m. and 8:00 p.m. get special brownie points. My boss literally checks whose car is still in the parking lot at 7:30 p.m. and I'm sure he notices my car is rarely there. No one checks at 6:30 a.m. Those early hours don't get you points in this culture." A colleague of hers who participated in the same focus group volunteered the theory that "it's some kind of macho screening device. When managers give a lot of weight to those early evening hours it becomes a way of discounting women, of shaking them off."

Some final thoughts: the ratcheting up of work pressures and the growth and spread of more extreme ways of working have serious consequences for women—and huge implications for the themes of this book. From an individual's perspective the growth in extreme jobs acts as a drag on a woman's progress, making it even more difficult for her to rise through the ranks or flourish in a top job. And from an organizational perspective, the growth in extreme jobs seriously hinders a company's ability to fully utilize its increasingly critical female talent pool. All of which is sobering. It's as though that male competitive model, far from fading, is morphing and becoming newly robust and vigorous as it feeds off the structural shifts of our age.

The truth is, those of us who are committed to women's progress on the work front have been battling a moving target. Think of the trajectory of workplace demands over the last thirty years. In the 1970s and 1980s, talented women, armed with impressive educational credentials, moved into professional and managerial positions and began doing well—at least in the early stretches of the career highway. Then, well-paying, high-level jobs got redefined. Workweeks lengthened and work pressures mounted in ways that made them newly inaccessible to women.

Our data captures trend lines over the last five years, but studies show that for at least twenty years there has been a steady escalation in the number of hours worked—especially among professionals. According to a recent study by economists Peter Kuhn and Fernando Lozano, among college-educated men working full-time, the percentage putting in fifty-hour weeks rose from 22.2 percent in 1980 to 30.5 percent in 2001.[30] This structural shift toward more intense and pressurizing ways of working is marginalizing talented women (and men) who have serious hands-on family responsibilities. Judith (whom we met in chapter 1) quit her job not because she failed to produce or perform but because work was encroaching on her life in intolerable ways. That's not to say that some women don't rise to the challenge of extreme jobs. Some immensely able superwomen do—especially those who don't have children. But many highly qualified, committed women don't. The 60 percent who are my concern in this book are undermined anew by the extreme work model.

I generally don't go in for conspiracy theories. In this particular case I don't think for a minute that a bunch of male executives got together in a smoke-filled room and invented a more burdensome work model with the expressed intention of leaving women behind—and shaking off the competition. But I do think that one immensely convenient, unintended consequence of extreme jobs is the way in which they reinforce and perpetuate male hegemony. Convenient, that is, for men.[31] But as we'll see in the next chapter, perpetuating male hegemony is already proving to be extraordinarily shortsighted as a confluence of circumstances constricts the talent pool and makes pursuing diversity the most realistic—and economically sensible—way forward.

4

The Business Case for Diversity

Regina was what you might call a superstar—one of a generation of high-achieving, highly educated young women who seemed destined to break glass ceilings. Her accomplishments were all the more impressive because she grew up in a housing project in Newark and was raised by a single mother. Regina won a full scholarship to Rutgers, graduated with honors, and went on to Columbia Law School, again on a partial scholarship. Upon graduation, she joined a highly prestigious New York law firm—"one of the firms that people in law school kill to work for," she recalls.

Regina settled in well and found her job exhilarating. She made a lot of money and enjoyed the status and standing that went along with her high salary. As a woman in a firm where "you could count the women partners on one hand," Regina sensed that she was part of a wave of change. She also liked the partners she worked with, and seemed, at least on paper, destined for partnership herself one day.

Instead, Regina left the firm when she was a fifth-year associate—just two years shy of the firm's seven-year partnership-track benchmark.

When Regina looks back on it all, she says her choice could have been predicted early on. "Like a lot of young associates, I found the prospect of making partner increasingly unattractive. You sacrifice seven years of your life to get this important promotion—and then getting promoted means you have to work even harder, since the junior partners put in more hours than the associates. At my firm, it was normal for people (associates and junior partners alike) to work seventy billable hours a week—which meant being in the office far more than that. I regularly put in fourteen-hour days during the week and went in for another ten hours over the weekend." Regina felt she had no control over her workweek and no prospect of control into the future, even as her career advanced. "I never wanted to work those kinds of hours, even before having children," says Regina, who by the time I interviewed her had married and was three months pregnant with her first child.[1]

Two months after leaving her law firm Regina took a job as a teaching assistant in a private school in Manhattan. Accepting this job entailed taking a 70 percent pay cut. So far the trade-offs involved in her career switch are working for her. "This is a job that I can see doing over the long haul," she says. Her one big regret: leaving her hard-won legal skill set behind her. "I spent ten years vesting in a legal career and I was good at it," she says wistfully.

THE COSTS OF ATTRITION

Regina's story is far from unusual. Indeed, it's emblematic of the "off-ramping" trends described in chapters 2 and 3: a great many highly qualified women do indeed leave extreme careers. This kind of downshifting not only affects individuals—dealing them out of top jobs and high salaries—it has serious ramifications for businesses. By conservative estimates, it costs a law firm between $200,000 and $500,000 to replace a second-year associate—meaning that every time five associates walk out the door, the firm loses more than a million dollars.[2]

Catalyst recently conducted a study of Canadian law firms that focused on the costs of losing women associates and found that the firms, on average, took 1.8 years to break even after a hire, and the average cost of losing a second-year associate was $273,000.[3] Regina's commentary on this study was to the point: "Losing so many female associates is expensive for big law firms," she said. "One would think they'd be doing everything in their power to retain this talent. If they offered flexibility, reduced-hour schedules, and perhaps more outlets for socially meaningful work, things would be different."

The fact is, losing skilled personnel is enormously expensive. There are the direct costs of finding a replacement—advertising expenses, campus recruiting efforts, headhunting fees, and the "opportunity cost" of time spent selecting and interviewing candidates. There are also significant indirect costs—the former employee's lost leads and contacts, the new hire's depressed productivity while getting up to speed, and the time coworkers spend guiding and training.

Both the American Bar Association and the American Society for Training and Development have crunched the numbers and found that the cost of replacing a professional is one and a half times the departing person's yearly salary.[4] Peter Hom, professor of management at Arizona State University's W. P. Carey School of Business, estimates the cost of turnover ranges from 93 percent to 200 percent of the departing employee's salary.[5] It all depends on the skill level. The rule of thumb seems to be the more senior the person, the higher the cost of replacing him or her. According to Anne Ruddy, executive director of WorldatWork, a global network of human resource professionals, the bill for filling the slot of a high-level executive is about three times the job's annual salary.[6] A recent study by Bliss & Associates, a management consulting firm, underscores the point that the costs of turnover are particularly high in client-facing and sales positions, ranging from 200 percent to 250 percent of annual compensation.[7]

Despite the steep costs wrapped up in high rates of turnover, few firms seem to pay attention—only 40 percent of companies even keep tabs on turnover rates. In an interview, Maury Hanigan of the Hanigan Consulting Group expressed surprise that there was so little awareness of the costs of losing talented employees: "If a $2,000 desktop computer disappears from an employee's desk, I guarantee that there'll be an investigation, a

big to-do. But if a $100,000-a-year executive with all kinds of client rela-
tionships gets poached by a competitor—or quits to stay home with the
kids—there's no investigation. No one is called on the carpet for it."[8]

EXPENSIVE LAWSUITS

The high price of attrition is not the only direct cost wrapped up in a
company's failure to retain or fully realize female talent. Take, for example, the costs associated with sex discrimination lawsuits. The numbers
can be eye-catching.

In July 2004, the Equal Opportunity Commission and Morgan Stanley reached a $54 million settlement in a sex discrimination lawsuit filed
on behalf of women at this Wall Street firm. The lawsuit, filed in September 2001, alleged that Morgan Stanley had engaged in a pattern or practice of sex discrimination since 1995 against Allison Shieffelin and a class
of other women, all employed in Morgan Stanley's Institutional Equity
Division. The charges included claims that Morgan Stanley regularly
excluded women from work-related outings, paid women less than their
male peers, and denied women promotions.[9]

The eventual settlement was structured so that Schieffelin—who initiated the EEOC's investigation by filing a charge of discrimination in
1998—was paid $12 million; $2 million was set aside to be spent on new
diversity initiatives in Morgan Stanley's Institutional Equity Division; and
$40 million was earmarked for distribution to eligible claimants. Sixty-
seven women came forward to participate in the claims process.

In another well-publicized case, also settled in July 2004, the Boeing
Aircraft Company agreed to settle a gender discrimination lawsuit covering twenty-nine thousand women who worked for Boeing between 1997
and 2004. The class action lawsuit was brought by twelve female employees who charged that they had been denied access to overtime work, promotions, management positions, training, equal pay, tenure, bonuses, and
other benefits and opportunities because of their gender. The plaintiffs
argued that Boeing's various compensation, promotion, and overtime
decision-making practices were tainted with "excessive" subjectivity and

managerial discretion and thus worked to systematically disadvantage female employees.[10]

In order to resolve the lawsuit, Boeing agreed to a consent decree, but did not admit to any fault or wrongdoing. Under the terms of the settlement, Boeing agreed to pay $40.6 to $72.5 million, to be divided among the named plaintiffs, other members of the class, and the legal team. The settlement also called on Boeing to change the way it determines starting salaries and to modify its performance evaluation systems so as to reduce the risk of gender wage discrimination reappearing.

Other high-profile sex discrimination lawsuits include Merrill Lynch, which has paid out more than $100 million in recent years, and Texas-based Rent-A-Center, which in 2002 agreed to a cash settlement of $47 million and significant changes in company employment practices.[11]

Lawsuits can be surprisingly effective in forcing change. Unlike attrition costs, they cannot be concealed or ignored. Sex discrimination lawsuits incur penalties that have "teeth." They grind on for years, often involve large sums of money, and generate negative media coverage that can undermine the most well-polished brand. No wonder lawsuits have a deterrent effect. Companies will go to some lengths to avoid a gender discrimination lawsuit—monitoring pay scales and fielding carefully balanced, diverse work teams.

STRUCTURAL AND CYCLICAL SHIFTS

Despite the importance of these various costs and expenses, they are not the prime drivers of the business case for gender diversity. More powerful arguments lie in the realm of broad-gauged structural shifts. The fact is, cyclical and demographic factors are aligned in new and alarming ways—and these macro trends are beginning to force action. The upper-echelon labor market is heating up at a time when highly qualified white males are in short supply and talented noncitizens are being drawn back home by robust economic growth rates in Asia. Who, then, will fill the talent void? The best candidates are well-qualified women who often have credentials, experience—and spare capacity.

McKinsey & Company first spotted these looming talent shortages. In 1998, at the height of the tech boom, this high-profile management consulting firm released a landmark report called "The War for Talent."[12] This study, which surveyed seventy-seven companies and six thousand business executives, makes the case that the most important corporate resource over the next twenty years will be human capital—specifically, the education, skills, and experience embodied in talented professionals. In this age of globalization, financial capital, infrastructural resources, and advanced technology are all readily available. Price might be a barrier, but access is not an issue. Thus, human capital, or "talent," has become the prime source of competitive advantage for companies around the world.

But if talent is the most important resource, it's also the one in shortest supply. The McKinsey study underscores the dangers posed by an emerging "demographic crunch" (a shrinking pool of employees in the prime thirty-five- to forty-five-year-old age group) and predicts that, for many companies, the search for talent will become a constant, costly battle. Not only will companies need to devise more imaginative hiring practices, they will also need to work harder to keep their best people. According to the McKinsey team, "today's high performers are like frogs in a wheelbarrow: they can jump out at any time."

Of the six thousand executives surveyed in the McKinsey study, 75 percent said they were chronically short of talent. Indeed, 40 percent of the companies surveyed said they were talent constrained in that they were unable to pursue growth opportunities because of a shortage of experienced, qualified employees.

The McKinsey study predicted that the war for talent would persist for "decades to come" as the demand for executives outstripped the available supply. The authors sounded a warning: "Everyone knows organizations where key jobs go begging, business objectives languish and compensation packages skyrocket." In short, companies ignore the talent imperative at their peril.[13]

Almost ten years later, McKinsey's warning has proved prescient— the war for talent has indeed escalated, spurred by an amalgam of factors:

robust growth, a tightening job market, demographic shifts, and increased global competition.

The job market is, indeed, tightening.[14] After a several-year-long jobless recovery, the market for highly qualified individuals is heating up. The job market for newly minted MBAs is indicative of trends at the high end of the labor market. The class of 2006 commanded starting salaries 17 percent higher than their colleagues in the 2004 class, and employers estimate that they will hire 18 percent more MBAs in 2006, compared with 2005.[15] One out of two new MBAs is now getting a signing bonus.[16] "It is the hottest market since the employment slump of 2001–2003 ended," according to Amy-Louise Goldberg, senior director at the search firm Leslie Kavanagh Associates, "and it's only going to get hotter."[17]

In a similar vein, data from the National Association of Colleges and Employers (NACE) shows that starting salaries for college grads ratcheted up in 2006—particularly in financial fields. The average offer for accounting and business graduates is up 6 percent, compared with 2005.[18] "Overall, the college class of 2006 is doing very well in terms of starting salaries" says Camille Lunkenbaugh, NACE research director. "Employers are facing more competition for new college graduates and that competition is translating into higher salaries."[19]

Today's booming search-firm industry confirms these trends in the job market—as might be expected, the headhunting industry tends to grow fastest when demand outstrips supply and companies need help finding key talent. After a slump in the early 2000s, search firms started to grow again in 2003. Since 2004, revenues at the big U.S.-based search firms have surged. Worldwide, the top twenty-five global recruiters added nearly a quarter-billion dollars to their top lines in 2005.[20] Korn/Ferry, for example, grew its North American business 30 percent in 2005 (the firm's second consecutive year of 30 percent–plus growth).[21] Stanton Chase International grew 40 percent. Steve Watson, chairman at Stanton Chase, attributes his firm's growth to "a continued improvement in the global business climate and an increasing need for upgrading management talent."[22] The fact is, over the last two years, executives across a wide range of sectors—real estate, IT, marketing, and financial services—have found themselves in heavy demand.[23]

The demographic trends driving this tightening job market are both broad and deep. To begin with, as baby boomers age and the smaller co-hort making up the "baby bust" generation hits its most productive years, the supply of mature talent, thirty-five- to forty-four-year-olds, is at a low ebb. Between 2002 and 2012, the population of thirty-five- to forty-four-year-olds in the labor force is projected to fall by two and a half million, a 7 percent decrease.[24] There are no countervailing trends to mitigate the emerging talent shortfall. In fact, as McKinsey pointed out in its seminal article, other demographic and economic trends are currently exacerbating the effects of the baby bust. By 2012 the workforce will be losing more than two workers for every one it gains.[25] According to AARP, as the members of the huge baby boom generation (78 million strong) move into their sixties, nearly 30 percent will retire—leaving more jobs open than there are workers to fill them, because of the smaller size of succeeding cohorts.[26] What's more, boomers who remain in the job market are likely to demand various accommodations. Indications are, they'll insist on much more flexibility and become more demanding of employers in terms of the nonpecuniary rewards of work. More than a third of those surveyed by AARP said they planned to work on a part-time basis during retirement for "interest and enjoyment."[27] A paycheck was important (38 percent of AARP survey respondents had ongoing responsibilities for a parent, spouse, or grandchild), but they were also seeking serenity, purpose, and fun.[28]

If the retiring baby boom generation poses problems for employers—creating both a shortfall of talent and a set of boomer demands—younger Gen X and Gen Y workers pose a different set of challenges. On the employment front, they are both skittish and picky. A study by the Florida-based staffing firm Spherion Corporation found that 51 percent of respondents under the age of forty said they would be looking for a job within a year, compared with 25 percent of those older than forty.[29] This "restlessness" among younger workers is due in part to the stresses and strains of an increasingly extreme work model. As discussed in chapter 3, high-level jobs negatively impact health and family relationships and are increasingly unsustainable. "Flight risk" is a real problem. Young women—and at least some young men—seek a better balance in their lives.

So who will make up the shortfall and take up the slack? In the past, immigrants have often acted as a "safety valve," bringing scarce, sought-after skills to the U.S. labor market. Indeed, in science and engineering fields, almost a quarter of high-echelon workers were born overseas. Given this reality it's understandable that talent-hungry employers might comfort themselves with the thought of hiring from abroad. The problem is, well-qualified immigrants are newly in short supply. Over the past few years the number of legal immigrants coming to the United States has fallen by a third. In addition, for the first time since the 1950s, enrollment of foreign-born students at American universities has decreased.[30] Applications to U.S. graduate schools dropped 12 percent between 2003 and 2006, with applications from China falling particularly sharply.[31] Twenty-five years ago 70 to 80 percent of foreign students stayed in the United States after receiving their degrees; now only 50 percent do.[32] This falloff in numbers is partly a result of the security climate. As a response to 9/11, the U.S. government reduced the number of green cards and temporary visas available to noncitizens. In 2003, for example, Congress cut the annual quota of temporary (H-1B) visas from two hundred thousand to sixty-five thousand. Visas were more plentiful in 2004 and 2005, but numbers are still down over a five-year period.[33] These reductions are counterproductive. This country can ill afford the loss of immigrants who play such an important role in filling the talent pipeline—that is, until we figure out how to better accommodate and utilize our own human capital.

But the challenges go beyond ill-considered policies. Even if visas were readily available, they wouldn't solve the talent shortfall since the number of highly qualified individuals available and potentially interested in coming to the United States is shrinking.

Because of high growth rates around the world (particularly in Asia), talented immigrants from third-world countries are increasingly being drawn back home. We're beginning to see a reverse brain drain as China and India become "destinations of choice" for their highly skilled nationals. Estimates are that India's economic boom could draw as many as 20 million Indian citizens currently resident in the United States and the United Kingdom back to their home communities, lured by opportunities that transcend what they can find abroad.[34]

Deepak, a graduate of the Indian Institute of Technology and Columbia University, explained his recent decision to move home:

> As recently as three years ago, I was set on becoming a New Yorker. I was climbing the ladder at a top-ranked management consulting firm and beginning to put down roots. I bought an apartment on Manhattan's East Side and acquired an American girlfriend. And then India took off. I figured that if I went back and got in on the ground floor of this boom the sky would be the limit. I would be able to create wealth in a way that's just not possible in the United States, where the most I could become was a highly paid professional. Add to that the comfort I would derive from being close to my family and being able to align my work identity with my cultural roots, and it becomes an unbeatable deal. So eighteen months later here I am back in Mumbai, the CFO of a rapidly expanding Indian-owned company.[35]

Deepak's story underscores the fact that into the foreseeable future, U.S.-based companies will be vying for talent in an increasingly global labor market. But it's not just competition in the marketplace. Governments around the world (but not in the United States) are beginning to get into the act, proactively seeking to attract key talent to their countries. In the summer of 2005 Australia launched a $2.3 million initiative to find twenty thousand skilled immigrants by hosting job expos in London, Berlin, Chennai (formerly Madras, India), and Amsterdam.[36] In a similar vein, in order to attract and retain talent, the European Union is considering a plan to offer citizenship to foreign students completing doctorates in Europe.[37]

These government initiatives are part of an official response to baby busts and burgeoning elderly populations. By 2050, France, Germany, Italy, Japan, Spain, Russia, and Australia—among others—will all have serious dependency issues as the ratio of workers to retirees shifts sharply in the wrong direction.[38] The United Nations predicts that in high-income countries, the proportion of the population age sixty and over will grow from 19 percent in 2000 to 34 percent in 2050, and in medium-income countries, from 8 percent to 20 percent.[39] Even China—because of its one-child policy—will face similar demographic shifts and will no longer be able to rely on a supply of hundreds of millions of young, inexpensive workers. India won't be caught in a labor shortage, but neither will it have workers to spare. That country's modestly declining birth rates will result in a population structure that's balanced across the generations.

Which brings us back to women. The multifaceted demographic crunch outlined in this chapter describes an urgent challenge: an emerging talent void different in scope and scale from anything we've faced before and anything we could have anticipated. Who would have thought that at the beginning of the twenty-first century, sixty-two countries would be contending with shrinking populations and weighty dependency ratios. We spent a good deal of the latter part of the twentieth century worrying about overpopulation! But however you position the problem, female talent needs to be a central piece of the solution. Indeed, women are splendid candidates to fill the talent void.

First, they've got the intellectual goods. Across the globe, the educational achievement gap between women and men is steadily widening—with women taking 55 percent of college degrees worldwide.[40] In the United States women now earn 59 percent of bachelor's degrees, 60 percent of master's degrees, and slightly more than half of all professional degrees.[41] They lag behind men in doctoral degrees but are catching up quickly. Fifty-three percent of law degrees go to women, as do 78.5 percent of graduate degrees in the health sciences.[42]

Second, women have an impressive amount of spare capacity—under the current rules of engagement women are not able to bring their full energies to bear. As we saw in chapter 2, 37 percent of highly qualified women take an off-ramp—they voluntarily quit their jobs for a period of time. Child-care issues (44 percent) and elder-care issues (24 percent) are the main triggers. But here's the rub. Although women spend fairly short amounts of time off-ramped (on average, two to three years), they experience huge difficulty reconnecting with their careers. The vast majority (93 percent) of off-rampers would like to return to work, but only 74 percent manage to do so, and only 40 percent succeed in returning to full-time, mainstream jobs.[43] In short, a great deal of talent is lost on reentry. If career trajectories were less rigid, if women were allowed to off-ramp or ramp down and then get a second chance to be ambitious, a great many more would succeed in staying in the labor market over the long haul. The potential here for expanding the talent pool is enormous.

LINKS TO PERFORMANCE

Let's say that you are a naval officer with a seemingly impossible task: a submarine has disappeared—somewhere. You have the coordinates for the last known position, but you have no idea how far or in what direction it traveled after that. Would you call in a few top experts on submarines, or would you assemble a team with a wide range of knowledge—mathematicians, marine biologists, and salvage workers, along with the submarine experts? Common sense would seem to favor the first option, but when this scenario actually played out in May of 1968—the *USS Scorpion* disappeared on its way back to its base at Newport from a tour of duty in the North Atlantic—John Craven, the man in charge, chose option number two. Craven figured that if a lot of people had a lot of different pieces of information and created a composite, they would end up with a pretty good idea of the submarine's location. And that, indeed, is what happened. The submarine was finally located 220 yards from the spot Craven's large and diverse team picked.[44]

The idea that there is "wisdom in crowds" is a notion developed by business writer James Surowiecki. His basic premise is that diverse teams make better decisions. Surowiecki assembles a great deal of evidence to show that homogeneous groups become progressively less able to investigate alternatives. Bring new and different people into an organization, and, even if they are less experienced, they actually make the group as a whole smarter, simply because what they know is not the same as what everyone else in the group knows.[45] A woman who grew up on the wrong side of the tracks and attended a small Baptist college has had very different life experiences from an upper-class white male who attended Yale. Introduce this woman into a group of Ivy League–educated men and the thinking will change. Any kind of difference—race, class, or gender—can have this kind of effect.[46]

According to Surowiecki, diversity expands the set of solutions and "allows the group to conceptualize in novel ways." Diversity also counterbalances what psychologist Irving Janis has called "groupthink"—the tendency of a homogenous group to staunchly put forth a wrongheaded set of ideas simply because everyone in the group thinks the same way.

Suroweicki's perspective is echoed in the Hudson Highland Group's recent study *The Case for Diversity: Attaining Global Competitive Advantage,* which stresses the importance of gender and racial diversity for companies operating in a global environment where clients and customers are unlikely to be either male or white.[47]

In this area of customers and markets, there is some interesting new thinking. Management guru Tom Peters recently declared himself to be an UTTER LUNATIC (his capitals) about the importance of women as customers. The data is dramatic. According to Peters women "are instigators-in-chief" of most purchases making 83 percent of all consumer decisions, including 50 percent of traditionally male categories such as cars, consumer electronics, and PCs; 80 percent of healthcare products; and 92 percent of vacations.[48] The conventional wisdom that management consultants urge on companies that "the customer is king" is actually dead wrong. The customer isn't king, she's queen.[49]

Companies that wish to be market-driven need to be woman-driven. Which is not to say that men are unable to understand women (many of the leading hairstylists and fashion designers are men, after all), or that male-dominated businesses have no access to information about women's needs and wants. Consumer products companies do bring women in for consultation and go to elaborate lengths to adapt their products to a woman-dominated marketplace. But this is not nearly as effective as having a significant number of women managers on the inside. Carlie Hardie, national marketing manager for Toyota's commercial vehicles and Camry in Australia, relates the reaction male management had to a concept her creative team presented for a Sienna advertising campaign. The campaign line was "take the family business class," and the story board showed a preschool locker room with backpacks hanging in the cubbies. Two of the backpacks sported "business class" tags. "I looked at it, and it hit me in the gut. It was perfect. But the guys, they didn't get it and didn't want it— even though 70 percent of car-buying decisions in Australia are made by women."[50]

As Peninah Thomson and Jacey Graham point out in their 2005 book *A Woman's Place Is in the Boardroom,* recruiting and promoting women to key positions allows companies to gain a competitive advantage because it leads to "deeper cultural adaptation to the marketplace."[51] Getting women in for consultation outsources female input. Getting women in top management embeds the feminine in the company's culture by feminizing the corporate persona. To use the words of management expert George Day, it's hard to weave "pervasive market orientation into the fabric of the organization" when the dominant gender of the market is unrepresented in the company's leadership.[52]

IMPACT ON THE BOTTOM LINE

One of the strongest arguments for gender diversity is, of course, the strongest argument for everything companies do: gender diversity links directly to a robust bottom line. Companies that increase the number of women in leadership positions perform better with respect to profits and shareholder value; companies that build diverse management teams have an edge on the client- and customer-development front; and finally, companies with a proven track record on the diversity front have an easier time attracting investors.

The link between gender diversity and corporate financial performance has been firmly established by Catalyst.[53] In a study that examined the financial performance of 353 *Fortune* 500 companies between 1996 and 2000, Catalyst found that both in the sample as a whole and across major industry categories, companies with the highest representation of women in their top management teams significantly outperformed competitors with the lowest representation of woman managers.[54]

For example, companies in the top quartile in terms of women's representation boasted a return on equity that was 4.6 percentage points higher than that of those in the bottom quartile (17.7 percent, compared with 13.1 percent). And companies in the top quartile posted a total return to shareholders that came in 32.4 percentage points higher than those in the bottom quartile: 127.7 percent versus 95.3 percent. These trends played out across all five industries analyzed. Within the categories of consumer discretionary, consumer staples, financials, industrials, and information technology/telecommunication services, the companies whose female management representation ranked them in the top quartile outperformed those in the bottom quartile, sometimes to an impressive degree. Top-quartile consumer staples and financial companies demonstrated a total return to shareholders that bested bottom-quartile companies by at least 80 percentage points.[55]

Catalyst is careful in its study not to posit a causal connection between gender diversity and financial performance. The study notes that a variety of initiatives interconnect and together create traction. For example, a leadership team that is "knowledgeable enough to leverage diversity is likely to be creating effective policies, programs, and systems, as well as a work culture, that maximize a variety of its assets and create new ones."

Two other studies buttress the case made by Catalyst. One, conducted over a nineteen-year period and published by the *Harvard Business Review*, evaluates the performance of 215 *Fortune* 500 companies and finds that, compared with median companies in each sector, organizations with a higher number of women executives have an edge with respect to profits—they performed 18 percent to 69 percent better.[56] A second study, undertaken by the University of California–Davis's Graduate School of Management, surveyed the two hundred largest publicly traded companies in California and concluded that having more women in leadership roles resulted "in a more profitable business."[57]

Customer needs and demands are a second powerful link between gender diversity and the bottom line. Companies that recruit and promote women and minorities and are able to field management teams rich in female and multicultural talent have a competitive edge in business development—they are more likely to win contracts and sign deals. The number of clients and customers concerned about this issue is rapidly increasing. In 2004, Roderick Palmore, general counsel at Sara Lee, the global consumer packaged goods company, persuaded the seventy in-house lawyers who worked for Sara Lee to sign a statement promising to use their hiring clout to promote diversity at the company.[58] Palmore also started to use diversity as one of several criteria with which to select and retain law firms serving Sara Lee.[59] General Electric, Lehman Brothers, Credit Suisse, Johnson & Johnson, and Reuters have also leveraged their concerns about diversity, using performance on that front as a criterion in the selection of outside counsel.[60] At a July 2005 conference on diversity, Wal-Mart informed its top one hundred law firms that of the five primary attorneys handling its business at these firms, at least one must be female and at least one must be a person of color. There could be no twofers: a woman of color couldn't count as two people. That same summer, Wal-Mart dropped two law firms—pulling ongoing work from them—because of unhappiness with the firms' lack of diversity.[61] In a similar vein, DuPont Corporation uses diversity as one of six criteria with which to select law firms. Recently, the company parted ways with a law firm that did not adequately support its diversity efforts. As of 2006, thirty of the thirty-nine law firms representing DuPont have either a woman or a minority as the lead lawyer in charge of the relationship.[62] Visa International, Del Monte Foods, Pitney Bowes, and Cox Communications have also begun requiring the law firms they work with to supply proof that women and minorities are fairly represented at senior levels.[63]

Which brings us to institutional investors, the third driver of gender diversity as a contributor to a robust bottom line. Institutional investors, especially nonprofit organizations and public employee retirement systems, are powerful financial players with an interest in promoting gender diversity. To give some sense of the scale and clout of these entities, the eighty-five largest public employee retirement systems hold assets of $2.37 trillion.[64] While some institutional investors are focused solely on financial performance and earnings, others see strong "social performance" as a critical factor in gauging the return on investment.[65] Social performance means sensitivity to issues of corporate governance and ethics, but it also means a commitment to diversity.[66] Many institutional investors also see diversity as a moral imperative that signals a firm's adherence to sound values and fits neatly into their mission and worldview. If you're a labor union committed to fair treatment and the "dignity" of work, it's an easy stretch to take up the challenges posed by gender and racial diversity. The Kinder, Lydenberg, Domini corporate social database confirms that diversity is important to institutional investors. Writing in the *Academy of Management Journal*, Richard Johnson and Daniel Greening argue that "fund managers believe that being responsive to women, minorities and communities will enhance [their fund's] legitimacy and reputation."[67]

CalPERS, California's $195 billion public employee retirement system, is a bellwether for today's activist institutional investor community, and it continues to press for gender diversity in its investment picks. On November 14, 2005, for example, CalPERS launched a strategy called Expanding Investment Opportunities Through Diversity. This initiative includes the hiring of a diversity consulting firm to help the fund reach out to women-owned and minority-owned money managers and brokerage firms.[68] The fund has a full-time staffer devoted to diversity, and an outreach program manager whose job it is to hold diversity fairs that "serve as a business and investment connection for those wishing to learn how to compete for investment opportunities with CalPERS."[69]

CalPERS is serious enough about diversity to be actively searching for women- and minority-owned firms with which to do business. Clearly, such an organization will look to place its money with a firm that can boast more gender diversity on its management team rather than less.

The association between gender equity and shareholder value, the increasing clout of diverse marketing teams, and the ways in which diversity can earn privileged access to investment funds are three factors that underscore the link between gender diversity and the bottom line. It's the rare CEO who's not susceptible to one of these pressures.

Business leaders do, in fact, find the business case for gender equity increasingly convincing. In a September 2006 interview, Niall FitzGerald, chairman of Reuters, put it succinctly: "This issue of diversity is newly at the core of a business. It's no longer a question of being nice, or being politically correct. Rather, it is an urgent, strategic necessity. Unless you reach out and tap into the widest possible pool of talent (more than half of which is women), you simply won't have the wherewithal to drive a strategy."[70]

Part Two

Models at the
Cutting Edge

The second half of this book is centered on solutions. On the face of it this is a daunting challenge. Chapters 2 and 3 outlined a deepening problem set. Not only are we battling an entrenched male model that's ill suited to realizing female talent, but we are dealing with one rendered newly robust and resilient by the growth of extreme jobs.

However, the analysis to date is also replete with good news. Chapter 4 developed a compelling, multifaceted business case for why companies may now be ready to mess with the conventional white male career model. Demographic shifts and global competitive pressures are creating a groundswell for action. This is a point of view bolstered by the track record of the Hidden Brain Drain Task Force. As mentioned in chapter 1, over the last three years, the thirty-four companies that constitute the task force have worked together to identify problem sets and sponsor cutting-edge research. More importantly, they have committed to spurring action on the ground and tackled the central challenge: how do you spearhead a second generation of policy capable of keeping talented women on the road to success?

Our June 2006 Hidden Brain Drain Summit—when change agent teams from thirty-four global companies gathered to share emerging best practices—was an important milestone. Over two extraordinary days these senior executives described setbacks as well as success stories and homed in on the key questions: Which policies and programs have the most traction? Is there a core package of options that constitutes a second generation of policy? And how can a company kick-start the process of becoming a second-generational player?

We were able to hammer out a collective vision. I'm not talking about a detailed or tight agenda here—the range of sectors and professions represented in the task force is too wide for that—but we did achieve a meeting of the minds. First, there was consensus on a core package: six essential elements that need to gain some real traction if a company is to fully realize female talent over the long haul. Second, there is a growing list of models at the cutting edge—some of them directly inspired by our new research—that can help a company get up and running. In essence, the emerging models of best practice described in chapter 5 through 10 provide a road map for companies embarking on a second-generational journey.

So what is this core package?

1. Establish a Rich Menu of Flexible Work Arrangements

These go to the heart of what women want most. As we saw in chapters 2 and 3, flexible work arrangements dominate women's wish lists—indeed, on the 2006 *Working Mother* magazine list of best companies to work for, flextime is the lead benefit offered by 99 of the one hundred companies on the list.[1] Reduced-hour options, flexible stop and start times, telecommuting, job sharing, and seasonal flexibility—time off in the summer, balanced by long hours in the winter—are among the policics and practices women yearn for. Many see flexible work arrangements as a lifesaver, eliminating the need to quit a hard-won, much-valued job. The case studies featured in chapter 5 (Ernst & Young, BT Group, and Citigroup) present a multitude of creative ways of reimagining when, where, and how work is done. It's important to note that in companies such as Citigroup, flexible work arrangements are not described as an accommodation to women's family lives; rather they are positioned as a business imperative—a powerful weapon in the battle to retain key talent.

Flexible work arrangements are likely to become even more important. With jobs becoming more extreme, an increasing number of talented women will both want and need the ability to ramp down a little. Having a baby or coping with a fragile parent is that much more difficult when workweeks ratchet up from fifty-five to seventy hours and spheres of responsibility become global. If 30-plus percent of talented women are currently opting for scenic routes, that proportion is likely to increase into the future as the performance challenges inherent in contemporary jobs continue to escalate.

2. Create Arc-of-Career Flexibility

Flexible work arrangements provide flexibility in the here and now— over the course of a day, a week, a year. But a related set of policies are enormously important to women: policies that provide flexibility over the arc of a career and allow a woman to ramp up after having taken time out of the paid workforce. These initiatives are quite new. Indeed, the case studies featured in chapter 6 (Booz Allen Hamilton, Lehman Brothers, and Goldman Sachs) got off the ground in 2005 and 2006 as a response to the "Off-Ramps and On-Ramps" survey data and are still at an early, experimental stage.

It should come as no surprise that arc-of-career flexibility is a brand-new concept. These innovative policies do, after all, represent a serious departure from the white male career model, which at its heart is dependent on lockstep, full-time employment. As we will see from the case studies showcased in chapter 6, a particular challenge for companies attempting to craft these types of flexibilities is that they are multilayered and multistep. Reattaching talented women involves creating more and better on-ramps for sure, but successful reattachment also depends on access to flexible work arrangements (many on-ramping women need flexibility) and on reconnecting to mentors and networks.

A word on these new and more complex forms of flexibility: as the case studies will reveal, senior executives driving these new policies are beginning to conceptualize work in different ways. Jobs are being unbundled and unpacked, clients are being shared, and work teams are being deployed in ways that allow responsibilities to be handed off seamlessly. All this is happening with the goal of allowing high-value, high-impact work to be done by experienced professionals working in "chunks" or "nuggets" of time.

3. Reimagine Work Life

Talented women also need work-life policies that offer accommodation for responsibilities associated with elderly relatives and reliant individuals outside the immediate family circle. As has already been shown, conventional work-life policies tend to focus on the nuclear family. For many years the best benefits—and finest support programs—within large corporations have gone to a specific demographic: employees who are married with young children. This doesn't work for half of all women. As we discovered in chapter 2, a large proportion of highly qualified women are childless—and almost as many are single. But if these women don't have two-year-olds they do (or will) have serious elder-care and extended-family responsibilities. The data shows that a significant number of women are forced to off-ramp because of an elder-care crisis.

The case studies featured in chapter 7 (Citigroup, Time Warner, and Johnson & Johnson) illustrate ways in which companies are beginning to honor and support work-life challenges that go beyond biological children and the nuclear family.

4. Help Women Claim and Sustain Ambition

The data presented in chapter 2 shows a serious fall-off in ambition as women move through their thirties. Confounded by the escalating pressures of extreme jobs and penalized for taking an off-ramp or a scenic route, many talented women downsize their expectations for themselves. This is a huge issue. An employer cannot promote a woman if she herself is not enormously vested in this endeavor. The case studies featured in chapter 8 (Johnson & Johnson, Time Warner, and General Electric) demonstrate how ambition can be sparked and rekindled through women's networks and other leadership initiatives.

Women's networks create a myriad of leadership development opportunities. At the simplest level they boost confidence by connecting women to their peers. All too often, executive women feel isolated—marooned in a sea of men. In addition, networks provide access to senior women who can act as mentors and role models; serve as a "showcase" for presentation and organizational skills; and expand business relationships—both within the company and on the outside.

5. Harness Altruism

As we learned in chapter 2, the aspirations of talented women are multidimensional and tend not to be centered on money. Financial compensation is important to women, but it's not nearly as important a motivator as it is for men. The data shows that while men list money as either the first or second priority on their wish list, women tend to rank this goal much further down on their list of career drivers. Career goals such as working with "high-quality colleagues," deriving "meaning and purpose" from work, and "giving back to society" tend to be top priorities for women. In focus groups women talked eloquently about the friendships they found in the workplace, the importance of being able to believe in the products they sold and the services they rendered, and their commitment to giving back to their communities (both their corporate community and those on the outside.)

The case studies showcased in chapter 9 (Goldman Sachs, Cisco, and American Express) demonstrate that recognizing and rewarding altruism gives an important lift to women's careers and cements loyalty to a company.

6. Reduce Stigma and Stereotypes

In many corporate environments, flexible work arrangements and other work-life policies and programs are heavily stigmatized, either through overt disapproval (a manager says quite openly that telecommuting will hurt a career), or because of subtler cues in the corporate environment emanating from gender-based stereotypes. For example, someone who has taken a reduced-hour schedule is simply never considered for promotion, or such an option is deemed suitable only for those who are not very ambitious, and in many companies this may be "code" for young mothers. Either way, flexible work arrangements—no matter how well designed or cutting edge—quickly become illegitimate or "off limits" to those with serious career ambitions. Naturally, this has a dampening effect on take-up rates. In focus groups, we found that women—often high-performing, ambitious women—routinely quit rather than take advantage of flexible work arrangement options that were on the books but had become stigmatized. In the words of one executive: "These policies label you as some kind of loser."

Reducing stigma and stereotyping is perhaps the most challenging element in this core package. Ask any HR director. They'll tell you it's relatively easy to create a set of exemplary policies and programs. But such initiatives are meaningless options unless they are supported and celebrated by senior managers in the corporate environment. As we shall see in chapter 11, one of the most effective ways of combating stigma is to "walk the talk" at the top. When senior executives take a scenic route and shout it from the rooftops—letting everyone in the office know they've done so—it can have a transformative effect on what is possible for everyone else. Suddenly, flexible work arrangements become legitimate—even desirable.

The case studies featured in chapter 10 (Lehman Brothers, Cisco, and Ernst & Young) show how companies are beginning to battle stigma and stereotypes head-on—and in so doing are kick-starting the process of transforming corporate culture.

A closing thought. I would like to stress that this core package is not a stand-alone deal. These six new initiatives are meant as add-ons to existing policies and programs. Large, progressive companies have already developed a valuable set of first-generation programs: they actively recruit well-qualified women and offer a conventional set of work-life policies—mostly focused on the nuclear family. But as discussed in chapter 1, this first round of policy and practice has gotten women only partway there. This first generation of policy served to make the white male model somewhat more accessible to women rather than creating alternatives to that model. It's this deeper agenda—the creation of alternative career models and alternative pathways to power—that lies at the heart of the second-generation challenge.

In hopes of encouraging other companies to take up this challenge—by adopting any or all the components of the core package—following each case study I've included a toolkit—a brief but succinct outline of how to institute the initiatives described in the preceding case. These toolkits are meant to give the reader, at a glance, a grasp of the essential elements needed to craft, launch, and sustain these efforts. I'm optimistic these toolkits will convince companies that these efforts are both doable and supportable.

5

Establishing Flexible Work Arrangements

At the core of corporate policies and practices that allow women to stay engaged with their career are flexible work arrangements. As we saw in chapters 2 and 3, flexible work arrangements dominate women's wish lists. Flexible start and stop times, seasonal flextime, reduced-hour options, telecommuting, and job sharing are among the policies and practices that wives, mothers, and daughters yearn for.

Of the six elements in the core package of second-generational policies, flexible work arrangements are the easiest to put in place—and the most established. In nearly all cases a company's bottom line will not be affected if a woman comes into the office a few hours earlier so she can be home in time to help children with homework or visit with a wheelchair-bound parent. Providing, of course, she makes up the time.

But women's lives also sometimes beg for a more "radical" flexible work arrangement—one that involves a reduced workload. Ernst & Young, for example, has been able to create flexible work arrangements that can accommodate a woman who wants to reduce her load to 60 percent of a full-time job. In fact, at Ernst & Young, it's even possible for a woman on a reduced-hour flexible work arrangement to be promoted—management recognizes that working fewer hours does not necessarily diminish a woman's leadership potential or intrinsic value to the company.

BT Group has been experimenting with flexible work for over twenty years and has found that flexibility isn't just "doable"—it's often accompanied by a leap in productivity. Fully 75 percent of BT's employees these days work flexibly—an astounding statistic—and three-quarters of those on flexible work schedules are men.

The basic tenets behind Citigroup's Flexible Work Initiative are enormously inclusive. When applying for a flexible work arrangement employees do not need to state their reasons. Instead, they are simply required to demonstrate their ability to deliver an approved work plan. Managers judge requests solely on business grounds. At Citigroup, flexible work arrangements are not "personal," they're about delivering the goods.

In three very different ways these companies have reimagined when, where, and how work gets done. All have demonstrated that providing a rich menu of flexibility is good news for the bottom line—decreasing turnover and allowing companies to retain key talent.

ERNST & YOUNG: FLEXIBLE WORK ARRANGEMENTS

Ernst & Young, a global leader in professional services, helps businesses across all sectors deal with a range of issues related to auditing, accounting, tax, and transactions. With 108,000 people in 140 countries around the globe, the firm logged revenues of $16.9 billion in fiscal 2005.

Lisa Kennedy, whose story was described in detail at the beginning of chapter 2, is a perfect example of how new forms of flexibility at Ernst & Young have actually begun to transform the company culture. Kennedy worked on a reduced-hour version of a flexible work arrangement for several years but still felt the need to off-ramp when she had her second child. Then, realizing that she missed the challenge that work provided, Kennedy on-ramped, working a reduced schedule that gradually increased from half-time, to 60 percent, then 70 percent, and finally 80 percent time. Last year, she made partner still working her 80 percent schedule.

Kennedy's success is due in no small part to her talent and dedication, but it was surely helped along by Ernst & Young's flexible work arrangements. Over the last ten years, flexible work arrangements have become pervasive at all levels at Ernst & Young—large numbers of junior and senior associates as well as a significant number of partners take advantage of these programs.

Kennedy stresses that flexibility is required from both parties involved in a flexible work arrangement—the employee as well as the firm. Kennedy makes sure she's adaptable; if she needs to be on-site or in her office for a client meeting, she's there, no matter whether it's Saturday afternoon or 7:00 Monday morning. On the firm's side, she says the commitment to flexibility is equally strong; "It's now part of the company's DNA," she says.[1]

So how did this company reconstitute its DNA? As early as the early 1990s senior management recognized that something was wrong. Turnover rates among female professionals at Ernst & Young were disproportionately high. Though entering classes of young auditors were composed of nearly equal numbers of men and women, only a tiny percentage of the company's partners and principals were female. Somewhere between first starting to work at Ernst & Young and the eight-to-ten-year mark (the length of time it took to accumulate the experience to be considered for partner), women were opting out of the company at an alarming rate. This was bad news on the business development front—high turnover rates meant lost continuity with key accounts and clients. Plus, there were the direct costs of attrition. Ernst & Young invested heavily in its female associates and incurred significant costs when these women left. Replacing a junior associate could cost upward of $100,000—the price tag was in the range of 150 percent of the departing employee's annual salary.

In 1997, after several years of battling high rates of attrition, Phil Laskawy—Ernst & Young's then CEO—decided to try to retain women by creating a culture of flexibility. It was a bold move, but it's been highly successful. Today, nearly 30 percent of women just below partner or principal level and 10 percent of female partners and principals are on flexible work arrangements. Indeed, estimates are that fully 82 percent of employees use some type of flexibility.[2] Largely as a result of this new flexibility, women's retention rates at Ernst & Young are equal to men's at virtually all levels.

Building Blocks of Change

Laskawy kick-started his flexibility initiative by creating a Diversity Task Force made up entirely of partners. He then sought the assistance of Catalyst, the nationally prominent nonprofit organization that consults with business on women's advancement. At Laskawy's request, Deborah Holmes, then director of research and advisory services at Catalyst, conducted scores of internal focus groups and one-on-one interviews at Ernst & Young before reporting back on the most important challenges facing women. Her top picks: an absence of work-life balance, a dearth of senior role models and mentors, and a lack of access to formal and informal networks. Holmes also told Laskawy that men as well as women were having trouble balancing their work and personal lives. Within the ranks of senior management, fully 60 percent of the women and 57 percent of the men were dissatisfied with the long-hours culture at Ernst & Young.[3]

In 1997, Laskawy created the Office for Retention, and hired Holmes as its first director. Her job was clear-cut: implement the recommendations she'd made as a Catalyst consultant. To demonstrate his personal commitment to this initiative, Laskawy gave Holmes an office on the executive floor of Ernst & Young's headquarters building in New York and had her report directly to him. He then accompanied her on visits she made to Ernst & Young leadership teams at local offices across the country, talking up the new initiative and showing by his presence its importance to the firm. Laskawy's high-profile involvement was deliberate—and highly effective. As we will see in chapter 11, when CEOs "talk the talk" and "walk the talk," they are able to accelerate action. Laskawy's personal involvement ensured that executives across the firm "got" the new campaign's message: institutionalizing flexibility and accelerating women's progress were not just fads but central to Ernst & Young's continued business success.

Holmes and her staff went right to work identifying four key challenges in the Catalyst research and selecting branch offices that would pilot new initiatives centered on those challenges. In 1997 Holmes launched four pilot programs at branch offices ready to spearhead change: Palo Alto and San Jose focused on work-life balance, Minneapolis focused on mentoring, Boston focused on women's external networks, and Washington, D.C., focused on women's networks within Ernst & Young. What the pilot programs had in common was process: each had a steering committee that included the area managing partner plus twelve to fifteen other client-facing professionals ranging from partner or principal to senior associate. In addition, there was a "solution team" comprising up to one hundred additional professionals who worked with a facilitator from Holmes's office. Over eighteen months each steering committee brainstormed potential policies and practices that responded to the challenge they had agreed to address, tested these policies and practices on their solution team, fine-tuned these new programs, and prepared them for firmwide rollout.[4]

Flexibility Today

The Office for Retention has been renamed the Office for Gender Equity Strategy (GES). It now has a staff of eight and is led by a senior client service partner, Billie Williamson. GES's mission is to develop and advance the women of Ernst & Young and propel them into leadership roles within the company and in the wider business community.[5] In response to what employees say they most need, a large amount of effort continues to be focused on flexibility. Thus, in addition to GES, Ernst & Young has a four-person Flexibility Strategy Team, also led by Williamson.

At the heart of the Ernst & Young vision is the idea that career and personal life are interdependent, and that the business's needs cannot be met if people's lives don't work. A core tenet is that flexibility is available to everyone, not just women or parents of young children.

Employees who need a flexible schedule can choose from a range of flexible work arrangements, including:

- *Compressed workweeks:* a full-time workload is condensed into fewer than five days

- *Flextime:* allows variation in the start and end of the standard workday

- *Reduced-hour schedules:* employees can work fewer days per week or fewer hours per day

- *Short-term seasonal arrangements:* employees work a full or reduced schedule for less than six months during the year

- *Job sharing:* two people voluntarily share the job responsibilities of one full-time position

- *Telecommuting:* performing a job from a site other than the office, usually from home

Flexible work arrangements can be mixed and matched at Ernst & Young. An employee might opt for a compressed workweek with flextime (staggered start and end times), or craft a reduced schedule that involves some telecommuting. Rather than have employees choose from a limited, fixed range of options, Ernst & Young has created a program that allows "customized" solutions that blend the needs of employees with those of clients and work teams. Flexible work arrangements are individually negotiated—employees sit down with their manager and work out an arrangement that meets their individual needs, the teams on which they work, and the clients they serve.

In addition to flexible work arrangements, all employees, with or without a formal arrangement, are equipped with the latest technology and allowed to work from home or any other remote location to accommodate personal needs and client deadlines.

Institutionalizing Flexible Work Arrangements

Ernst & Young has developed some creative ways to institutionalize flexible work arrangements so that they take root and become sustainable. Early on the company created a flexible work arrangement database that featured information on the specific arrangements negotiated by hundreds of employees. Today Ernst & Young's Achieving Flexibility intranet site is particularly important—helping employees navigate the best arrangement for them and featuring advice for managers on how to support flexibility and enable virtual teams. A central theme of this Web site is that flexible work arrangements should not affect an employee's opportunity for advancement, because it is not hours billed that determines upward mobility but quality of work.

The Cost-Benefit Logic

A recent firmwide survey of Ernst & Young employees who have a flexible work arrangement confirms that "two-thirds of the people using flexible work arrangements view them as a reason for staying or joining the firm." In addition, between 2002 and 2005, 84 percent of women who took maternity leave at Ernst & Young returned to their careers at the firm. This impressive number demonstrates that Ernst & Young women believe they can have a dynamic career and a successful family life.

But it's not just a question of well-being—happier employees with more balanced lives staying with the company longer; there are demonstrable cost savings as well. According to Holmes, who now heads up Corporate Social Responsibility at Ernst & Young, increased rates of retention among female professionals yield savings of $10 million per year.

Flexible Work Arrangements

Ernst & Young has rolled out multiple versions of flexible work arrangements and encourages flexibility at all levels—a hedge, it believes, against losing a disproportionate number of young and talented female employees. Some ten years ago, Ernst & Young's leadership grasped that although each entering class of auditors had for years been split about evenly between men and women, only a tiny percentage of its partners and principals were female. The solution, thought former CEO Phil Laskawy, lay in making flexible work arrangements part of Ernst & Young's culture.

To accommodate individual needs Ernst & Young has devised numerous flex work arrangements. Some employees work a nontraditional day or week; others compress full-time work into fewer than five days. The firm has also adopted seasonal arrangements: employees might work a normal schedule for most of the year, followed by a period of time off and then back to a conventional schedule. Employees can work a reduced schedule and still be serious contenders for promotion.

Today, nearly 30 percent of women on the rung just below partner or principal work flexibly. Ten percent of all female Ernst & Young's principals and partners work flexibly.

The Business Case

Ernst & Young was experiencing disproportionately high turnover among female employees. Turnover in client-serving roles meant lost continuity on engagements. On top of losing talent the firm had invested in developing, Ernst & Young incurred costs averaging 150 percent of a departing employee's annual salary just to fill a vacant position.

Ernst & Young credits flexible work arrangements with improved retention of female professionals. Between 2002 and 2005 for example, 84 percent of women who took maternity leave returned to their careers at Ernst & Young. A recent survey of Ernst & Young employees participating in flexible work arrangements confirms that two-thirds would have left—or not have joined the firm at all—had it not been for flexible work arrangements. At virtually all levels of Ernst & Young women's retention rates now equal men's. That means a demonstrated savings of at least $10 million annually in costs associated with replacing employees, as well as hard-dollar savings associated with retaining know-how, relationships, leads, and contacts.

Getting Started

- Understand the root causes of attrition. Ernst & Young, for example, conducted focus groups and one-on-one interviews with men and women, identifying challenges most associated with high turnover.
- Win top leadership commitment to transforming the culture, not just to implementing a program.
- Assume that *all* jobs can be done flexibly.
- Match each major challenge—life balance, mentoring, networking—to a pilot initiative. At Ernst & Young, a selected local office developed and perfected a single program.
- Work out a time frame for a pilot program, followed by a rollout to the remainder of the organization.
- Run the metrics. Ernst & Young, for instance, estimates that the increased retention saves the firm at least $10 million in hard costs.

Critical Elements

- *Strategic drivers.* Ernst & Young sees its central challenge as creating a variety of flexible work arrangements to support its business strategy.
- *Stigma in retreat.* The company has transformed the culture so that a flexible work arrangement no longer negatively impacts an employee's opportunity for advancement.
- *Commitment at the top.* The director of the firm's Office for Gender Equity Strategy reports directly to the vice chairman of client service and she is supported by a staff of seven. A four-person Flexibility Strategy Team ensures that flexibility is available to everyone—not just women or parents.

- *Flexibility on both sides of the equation.* Each flexible work arrangement is a custom blend of the needs of an individual and the needs of the work teams and the clients. To provide guidance in making flexibility work for the individuals and the firm, Ernst & Young has built an intranet site which provides support and assistance to employees and managers.
- *Technology at one's fingertips.* All employees are equipped with the technology to enable full mobility: laptop computers, cell phone, an office phone system that can bounce to any phone line, instant messaging, e-mail, voice mail.

BT GROUP: FREEDOM TO WORK

With 102,100 employees and £18.6 million in revenues, U.K.-based BT Group, formerly known as British Telecommunications plc, is one of the world's leading providers of communications solutions and a cutting-edge company in the realm of flexible working. The company has pioneered a variety of flexibility programs and become a driver of change in the public sector, helping craft legislation on the flexibility front.

BT's first all-out initiative, Freedom to Work, was started during the late 1990s as a way to boost performance in a rapidly changing global environment. BT traces the roots of this program to the Cardiff Software Engineering Centre, where in 1998, a team of nine men and nine women were struggling to finish a debugging project tied to the millennium switch-over. These employees weren't merely working against a fixed deadline (not being prepared by January 1, 2000, would spell disaster); they were also collaborating with colleagues in Calcutta, India, whose work schedules were dictated by their own time zone—which was an awkward five hours ahead of Wales. The crack-of-dawn hours demanded by this situation were encroaching on the Cardiff team's quality of life.

Realizing that the hardships endured by this group were affecting the quality of their work, BT came up with a plan: the company would provide technology and support, and Cardiff team members would be allowed to work whenever and wherever they wanted. There were only two provisos: each team member had to create a reasonable work schedule that fit around the needs of other team members, and all were required to maintain a high standard of work, including meeting the project deadline.

Results, in terms of hard numbers, were impressive. The Cardiff team took fewer sick days, were more productive, and accomplished more over a shorter time period than similar BT teams. Flexible hours had the huge advantage of allowing them to deal better with multiple time zones and work closely with colleagues in Calcutta who played an important role in the debugging project—which was finished ahead of schedule. Another plus: the Welsh team forged a lasting, productive collaboration with their counterparts in India. The strategy was such a success that the line manager of the project became a vocal spokesperson for the plan within the company, encouraging other managers to adopt Freedom to Work.

As far back as the early 1980s BT management was thinking about implementing some kind of flexibility program. At that time the company was predicting a global telecommunications boom, and this alerted management to the urgent need for 24/7 service availability and much more flexible ways of working.

By 1986 three hundred to four hundred BT employees were working exclusively from home, but it wasn't until the Freedom to Work initiative was developed in Cardiff that flexibility really got off the ground. (This initiative is now embedded within the larger Achieving the Balance program.)

Over the years Freedom to Work has become an extremely large-scale initiative. Increasingly, employees are encouraged to develop their own "customized" versions of flexibility, working with their various bosses to decide on the approach that blends their work responsibilities with their lives at home. They look at both their own personal needs and the needs of their work unit or team—always factoring in the implications for customers.

Jyoti Blew, who has been with BT since 1987 and has two young sons, says that without Freedom to Work she would not have been able to continue working. After her second child was born, Blew came back to BT without a specific position but then saw an internal posting for a job as a field manager. She was wary of applying for the position since field manager jobs tended to be filled by men. Her manager encouraged her, however, since the position offered the flexibility she needed. Blew got the job and with it the flextime that allowed her to balance work and family obligations. Blew has an office at BT but also has broadband at home, allowing her to split the week up by working from home some days and going into the office whenever she needs to. Blew credits her manager with encouraging a flexible schedule. "He tells me what's important is how I manage my team and my time so that work gets done," says Blew.[6]

BT's flexible work initiatives have yielded amazing results. Company-wide, turnover is an astonishingly low 3 percent—saving the firm £5 million a year by not having to replace departing employees. After a maternity leave, 99 percent of BT's female employees return to work—compared with the U.K. average of 47 percent. Partly because the needs of working moms and dads are so well accommodated, the average number of sick days taken by BT employees has fallen to only three days a year, in sharp contrast to the U.K. average of eleven days per year. Equally impressive is the fact that since 1998 productivity for flexible, home-based workers has risen steadily, sometimes as much as 30 percent a year. In addition, since 10 percent of BT's flexible employees work entirely from home, the company has been able to reduce its need for office space and has saved an additional £70 million a year. A final plus: flexible work arrangements are "green"— that is, they cut down on employee transportation needs. BT's flexible and home workers save £10 million a year in fuel and other transportation costs, and experts estimate that this reduction in travel lowers carbon dioxide emissions by 54,000 tons a year.

Caroline Waters, BT's director of People and Policy, touts an unexpected benefit of flextime. Given that members of a team often work staggered hours they don't mind fielding calls from home. "When one employee calls another at home to ask a question, the employee receiving the call is usually open to talking about a work-related matter even if he/she is not officially on the job at that moment," Waters says. "In this way, more real work is accomplished than when all employees are at their desks for a standard workday."[7]

As Freedom to Work has taken hold across the company BT has worked hard to ensure that the program is available to all employees. Bringing the engineering department on board has proved to be a particular challenge. These employees are the primary customer link (visiting clients' homes to install and repair BT products), and BT has created a situation where these employees are able to maintain—and even improve—their customer service record while enjoying the benefits of Freedom to Work.

Working with the engineering field teams, BT tested an initiative called Self Motivated Workers. This called for teams of engineers who had been given flexible schedules to target an enhanced level of productivity. Each worker within a team would then decide what his or her contribution would be. Some opted to start their rounds earlier in the day; others chose not to begin their workday until late morning or midafternoon. It turned out that productivity was boosted by these varied arrangements because a greater number of workers were available during early morning and early evening hours when customers were most likely to be at home.

Self Motivated Workers has recently been rolled out nationwide, with impressive results. The company has been able to service an additional 1 million customers a year with the same number of engineers. Plus, customer satisfaction has risen by 7 percent—a metric that's hugely important to the company.

When asked to pinpoint why Freedom to Work has been so successful at BT, Waters mentions the importance of scale (an astounding 75 percent of all employees at BT now work flexibly) and the high-profile role played by men. More than three-quarters of those working flexibly are men. Indeed, the percentage of those using flexibility at BT is in direct proportion to the company's three-to-one male-to-female ratio. Across the board it seems, workers, irrespective of gender, are taking advantage of the new flexibility programs. These facts have helped enormously in getting rid of any stigma surrounding flexible work options, thus transforming the BT culture.

Waters also talks about the importance of trust. "Workers are entrusted to make good decisions and troubleshoot their own problems—without interference or help from management. We've learned that we, as a company, don't always need to be there to solve problems. If managers have confidence in employees they're capable of anything," she adds.

One of the unusual aspects of BT's Freedom to Work program is the traction it has produced in the public sphere. BT was heavily involved in shaping the United Kingdom's Employment Act of 2002. The company both provided some policy ideas and helped garner the support that ensured passage of the bill, which went into effect in April 2003. Since that date parents in the United Kingdom who look after young children have the statutory right to apply to work flexibly no matter what company employs them.

TOOLKIT

Freedom to Work

BT traces its Freedom to Work program to a Cardiff team, which, in 1998, pioneered a radical approach to flexibility. Today, employees are encouraged to develop their own flexible work options wherever practical. They can balance working from home with long and short days at the office, or accrue blocks of vacation time to use during school holidays. Freedom to Work creates opportunities for employees with caretaking obligations, and for those returning to work after maternity leave.

One of the interesting by-products of Freedom to Work is its impact on government policy. It provided the model for Britain's Employment Act of 2002. The legislation took effect in April 2003 and gives parents of young children the right to request flexible work arrangements no matter where they work.

The Business Case

Since implementing its flexible working strategy BT has seen labor turnover drop to 3 percent per year. After maternity leave, 99 percent of BT women return to work (compared with the U.K. average of 47 percent). This saves the company £5 million a year by not having to replace new moms. Perhaps because the needs of working parents are accommodated, sick days for BT workers have fallen to three days per year—a sharp contrast to the U.K. average of eleven.

For home workers, productivity has risen steadily since 1998—some years as much as 30 percent. Meanwhile, with a large population of employees working outside the office, BT has been able to give up acres of office space, saving £70 million a year. Other savings focus on cutbacks in employee transportation needs. BT's flexible and home workers save £10 million a year in fuel and other transportation costs.

Getting Started

- Think about the direction of your business and how to opportunistically link flexibility with business strategy.
- Start with a pilot and then roll out your flexibility initiative across the entire workforce—not just to high-potential employees or minority groups.
- Vigorously document the metrics associated with flex work in order to construct a robust business case.

Critical Elements

- *Strategic momentum.* The needs of BT's increasingly global business drive its flexibility programs.
- *Trust and cooperation.* These programs are based on shared assessment, collaboration, and trust. To get started BT employees consider whether flexibility will be a plus for their coworkers and customers as well as their families. If the answers are positive, then employees and managers review the flex-hour request together.
- *A tipping point.* Inside BT there is a sense that the culture has shifted—with 75 percent of BT workers now working flexibly. Flex has become the norm, transforming the culture and eliminating any stigma associated with flexibility.
- *Gender stereotypes on the wane.* At BT men are as likely to avail themselves of flextime as women. Indeed, more than three-quarters of those who work flexibly at BT are men.

CITIGROUP: FLEXIBLE WORK INITIATIVE

In July 2005, just days before her son Matthew was born, Patricia Lennon started her maternity leave, fully intending to return to her job at Citigroup. However, after several weeks of motherhood, Lennon knew that an 8:00 a.m. to 7:00 p.m. workday—the kind she put in at her job before she became pregnant—would be extremely challenging for her. However, staying home would be impossible as well: not only did her family need her income, Lennon enjoyed her job enormously.

Her timing turned out to be perfect. Just as Lennon's maternity leave was ending, Citigroup rolled out its job-share plan—and, as luck would have it, Lennon's job was perfectly suited to the new program.

Before her leave Lennon's job had been restructured (for business reasons) so that instead of managing people she was now managing projects—which made her job easier to unbundle and divide. A second piece of serendipity: Christine Cokeley, another working mother with whom Lennon had collaborated in the past, was looking to work reduced hours too. She was the natural "other half" for a job share. Lennon's manager was not merely supportive of the job-sharing idea—she was eager to sponsor it. A job-share arrangement would mean she could keep two experienced, well-regarded employees.

The application process for the job share was relatively simple. Lennon and Cokeley laid out how the job would be divided, which one of them would do which tasks, and how they would share time in the office. Since the job didn't require a 9-to-5 workday presence they decided that Cokeley would work from 8:00 a.m. to 3:00 p.m. Mondays through Wednesdays, while Lennon would work the same hours Wednesdays through Fridays. Wednesday became the overlap and "handing-off" day.

Citigroup's job-share plan has allowed Lennon to become a winner on all fronts. Her half-time schedule allows her to meet her financial obligations, stay involved in work she's passionate about, and spend real time with her son. "It's a win-win," she says. "I can make a difference at work and I can make a difference at home."[8]

Crafting a job share may have seemed like a cinch to Lennon, but for Ana Duarte-McCarthy, Citigroup's director of Global Workforce Diversity, implementing a firmwide Flexible Work Initiative has been extremely challenging. Citigroup, the world's largest financial services company, manages about 200 million customer accounts worldwide. Mergers in the banking industry over the last ten years have brought a variety of new companies into Citigroup. Each had a different version of flexible work and a different version of what such a program should include. Not only was there no consistency to the various policies, data from Citigroup's internal "Voice of the Employee Opinion Survey," which is fielded annually, suggested that many employees were unhappy with the existing flexible work options. In general, "flextime" was considered an ad hoc, under-the-table kind of deal, something offered only to favorites.

Duarte-McCarthy's challenge was to merge the myriad flexibility programs scattered across Citigroup and create a Flexible Work Initiative that was consistent and "arm's length." Flexibility would no longer be viewed as a personal accommodation but rather as part of a business strategy that focused on retaining and fully realizing key talent. Duarte-McCarthy was intent on expunging the negative view that had traditionally surrounded flexibility at Citigroup.

She faced some immediate problems. The company did not have the internal resources to design and drive a firmwide flexibility initiative, so she turned to Boston-based Work Family Directions, a consulting group that specializes in helping companies set up work-life programs. Work Family Directions created an action plan and laid out what Citigroup needed to do to ensure that the new Flexible Work Initiative achieved its mission of reaching *all* employees.

Another problem area was designing a comprehensive and accessible Web site. Given its global scope the new initiative needed a rich site that would showcase information in a variety of languages—Citigroup is a truly global company with three hundred thousand workers in one hundred countries around the world. Without a multilingual approach management would never be able to claim that flexibility was available to everyone, regardless of location.

The Web site has, in fact, proved to be enormously useful—providing tips and guidelines for managers and employees alike. In its first six months (September 2005 through March 2006), it received 1.3 million hits. Users seem to find the sample work plans particularly helpful. These are designed to assist employees figure out how to develop a feasible arrangement. How can you convince a boss that you will continue to deliver? What does a strong flexible work plan look like? In addition to sample work plans the site features role models and success stories: employees who are thriving on flexible work plans. These stories come from around the world—proving that the Flexible Work Initiative is not U.S.-centric but a global reality.

As Duarte-McCarthy developed the Citigroup flexibility initiative, she recognized that the initiative must itself be flexible. As is the case at Ernst & Young, Citigroup's Flexible Work Initiative comprises five component parts that can be mixed and matched:

- *Flextime:* flexible daily start and end times

- *Remote work:* either a partial or a fully remote work schedule, which involves employees working from home or at satellite offices

- *Compressed workweek:* a full-time work schedule condensed into fewer than five days per week

- *Job sharing:* two employees sharing responsibility for one full-time job

- *Part-time or reduced schedule:* employees working fewer hours than the standard workweek

Since the new initiative was rolled out in September 2005 there has been a surge of demand for flexible work at Citigroup. The firm has done a good job tracking the numbers—which are impressive. In the first year of the program more than forty-nine hundred employees applied to work flexibly. Most of the applicants were successful—only 9 percent of the requests were declined. So far most applicants have been U.S.-based employees, but this is changing as materials are translated and Citigroup figures out how to mesh its Flexible Work Initiative with local labor laws. Fifty-seven percent of employees requesting flexibility are high-echelon workers ("exempts" in U.S. parlance). Thirty-four percent of applicants have been men.[9]

A key goal of Citigroup's Flexible Work Initiative has been to reduce the stigma associated with flexibility—otherwise there is a danger the company will end up with an impressive set of programs that look great in the employee handbook but are rarely used. The strategy here has several parts. First, the new Flexible Work Initiative is open to all employees and is not "reason based." Employees who apply for flexible work do not have to say why they want this arrangement—they don't need to be looking after a new baby or a frail parent. Instead, they are asked to justify their request by creating what amounts to a feasibility plan—they must provide their managers with a list of current deliverables and a work plan that lays out how they aim to deliver great results within a flexible schedule. According to this work plan (and recent performance reviews), managers then determine whether or not to approve the request for flexibility.

Stigma is also reduced by promoting flexibility as a business tool that increases employee engagement and productivity, increases retention, decreases turnover, and cuts real estate costs—with more people working remotely, Citigroup has fewer offices to maintain. The business case for flexibility has become a drumbeat at Citigroup. Chuck Prince, Citigroup's chairman and CEO, is constantly reminding people that flexible work is not a personal accommodation, but a business imperative that's good for the bottom line. Indeed, Prince promoted the concept of flexible work in the five-point strategic plan he rolled out in March 2005. This plan is Citigroup's strategy for bringing about the changes needed to reach the goal of becoming the most respected financial services company in the world.

Finally, stigma has been reduced by a top-down, comprehensive communication strategy—which has included Webcasts by Prince and quarterly reporting on the Flexible Work Initiative's progress to heads of business units around the world.

Patricia Lennon doesn't know anyone else at Citigroup who is sharing a job—but she sees people working flexibly all around her. "Some people are coming in earlier and working from 7:00 a.m. to 3:00 p.m. so they can pick their children up from school," she says. "Others begin earlier, or work later, and take an extended lunch hour to transport their children from school to after-school activities." Still, Lennon is aware that not every job can be split down the middle or done on a reduced-hour schedule. "I don't think we'll see Chuck Prince in a job share," she quips. Lennon cautions that allowing an employee to arrange a job share or design a flex option can be risky for management. "Your manager is relying on you to make sure everything is covered. With a part-time or job-share position it's incumbent on the employee to deal with a lot of logistics that aren't present in a full-time job. When you think about it from that angle it's amazing that my manager—and the company—are not only on board, but are taking extra steps to help me out," she says.[10]

Lennon is so appreciative she's has written a thank-you note to Ana Duarte-McCarthy. She regards herself as a role model—if she can make her job share a success, job sharing will be seen as more viable and therefore more readily available for other employees.

Duarte-McCarthy, the driving force behind this new program, recognizes that there remain significant challenges the firm must address to ensure an efficient and effective program. Managing flexible workers is one of them. People management is challenging even when all employees spend the entire day, every day, in the same location. Managing staff on flexible work plans when they are not in the office much of the time can be even more daunting—especially at a time when performance pressures are escalating. To address this, Citigroup is providing managers with extensive training so that they can become supportive of flexible work and understand the link between flexibility and business objectives. This training program has been rolled out globally.

TOOLKIT

Flexible Work Initiative

Citigroup's Flexible Work Initiative was launched in September 2005. One of its distinctive features is that employees who apply for flexible work do not need to give a reason for their request. What they do need is a list of current deliverables and commitment to a work plan. Factoring in past performance and the strength of the work plan the manager then decides whether the request should be approved.

To date,more than forty-nine hundred employees have applied to work flexibly. Most are U.S.-based, but that is beginning to change. Preliminary feedback suggests some interesting trends among applicants. Fifty-seven percent are high-echelon workers. More than 30 percent are men. Only 9 percent of applicants have had their request for flexibility turned down.

The Business Case

The Flexible Work Initiative has had the visible support of Chuck Prince, Citigroup's chairman and CEO, who views flexible work not as a personal accommodation but as a business imperative that will increase employee productivity and enhance retention. Indeed, in 2005 Prince promoted the concept of flexible work in his five-point plan—Citigroup's strategy for bringing about the changes, both large and small, that the company needs to reach its goal of becoming the world's most respected global financial services company.

Getting Started

- In a postmerger environment of multiple flexible work programs, evaluate each arrangement, including its associated metrics. Aim to identify best practices and barriers to success.
- Understand employee attitudes toward existing programs. At Citigroup, employee feedback suggested that flexible options were regarded not as actual

policy and practice but as ad hoc personal accommodations for select employees. Citigroup has worked to change that perception.

- Know your employee base and identify the tools needed to sustain a program. To support its commitment to offering flexible work to all employees around the world, Citigroup is building a robust multilingual intranet site dedicated to best practices in the flexible workplace.

Critical Elements

- *Flex is flexible.* Citigroup's flexible work model is itself flexible, offering several variations, including flextime, compressed workweeks, remote work, job sharing, and part-time work. To date, the most frequently requested form of flexibility has been "partially remote" arrangements that involve working outside the office on certain days of the week.
- *A wide pool of beneficiaries.* To reduce stigma and encourage all employees to see themselves as stakeholders, Citigroup has positioned flexible work as a business imperative and designed a comprehensive communications strategy that involves senior management. In addition, Citigroup has created a framework for applicants that is not reason based—employees do not need to say why they want to work flexibly. This enormously expands the pool.
- *An inventory of challenges.* Citigroup has identified barriers—including external challenges like the multiplicity of laws in the countries in which it operates. Internal challenges include the ambivalence of managers who are simultaneously asked to deliver on ambitious performance goals while also driving flexible work as a business imperative.

6

Creating Arc-of-Career Flexibility

The flexible work arrangements and policies described in the previous chapter—flextime, telecommuting, job sharing, and so on—get us partway there. But they don't go far enough. Flexible work arrangements are static: they're all about carving out partial relief in the here and now, allowing employees to ratchet down the pressure and craft a "scenic route." Valuable as they are, flexible work arrangements don't deal with the longer-term, more recalcitrant problems. As we saw in chapter 3, high-impact extreme jobs don't lend themselves to scenic routes and the spread of these jobs has forced many highly credentialed women off the career highway. For these complicated challenges, we need more thoroughgoing and dynamic forms of flexibility.

Arc-of-career flexibility takes into account the span of a woman's work life, acknowledging its nonlinearity and discontinuities. This kind of flexibility allows a woman to "ramp down" when necessary and then "ramp up" without the frustration of an extended and often fruitless job search. At its core, this type of flexibility is all about reattachment without unfair penalties or punishments. Arc-of-career policies recognize that many women need a second shot at ambition—at age thirty-three, forty-eight, or even fifty-four.

These more sophisticated forms of flexibility are newcomers to the scene. Over the last few years a small number of companies—many of them members of the Hidden Brain Drain Task Force—have started to design and implement programs that target off-ramping and on-ramping women, experimenting with initiatives that help ambitious women stay with their careers. Booz Allen Hamilton's Adjunct program, launched in April 2005, provides high-level, part-time work for women who want to ramp down, keeping them in the loop until they are ready to ramp up. Lehman Brothers' Encore program, launched in November 2005, and Goldman Sachs's New Directions program, launched in May 2006, welcome back highly qualified women who have left the financial sector and now want back in. These programs are still quite small in scale yet they have enormous potential for expanding the talent pool. As we saw in chapter 2, 93 percent of women who off-ramp want to go back to work, but only 40 percent of these women succeed in finding mainstream jobs. Clearly, a great deal of talent continues to be lost through bars to reentry. These new initiatives have the potential to help curtail that loss dramatically.

BOOZ ALLEN HAMILTON: ADJUNCT PROGRAM

Ilona Steffen-Cope is one of the women whose work-life conflicts pushed Booz Allen Hamilton, the global strategy and technology consulting firm, to institute policies that afford arc-of-career flexibility. A principal at Booz Allen's San Francisco office, Steffen-Cope began commuting from Vancouver about the same time she became pregnant with her first child. (Her commute was necessitated by a shift in her husband's career.) Commuting between Vancouver and San Francisco—which are 800 miles apart—was a challenge in itself, but the logistics of Steffen-Cope's life were further complicated by the fact that her principal client was based in Tennessee. This resulted in a three-pronged existence for Steffen. "I was spending five days a week in Tennessee with my client, then stopping in

San Francisco on my way home to touch base with my office," she says. "All in all I had a ten-hour commute door to door."[1]

As she neared the end of her pregnancy it became obvious that her job was becoming untenable. Not only was Steffen-Cope not allowed on a plane during the last month of pregnancy, she had a new baby to plan for. So she signed up to participate in Booz Allen's Ramp Down/Up, Internal Rotation programs—initiatives at the company that allowed high-performing employees to ramp down and work on special projects that were not client facing. So when Steffen-Cope returned from maternity leave she became a part-time worker in the Internal Rotation program where she was deployed on a variety of intellectually challenging tasks—proposal writing and the like. It suited her needs perfectly because this internal staff role was not subject to client demands, which are inherently unpredictable. Project work kept her skills and contacts fresh, but at the same time permitted her to spend a great deal of time with her new baby.

Somewhere down the road, Steffen-Cope wants to ease back into full-time work. "I plan to return, but I'll need to get a nanny up to speed, and since I'm nursing it will be a while before I can be away for a week at a time," she noted. Steffen-Cope was confident that when she was ready Booz Allen would allow her to gradually ramp up to full-time work. She had a new sense of loyalty to her company. "Given my recent experience, there's nothing I wouldn't do for this firm," she said. Which is, of course, exactly the attitude the company was looking to generate with its Ramp Down/Up, Internal Rotation programs.

But creating part-time work for high-performing employees isn't easy to do in some of Booz Allen's lines of business. In its private-sector management consulting arm, Booz Allen has had serious problems retaining female talent—as have other firms in this sector. The firm's government consulting arm is a different reality. In the public sector there is less pressure and a greater measure of predictability, and here Booz Allen has been able to do a good job retaining and promoting women.

As Ann Bohara, adjunct professor of management at the Wharton School, has pointed out, private-sector consulting throws off serious challenges for women—not the least of which is the career model itself, with its "tough" advancement track. In an interview, Bohara, whom Booz Allen hired to head its work-life balance initiatives, described a fiercely competitive winnowing process.[2] At the end of the first year about 20 percent of the new class of associates is cut from the company's roster. The top 80 percent then stay on to battle it out until the next round of eliminations. If associates make it through seven years of such competition they generally will make partner. But it's a treacherous seven-year period, and one that many women—especially would-be mothers— aren't willing to pursue, at least in part because this period tends to clash and collide with the imperatives of the biological clock. It's hard to wait until you've made partner before attempting to have children—by that stage in the game you may well be thirty-five or thirty-eight years old and beginning to confront fertility problems.

So how do you create a little ebb and flow in this career model? How do you craft some "time out" and then make sure high-potential women have a second shot at ambition? In short, how do you create state-of-the-art off-ramps and on-ramps?

In 2004 DeAnne Aguirre, senior vice president at Booz Allen and managing partner of the western region, decided to take on this challenge. Booz Allen had recently joined the Hidden Brain Drain Task Force, and in October 2004, just after a task force meeting focusing on off-ramps and on-ramps, Aguirre began to see a way for her firm to stem its female exodus. As she developed the new program along with her colleagues, she drew inspiration from three sources: the experience of women in Booz Allen's Ramp Down/Up, Internal Rotation programs; ideas she'd gleaned from task force meetings; and discontinuities in her own, highly successful career path.

Over the sixteen years she'd spent at Booz Allen Aguirre had ramped down and ramped up a total of eight times. She'd taken a year off to get an MBA at Stanford University. Soon after, her husband's job had taken her to Brazil for a year where she had to restart her consulting business. Soon after that, she became pregnant and took a four-month maternity leave. Two years later, her husband's job transplanted the family to New York

City. She then had twins and took another three-month maternity leave. At this point in her life, the family load was significant and she took an internal rotation job that not only allowed her to have a more predictable schedule, but also exposed her to senior executives at the firm. This lasted for three years, until the family moved to San Francisco—a shift that was again necessitated by her husband's career. Two years after that, she took another four-month leave when her fourth child was born. After this maternity leave she ramped up gradually—working 50 percent of a full load after two months and then slowly increasing to 100 percent over the next two months. The stunning truth is that despite all these off-ramps and on-ramps Aguirre had the talent and grit to become a huge producer and valued leader at Booz Allen. She is now the highest-ranking female in the private-sector business—the first woman ever to make senior vice president in this division of the firm. One thing's for sure: Aguirre knows first-hand the challenges posed by career breaks and the difficulties wrapped up in needing to start again—and again.[3]

Aguirre's experience—though eye-catching in its variety—is not atypical. An internal poll at Booz Allen demonstrates that Aguirre's work trajectory is fairly typical for women in senior positions. The data shows that, on average, women deal with eight career interruptions during the sixteen years it takes them to progress from associate to senior partner, while men deal with approximately two.

For all these reasons Aguirre decided to develop a new program—to build on the Ramp Down/Up, Internal Rotation initiatives and create a program that allowed women to rejoin the Booz Allen family even after they "quit." Piggybacking off an idea floated at task force meetings—that women who quit need two-day-a-month jobs—Aguirre proposed that Booz Allen create an Adjunct Program that offered part-time contract work to off-ramped women (and men) and make it available to valued alumni.

Aguirre's idea was the right solution at the right time. Booz Allen's private-sector business had downsized after the tech bubble burst, but in 2003 the firm was back in growth mode, dealing with a surge of new business—and a burgeoning staff shortage. Eager to recruit experienced talent, the company was ready to pilot the Adjunct program.

As one might expect, chunking out nuggets of high-impact work that could be done by part-timers proved to be a particularly challenging part of this new initiative, and Aguirre found that she needed to drive a whole new way of looking at work. Standard management consulting jobs were unbundled and divided into "bite-size" chunks that could be done by an employee who was telecommuting or spending short stints of time in the office—or a mix of both. And work teams were pushed to become more collaborative as full-time workers and part-time contract workers learned to hand off assignments seamlessly. Ultimately, Booz Allen was able to create a pipeline of bite-size projects that were appropriate for adjunct workers—proposal writing and in-depth research lent themselves particularly well to being packaged in chunks.

In early 2004, Booz Allen reached out and offered adjunct positions to 148 individuals. Ninety-nine accepted—59 alumni and a variety of others, some of them referrals from current employees of the firm. These new adjunct roles comprised part-time positions that ranged from a few days a month over the life span of a long project, to short bursts of intense activity around some urgent deadline. When the Adjunct program started, this new breed of worker received a fee but no benefits. The firm is now considering adding a whole list of benefits: career planning, mentors, an annual conference, a training allowance, and partial health coverage. A year after its inception, two adjuncts had already ramped up to full-time. Exactly the result Booz Allen wanted to see from the program.

The Adjunct program continues to be disproportionately used by female professionals. Overall Booz Allen is 20 percent female, but the adjunct program has a 2-to-1 female-to-male ratio. The reasons are obvious. As we saw in chapters 2 and 3, women deal with more family responsibilities than men and are thus more likely to want to ramp down. However, despite the predominance of women in the Adjunct program, Aguirre did not want this initiative to be seen as merely an accommodation to women's lives, and was careful to position it as a business imperative—part of Booz

Allen's variable staffing model. During upswings and downswings in the business cycle adjunct workers can potentially either expand or contract capacity at the firm. In the early months of the program Aguirre analyzed profit margins generated by adjunct workers and found them to be pulling their weight—contributing equally to the firm's overall results.

From Bohara's perspective, the main "value" delivered by experienced women in the Adjunct program has to do with continuity in client relationships. Stellar customer service in the management consulting business is about building long-term, in-depth, "trust-filled" relationships with clients and making them feel looked after and catered to. To deliver this kind of excellence, a company needs to be able to produce continuity and consistency—the same professionals providing services for the same clients over time. "Management consulting has no product, no manufacturing line," says Bohara. "It's all about people and brainpower. Finding the right people and keeping them is absolutely crucial. When one walks out the door it's analogous to losing a valuable product line."[4]

TOOLKIT

Adjunct Program

Private-sector consulting revolves around tight deadlines, 24/7 client demands, and lots of travel. The trajectory of careers in this sector is particularly difficult for women. Those who progress through the "up or out" assessment process will be in their mid-thirties before they can be considered for partner. These years of overload and overwork are the same years that women feel the pull of family. The consequence is that women are dramatically underrepresented in the senior echelons of the management consulting profession.

Seeing that the career model was making it difficult to retain key talent, Booz Allen Hamilton took steps to rectify the situation. The firm joined the Hidden Brain Drain Task Force, with senior vice president DeAnne Aguirre as the point person. She was the right person at the right time. In her sixteen years at Booz Allen, Aguirre reckons she has ramped down and ramped up a total of eight times. All along she remained attached to Booz Allen—but it wasn't through a formal program and it wasn't easy. The firm wants to make it possible for more women like Aguirre to stay.

In 2004 Aguirre reached out to 148 qualified off-rampers and hired 99 of them to be part of a new Adjunct program at Booz Allen. This program, which builds on previous Ramp Down/Up, Internal Rotation initiatives, is designed to provide part-time, high-impact work for individuals who need to ramp down their professional commitments. The idea is to retain high-performing women who otherwise would quit.

The Business Case

Retaining an experienced cadre of talented consultants is one of the most difficult challenges in management consulting. Delivering excellence requires continuity in the client-consultant relationship—which underscores the importance of retention. When an employee walks out the door, it is analogous to losing a valuable product line. Moreover, the inherent flexibility of the Adjunct program does more than bring attrition rates down—it can aid the bottom line by creating a variable staffing model. Adjuncts can temper the business cycle. A final plus: the Adjunct program has already garnered great press and may well prove to be a powerful recruiting lure.

Getting Started

- Create leadership buy-in by linking to initiatives already embedded in the corporate culture. At Booz Allen, for instance, the Adjunct program was positioned as an innovative way to improve the firm's long-standing diversity index.
- Stimulate internal demand for the program. At Booz Allen Aguirre focused attention on the challenge of unbundling management consulting jobs and chunking out "bite-sized" pieces, thus creating an appropriate work stream for adjuncts.

- Identify different types or categories of talent—including men—who want to be part of this adjunct workforce. At Booz Allen, current employees wanting to ramp down as well as off-ramped individuals wanting to ramp up were offered this opportunity.
- Create a standard employment contract defining the terms of the relationship.

Critical Elements

- *Visionary leader.* The Adjunct program would not have gotten off the ground without the passionate commitment of Booz Allen senior vice president DeAnne Aguirre who spearheaded the initiative.
- *A variable staffing model.* The Adjunct program has, in effect, combined current and former employees into one highly flexible labor pool that helps Booz Allen deal with the peaks and valleys of the business cycle.
- *Pieces of a puzzle.* The Adjunct program is part of a rich menu of flex options (including the Ramp Down/Up and Internal Rotation initiatives). This firm believes that what works for one person might not work for another.

LEHMAN BROTHERS: ENCORE

Susan Siverson was tapped by Lehman Brothers to be an early participant in Encore—an on-ramping program launched in November 2005 to welcome back women who had left jobs in the financial sector. In an interview Siverson explained why she off-ramped.

"I was going crazy. Baby twins. Flying to London. Multiple nannies. This going-back-to-work thing wasn't working for me," said Siverson about her post–maternity leave return to work at the investment bank she'd been employed at for nearly eight years.[5] Her mentor arranged for some flextime, but Siverson still found herself traveling to London on a regular basis. Not wanting to do two jobs badly, she decided to devote herself full-time to motherhood—at least for a while.

A few months later, Siverson was invited to the launch of Lehman Brothers' Encore program. She felt that she wasn't yet ready to go back to work but, she reasoned, it wouldn't hurt to attend the event and find out what this program had to offer. "I didn't have any immediate expectation of using it," she said, "but the concept sounded interesting." When she got to the event she realized that the other attendees had come with more focused aims; several, in fact, were regarding the day as a sort of job interview. Siverson didn't feel nearly as committed. Yet by the end of the presentations she was ready to jump on board and join the program.

Where did her enthusiasm come from? "Lehman set the right tone," Siverson explained. She thought the program would have a soft-focus "working moms" approach. Instead, she says, "Lehman did much better—appealing to our intellect and professionalism. Though many of us happened to be moms, the event was all about business—how to reenter the job market, how to buttress confidence, how to have a successful nonlinear career. I had never experienced anything like this before," she recalled. The Encore event convinced her that although part-time work hadn't panned out for women friends at other companies in the financial sector, Lehman was newly able to allow her to rejoin the workforce on her own terms.

Which is exactly what happened. Siverson and Lehman worked out an arrangement whereby she undertakes some specific management consulting projects. Siverson has created strict boundaries around her time and responsibilities. She works two days a week. The day before she goes into the office, she receives an e-mail detailing precisely what she's expected to accomplish. So far, it's working well. "A year ago, if I had wagered that I would be working now—and loving it—I would have lost the bet. But Lehman has made me a winner," Siverson said.

Siverson's experience shows why Lehman Brothers' Encore program has created such buzz on Wall Street and in the media. Where did it come from? What were the drivers?

Like many other Wall Street firms Lehman has begun to feel the pinch of losing experienced female talent. As a top-tier investment banking firm with almost twenty thousand employees and a stellar recent track record on the profits front, the company has had no problem recruiting newly minted female associates and analysts. However, around year five, female attrition rates begin to rise, peaking in year ten. "Retaining key female talent is a real challenge for the investment banking sector, which is why we are enormously committed to Encore," says Joe Gregory, Lehman Brothers' president and chief operating officer. "This program is critical to helping Lehman Brothers tap into the widest, richest talent pool."[6]

According to Janet Hanson, a managing director at Lehman, "Solving the female talent exodus took on greater urgency in 2003 when Wall Street's post-9/11 slump finally ended." Business units whose hiring had been flat suddenly surged, and Lehman's leaders realized they needed additional experienced talent. "We needed people with a track record," said Hanson.[7] So Lehman went looking for people who could bring established skills and connections to the table. The company knew there was plenty of talent out there—particularly women who had off-ramped. But how do you reach out to these women and interest them in a second career?

Guided by these market conditions, Anne Erni, Lehman's chief diversity officer, designed and launched Encore to "legitimize women who have off-ramped and create a new stream of experienced talent for the firm."[8] Gregory threw his weight firmly behind the program because he knew it made good business sense. In contrast to new recruits straight from college or business school, off-ramped women would bring many more skills and a wider range of contacts to the job. Financial incentives for the company included savings around the costs associated with luring high-level talent from other companies, costs that could include headhunting fees and the spiked salaries often needed to attract talent that's well situated elsewhere.

Because senior management saw off-ramped women as potential assets, they gave Erni's brainchild a green light. She received ample funding with which to start the program, enough to pay for a full-time recruiter-manager, a diversity-oriented search firm, and customized "reskilling" to bring the new on-ramping recruits up to speed.

Encore is not a job fair in disguise. There's never the promise of an interview with Lehman to those who are invited to the Encore events, let alone a job offer. Rather, the program is a way of putting impressive résumés into the company's talent pipeline. The women Lehman can't use won't have wasted their time either: Encore events are inspirational for those who attend, reinforcing women's professional identities.

"In designing Encore, we relied on Hidden Brain Drain Task Force research showing that most off-rampers are trying to reenter within two years of taking their initial leave," Erni says. "For our first event in November 2005 we sent out 180 invitations to women who had been out of the workforce for three years or less. We also stipulated that they needed to have had at least five years of experience before they off-ramped." Seventy-five seats were available at Encore's first New York City–based event; 71 of those seats were filled. Approximately half the attendees were former Lehman employees; the rest were contacted through a Lehman employee or through a friend of a Lehman employee. Two women flew in from California to attend the event; two others made their way to Lehman's New York offices from Vermont and Washington, D.C. The firm dubbed this first event "Re-Igniting Your Story." It was structured as a mix of updates from the financial sector, self-assessment, and networking opportunities, bracketed by breakfast and lunch.

This mix of substance and support was precisely what most of the women in attendance had come to Lehman to find. Many said they were attempting to return to their careers because they'd missed the camaraderie of the workplace. "Re-Igniting Your Story" gave them a dose of what they'd been missing, and some practical tools to help them bring this sense of fellowship back into their lives on a more regular basis. "The event was fantastic," says entrepreneur Cynthia Borcherding, whose résumé included twelve years of international experience in the reinsurance industry and a recent MBA from Duke University's Fuqua School of Business. She'd off-ramped three years before the Encore event and was encountering unexpected hurdles returning to her career. "The Encore people seemed to understand where I'm coming from. They're looking at women who have had nonlinear career paths, and saying, 'We know you have amazing credentials and valuable experience and we're trying to attract you to our company.'"[9]

The November 2005 Encore event began with a panel discussion titled "Since You've Been Gone," during which four Lehman managing directors discussed trends in the financial sector. The conversation ranged from the intensified regulatory climate to the rise of derivatives. Then a gong sounded and the tenor of the day changed as one of the facilitators told a fairy tale about a princess who was "trapped in her own story" until she figured out a way to "leave this inconvenient story and write one of her own."[10] The women listening nodded their heads and smiled. After a brief talk about what makes a compelling tale, the facilitator instructed everyone to pair off and begin writing their own stories in ways that would interest potential employers.

The event was enormously successful. Fully 98 percent of attendees wanted to learn more about potentially working at Lehman, and an Encore e-mail address was set up to field résumés. Two internal recruiters were assigned to Encore to make sure these résumés weren't buried at the bottom of a pile on some hiring manager's desk. Screening sessions were then set up with the majority of women who submitted résumés, which resulted in a number of follow-up interviews and, to date, twenty hires.

A graduate of Wharton, Melissa Eisenstat off-ramped in 2004 after an impressive ten-year career in equity research and seven years in the tech industry. Her last position was president of Palladian—an independent equity research firm. She stepped out in early 2004—partly because she couldn't get behind the firm's new business plan, and partly because she wanted time out for a project close to her heart: playing the cello full time. In Eisenstat's words:

> So that's what I did. I devoted two years to the cello—making it the centerpiece of my life. I did the total immersion thing: thirty hours a week of practice, chamber music, orchestra, and a solo recital. I didn't become a star—no one was calling me to substitute for Yo-Yo Ma—but I became good enough that I could have made a living playing the cello. This kind of progress gave me an enormous sense of accomplishment.

But by the fall of 2005 I was ready to go back. I knew I did not want to be a professional musician scrambling for the next gig. Music for me was an avocation, not a vocation. I missed the excitement, the rigor, and the rewards of the financial sector. So I worked my network and was invited to the first Encore event in November 2005.

To tell the truth I initially had a mixed reaction to the program. I was intrigued and impressed, but also skeptical. I looked around that room, chock-full of immensely talented women and I thought to myself, "How can this firm follow up with over a hundred women? This is just one of those feel-good events—long on lip service, short on delivery."

Boy, was I wrong. Not only did Erika Irish Brown and Rebecca Hornstein [members of Encore's Diversity Lateral Recruiting group] work with me—painstakingly scoping out my experience and skills, attempting to make a match with opportunities at the firm—but over the next eight months I was offered three different potential job opportunities at Lehman. The third one fit like a glove. In August I accepted a job as Vice President of Product Management—and am now working with equity analysts to help them polish their stock pitches to the institutional sales force. It's a great job—and one that has all kinds of growth potential for me.

Melissa is well aware of how lucky she was to have found Encore:

I was interviewing on the outside during the months I was talking to Lehman, and I have to say it was tough. Prospective employers were suspicious on two grounds. They kept questioning whether I could "cut it" after a two-year break—the field had changed so much. They were also nervous about my being "overqualified." Would I be happy coming in at a lower level? No matter what I said it was hard to put this fear to rest. My new job has a compensation package that is less than half the salary I was earning in my last job. That's fine with me. I know I need to prove myself again. This firm has given me that chance.[11]

Looking back on the launch of the Encore program, Anne Erni identifies two key hurdles: internal skeptics who had doubts about the wisdom of hiring individuals with gaps in their résumés, and figuring out how to create flexible work arrangements for off-rampers. Support from top management was crucial in winning over the skeptics, and successful integration of flexible work arrangements often depends on the availability of a range of options. So Erni decided to be flexible about flexibility—on-rampers would be told that the firm was open to all kinds of arrangements that would be negotiated in dialogues with managers. While not prepared to reengineer entire job categories, Lehman was newly willing to reshape individual jobs for the right applicant.

The Encore event in New York was so successful that it was replicated in London in February 2006. Again, the response was impressive. Forty-nine off-ramped women showed up for an event at Lehman Brothers headquarters on Canary Wharf to listen to senior executives talk about what had happened in the banking industry since they left. As participants in New York had done, the women in attendance then wrote their own stories. Subsequently, thirty women started conversations with Lehman Brothers about potential positions at the firm. To date, there have been four hires.

Encore is currently expanding its scope. Although it was developed as a tool for recruiting talented women, Encore is now gender neutral, with off-ramped men now interested in the program.

Brooks Dougherty is a case in point. A Dartmouth grad with an MBA from Tuck, Dougherty off-ramped in 2002 after a nine-year career in the financial sector that culminated in a position as lead manager for the highly successful Zurich Scudder Technology Innovations Fund.

His decision to quit for a while was partly a result of a buy-out—Deutsche Bank bought out Zurich Scudder Investments, and as part of that deal, it bought out the partners, including Dougherty. But his decision to turn this watershed moment into a several-year off-ramp was a function of family circumstances. Divorced, with four children, ages six to sixteen, Dougherty was newly faced with heavy responsibilities on the parenting front. In 2002 his ex-wife had become seriously ill and needed medical treatment, so just after the Deutsche Bank buy-out, Dougherty took custody of the children for a period of four years and committed to being a hands-on, full-time dad. One son in particular needed special parental attention; diagnosed with ADHD, he needed extra support in developing the coping skills necessary to succeed in school.

Three and a half years later, with his family stabilized, Dougherty was ready to return to his career. After some discouraging initial soundings, he realized he needed some help and enrolled in the Tuck School's on-ramping program Back in Business. He figured that after a four-year break, he particularly needed the re-networking opportunities offered by this program. Through Back in Business, he learned of Encore and attended the second New York event on November 8, 2006.

As Dougherty begins to hit the job market "for real," he's impressed with how hard it is to find an on-ramp. Like Melissa he finds he is struggling with the perception that his skills are out of date and that he is overqualified. Would he really be content with a lesser position—and a much smaller compensation package—than he had grown accustomed to?

Even more problematic is what one potential employer described as "his lifestyle choices." Dougherty sees this as "the elephant in the room." Often the whole subject of his stint as an at-home dad is avoided. But he knows it looms large with headhunters and employers alike—a source of discomfort and suspicion. What kind of loser is he—putting his children at the center of his life for almost four years!

Dougherty is enthusiastic about his experience so far with the Encore program. "Here's a place where I can exhale and not feel I've done something bad. Will the program work for me? I hope so. But even if it doesn't actually produce a job it's already done wonders for my confidence and sense of worth. I know it will jump-start my job search."[12]

TOOLKIT

Encore

For years, Wall Street and the City have viewed high female attrition rates as an unfortunate but unalterable fact of life. But times are changing. In 2005 Lehman's chief diversity officer, Anne Erni, developed a program called Encore—to welcome off-ramped women who wanted a new road back into the financial sector, but also to give her firm access to a new and significant pool of talent. Lehman president Joe Gregory threw his weight behind the idea because it made business sense.

The first Encore event was held in New York in November 2005. Invitations were sent to women who had at least five years of experience in financial services, had been out of the business for three years or less, and had an interest in rejoining their careers. Seventy-one women attended. Feedback after the event was overwhelmingly positive. Fully 98 percent of attendees expressed a desire to learn more about coming to work at Lehman. In the months following the event, Lehman hired twenty of these women through the Encore program.

The Business Case

Lehman's Gregory calls his reasons for backing the Encore program "selfish." He notes that out of every newly recruited class at Lehman, only 30 percent of the women will still be with the firm five years down the road. He calls this "a brutally inefficient use of talent." It is expensive to lose so many great women. High rates of attrition among women are a trend across Wall Street and Gregory points out that off-ramped women constitute "a large underutilized talent pool."[13] Lehman wants to tap in.

Meanwhile, the Encore initiative is serving as a recruiting tool at business schools, where, in recent years the number of women going into the financial sector has been falling. "If we can prove as a company that we respect the non-linearity of women's careers," says Anne Erni, "more women may consider pursuing a career in investment banking."[14]

Getting Started

- Gauge what you most need on the talent front—what skill set, what level. Lehman realized it needed to recruit more experienced professionals.
- Identify a variety of avenues through which to find a substantial pool of potential on-rampers. One source could be your organization's alumni database. Lehman also sourced through an informal friendship network and through referrals. Candidates were then assessed through introductory screening sessions.
- Identify both line and staff jobs that can be done flexibly by the on-rampers. Lehman isn't ready to reengineer all jobs immediately but is willing to tinker with specific jobs that make a good fit with Encore participants.
- Create a feedback loop. Lehman not only surveys attendees at its Encore events, but maintains a dedicated e-mail box for capturing feedback as well as résumés.
- Have a system in place to solicit résumés, line up interviews, and track results. Establish credibility by announcing hirings from the talent pool you've created.

Critical Elements

- *An asset-based model.* Lehman's senior managers viewed off-ramped women as an untapped asset—this made it easier to give the Encore program the resources it needed.
- *Tone at the top.* The visible support of Joe Gregory (president and COO) for what he perceived as a business opportunity—not a diversity program— was showcased internally and to Encore attendees.
- *Branding and image.* Lehman has capitalized on the brand-building and recruiting opportunities offered by Encore.
- *Advocates on the inside.* Encore's champions have worked hard to convince skeptics and to craft flexible work options for on-rampers.

GOLDMAN SACHS: NEW DIRECTIONS

David Crawford, vice president of the Human Capital Management Division at Goldman Sachs, the global investment bank, and a recruiter for the firm, often wondered what happened to the women who left Goldman Sachs after their maternity leaves ended. "But a typical recruiter only looks at a typical résumé, which—to be worthy of attention—is continuous. So I hadn't seen any from Goldman Sachs alumnae," Crawford said. "Their résumés weren't making it to my desk."[15]

So Crawford was enthusiastic and supportive when Melinda Wolfe, managing director, Global Leadership and Diversity at Goldman, started exploring the idea of developing a program for off-ramped women. Inspired by her involvement with the Hidden Brain Drain Task Force, Wolfe knew there were many talented women trying to find a way back onto the career highway. She wanted her firm to have first pick of this treasure trove of talent. Wolfe saw a chance for Goldman Sachs to fill a market niche by viewing a gap on someone's résumé not as a negative but rather as an opportunity to attract new and needed skills. Costs-of-attrition data bolstered the business case for an on-ramping program. Industry research indicates that when a skilled employee leaves, it can cost upward of 150 percent of that employee's salary to hire a replacement. "In addition to direct costs, you lose leads, contacts, and institutional knowledge," explained Crawford. "And you have to train the new person and orient them to Goldman's culture."

Another plus, on-ramping women would add depth, creativity, and diversity to Goldman's labor force. Well-versed in the work of James Surowcicki (see chapter 4), Wolfe understood that the more heterogeneous the group, the richer the brew. Thus a team that included on-rampers would have a wider and deeper perspective than one that consisted of newly minted MBAs.

An immediate hurdle facing Crawford and Wolfe was designing a program "authentic" to Goldman Sachs. "We wanted to find women who were interested in returning to work full-time—not that we wouldn't offer flexibility—but in the main we wanted women who were committed to reentering the work force at full throttle," Crawford explained.

The Office of Global Leadership and Diversity teamed up with the company's Recruiting and Wellness department to craft a nearly daylong event to launch the new on-ramping program, which was to be called New Directions. As Wolfe described it, the name underscores the fact that the program could give on-ramping women a new compass, showing them the way back to their careers.

As Wolfe started to plan the event a serious challenge emerged: where to find appropriate invitees? Since there is no formal job market for on-ramping women, there are no obvious places to look. Elana Weinstein, vice president for Global Leadership and Diversity at Goldman, says that initially they generated a list by reaching out internally through the company's own Women's Network. "We told members that if they knew of someone, send her along—and we got a huge response," Weinstein says.[16] Applicants also came in via other avenues: the company approached the Forté Foundation, a nonprofit organization that reaches out to current and prospective women business leaders and asked for a list of referrals. The ground rules for invitees were simple: women had to have been out of the workplace for no more than five years and had to have left their jobs in good standing.

Each invitee received an e-mail from Goldman Sachs's Office of Global Leadership and Diversity, with a link to a Web site that had logistical information about the event and a registration form. If invitees wanted, they could also include their résumé. They were asked a few simple questions, such as whether they were looking for full- or part-time work, and whether they needed flexibility. "We weren't judging women by their registration information. Admission was on a first-come, first-served basis," Weinstein explains. The number of places was limited—the program's designers knew that too big an event would be impersonal and wouldn't create the ambiance they wanted. Eighty women were accepted, with the expectation that there would be a large drop-off at the last minute. "But the room was still packed. We had sixty-five women!" Weinstein comments enthusiastically.

One of those women was Aviva, who started working as a trader on Wall Street in 1989, a time when female traders were few and far between. Her most recent job had been at Goldman Sachs, but after her second son was born—she had three boys, ages three, six, and ten—she felt she needed to be at home with her children. Two years previously, Aviva started thinking about going back to work, focusing at first on part-time opportunities. "But the jobs I was offered weren't appealing. Nothing was demanding enough for someone with my background," she remembers. "I guess I wanted to have my cake and eat it too; I said I wanted to work only three days but what I really craved was the challenge and excitement of a full-time commitment. I missed the intellectual stimulation, the adrenaline rush, the feeling you get from being a player."

Aviva attended the New Directions event and thought it was a great tool for women who wanted to return to Wall Street. She hoped she would meet women like herself—women who loved being moms but still wanted a high-impact job. "When I was at home, I didn't meet any women who wanted to on-ramp and I thought maybe there was something wrong with me, but at New Directions I felt as if I could have been looking in the mirror," she says. "It helped me get focused. I started to think about full-time and I realized I could bring a lot to the table." When the Goldman Sachs recruiters met Aviva they immediately realized the value of her trading background. She has just been hired to a high-profile job in the equities department.[17]

Aviva is immensely grateful for Goldman Sachs's willingness to embrace her desire to restart her career. "I thought getting a job might be difficult because of the big hole in my résumé. But during the interviews, it never came up. No one said, 'Why did you leave?' I never felt as though I was being given 'bad marks' for having taken time out." Instead, she says, "Goldman wanted to talk about why I was a good fit for several positions at the firm. Here's when I felt the power of New Directions," says Aviva. "Imagine, I was weighing the pros and cons of more than one position! Not only did Goldman offer me a job, the firm offered me a choice of jobs."

As Aviva eloquently testifies, among on-ramping women, New Directions is already seen as a great success. Attendees at the May 2006 event particularly appreciated the involvement of senior management. At the luncheon session two Goldman managers were seated at each table, providing attendees with a chance to introduce themselves to the company. At the same time, managers could catch a glimpse of the impressive credentials of the women who were being drawn into the Goldman fold through New Directions.

"In addition to pulling in senior men, we made sure to have senior female managers at the event," said Crawford. "Senior women send a strong message—besides which, down the road, they might well be in the audience!"[18] Female managers resonate in special ways, but the presence of male managers was also powerful. Their attendance sent the message that the firm was serious—from the top down—about this pioneering approach to exploring the off-ramped talent pool.

In addition to the presence of top management, this first New Directions event had other distinctive elements: it was sprinkled with distinguished speakers—Myra Hart, a former Harvard Business School professor and an authority on women's career paths, led the luncheon discussion; and it showcased a panel of Goldman Sachs female executives who themselves had successfully on-ramped at the firm.

Wolfe sees New Directions as a program that's still evolving. First, Goldman is staging a second event in New York due to the outstanding response to this initiative. In the six months from May to October 2006, 155 more women have expressed interest in attending the program. Goldman is also taking the program to other company locations around the world—kicked off by a London launch in September 2006. Down the road Wolfe and her team envisage a rich pipeline of talented women brought in through the program, filling vacated or newly created positions at Goldman Sachs.

TOOLKIT

New Directions

Inspired by her work with the Hidden Brain Drain Task Force, Melinda Wolfe, managing director, Global Leadership and Diversity, began developing a program that would put off-ramped women back into the Goldman Sachs talent pipeline. Gaps in a résumé would no longer be considered a negative. Instead, recruiters would consider what the individual had done before and while she was away from her career.

The immediate challenge was designing a program that reflected the Goldman Sachs philosophy and culture. Flexibility would be an option, but the primary targets of the new program would be women who wanted to hit the ground running. The name of the program, New Directions, was meant to indicate that Goldman was providing a compass, showing women the way back into high-impact careers.

New Directions was launched in May 2006, when sixty-five women attended a substance-packed event at Goldman's New York headquarters. The program has been enthusiastically received and is being rolled out globally.

The Business Case

Goldman Sachs has determined that when a skilled employee leaves, it costs 150 percent of that employee's salary to hire a replacement. In addition to direct costs, the firm loses leads and contacts, and the new recruit has to be oriented to the Goldman culture. As well as saving on turnover costs, on-ramping women add another layer of diversity and creative depth to the firm—the more heterogeneous the professional team, the more "out of the box" strategic thinking.

Getting Started

- Proactively seek out suitable participants. Goldman reached out to off-ramped alumnae, but Wolfe and her team also made huge efforts to reach other women by partnering with nonprofit organizations with access to this talent pool.

- Include in the initiative organizations within your company that can provide meaningful content and support—and have a vested interest in making the program a success. Goldman brought in its Women's Network (to solicit referrals), its alumni networks, its recruiting arm (which was interested in filling the pipeline with great candidates), and its wellness program (which had a stake in demonstrating that off-ramping and on-ramping are viable life choices at Goldman).

- Find blue-chip speakers and showcase success stories. The people involved in New Directions events have been top-notch: Harvard Business School professors and other well-known experts in the field. Tapping into some "home-grown" on-ramping successes was an inspired thought, since attendees were moved by these women's stories.

- Involve your key players. Senior managers who attended the launch saw first-hand the caliber of the on-ramping talent pool.

Critical Elements

- *A differentiated product.* New Directions was primarily looking for people to return full-time, which distinguishes it from other programs.

- *A wide net.* Working with nonprofit partners Goldman was able to tap into a larger, richer talent pool.

- *Access to decision makers.* Attendees at the New Directions events were given access to senior executives who might have a say in hiring.

- *Role models.* Panels provided New Directions attendees with real-life examples of women who had on-ramped at Goldman. These women became instant role models. The subliminal message: "If she could do it, so can I."

- *A market vantage point.* To reinforce its commercial orientation, New Direction events gave women critical information on trends and changes in global financial markets.

7

Reimagining Work Life

Many of the standard work-life policies offered by companies were designed with a specific demographic in mind: married with children. For decades the best benefits—and finest family support programs—in large corporations have been devoted to this group of employees.

For more and more workers this narrow focus just doesn't cut the mustard. As we saw in chapter 2, a large proportion (44 percent) of highly qualified women are childless.[1] Indeed, fully half of professional women ages twenty-eight to forty don't have children.[2] Some will undoubtedly become older moms, but given the fact that 39 percent of forty-one- to fifty-five-year-old professional women in our survey don't have children, we can assume that childlessness is a conspicuous reality among women in high-level, high-impact jobs.[3] In addition, a large number of highly qualified women are single—nearly a third of the women surveyed are currently not married, and this figure rises to 37 percent among African American female executives.[4]

But if a significant proportion of highly credentialed women don't have husbands and two-year-olds who need their care, they still have serious caregiver responsibilities. A substantial number (24 percent) of professional women off-ramp because of an elder-care crisis. The fact is, if a talented woman is not derailed by a two-year-old at age thirty-five, she may well be derailed by an eighty-two-year-old at age forty-five.

A recent *New York Times* article by Jane Gross described the plight of midlife professional women scrambling to care for frail, elderly parents and failing to find much in the way of help.[5] According to AARP, more than 20 million employees (50 million individuals overall) are now caring for aging parents, and women account for 71 percent of those devoting forty or more hours a week to this task.[6] The mommy track has now been joined by the *daughter track*—Gross's term for professional women hemmed in by the responsibilities of daughterhood.

One additional dimension of the problem has come to light. In 2005, the Hidden Brain Drain Task Force undertook a study of the challenges faced by minority executives and found that professionals of color—particularly women—routinely take on responsibility for needy young people in their extended families and their communities. To a much greater extent than their white colleagues they reach out and give back as "big sisters," godparents, and honorary aunts.[7] The circle of care seems to be particularly wide for African American female professionals.

The case studies featured in this chapter (Citigroup, Time Warner, and Johnson & Johnson) demonstrate that companies are beginning to realize that professionals—particularly women—have responsibilities that go beyond biological children. Employees these days need help and support that extends past—sometimes well past—the nuclear family.

CITIGROUP: ELDER CARE MANAGEMENT SERVICES

Sam Rubino, head of Employee Networks and Strategic Dependent Care Programs at Citigroup, likes to think big and anticipate the future. In 2001 he was taken aback by demographic data, shared at a conference he attended, showing that approximately 25 percent of the U.S. workforce was involved in the care of an older family member. What's more, over a five-year time frame, this number was expected to double. Given his role at Citigroup, one of the largest financial services companies in the world,

Rubino was well positioned to realize that the impact of this escalating load of care could have serious consequences for companies. As longevity increased, ever larger numbers of workers would need help caring for elderly family members, and if such support was not forthcoming, employees would surely spend at least part of the workday distracted and anxious—absenteeism would spike. Rubino also understood that the employee pool most affected by these trend lines would be middle-aged female employees. According to a study published in the *Journal of Gerontology*, women in midlife disproportionately take on the care of frail or disabled family members.[8] Because midlife is also the time when rates of female participation in the labor force peak, many women are faced with particularly difficult trade-offs: how to balance a career that had been put on hold for children but is finally taking off with a new round of caregiving responsibilities—this time centered on elders.

When Rubino began to wrestle with these trend lines, rudimentary support for U.S.-based employees dealing with an elder-care crisis was already available through Citigroup's employee resource and referral services. Although this capability was useful, providing tips on elder care and information about what to look for in assisted living arrangements, Rubino knew it wasn't nearly enough.

Therefore, to expand its offerings, in 2003 Citigroup asked Ceridian Corporation, the company that already provided Citigroup's resource and referral services, to roll out a program, called Elder Care Management Services, that would go one step further. This new program offered Citigroup's U.S. employees up to six hours of free consultation each year to help them evaluate and assess living and wellness needs for older family members.

This program enables employees, their siblings, and elderly relatives to consult with a trained professional about eldercare options, either by phone or in person. The specialist then makes on-site visits to assess whether the elderly family member would benefit from special equipment or alternative living arrangements. This specialist is also available to investigate a variety of alternative or assisted living facilities in a given geographic area and provide the employee with a written assessment of the chosen options' pros and cons. Other benefits include a check-in service to monitor an elderly relative's condition, and a management service that coordinates the various pieces of the support package for the older relative.

Professional assistance may also be tapped to help employees better navigate the morass of insurance and billing issues that frequently complicate senior care. Citigroup's program can even arrange for respite care to relieve a primary caregiver.

To date, employees who avail themselves of this new program average between four and six hours of use per year.[9] Despite this modest figure Citigroup's initiative has paid off in terms of intangibles—caregivers with elder-care responsibilities feel newly supported. In the rare case where an employee requires more than the allocated six hours, the company has provided additional help at no cost to the employee.

"The private sector must understand the complex needs of today's professionals grappling with responsibilities to parents as well as to children," says Rubino.[10] Citigroup believes that an impressive amount of lost productivity is associated with elder-care responsibilities. Absenteeism and tardiness tend to spike, and at least some valued employees are forced off-ramp by elder-care crises.[11] The anecdotal evidence is compelling and has helped decision makers at Citigroup drive this new program. Ana Duarte-McCarthy, chief diversity officer at Citigroup, sums up the situation: "We all know how personal problems can undermine professional activity. It's difficult for an individual to concentrate on work when they have an ailing parent or relative who's not coping. We recognize that from time to time these concerns become priorities in a person's life. Hopefully our Elder Care Management Services address these issues and help employees manage these worries."[12]

Citigroup employees are using all aspects of this program. Thirty percent of the need has been for assessment of living situations, 22 percent for consultations, and 21 percent for care reports to the family. The average age of the relatives in need of assistance is eighty. The majority of the requests target elderly mothers (55 percent) and elderly fathers (26 percent). The remainder targets parents-in-law, grandparents, and spouses/partners.

Citigroup publicizes its Elder Care Management Services internally three times a year: just after the winter holidays (Christmas, Hanukkah, Kwanzaa), after the spring holidays (Easter, Passover), and at the end of the summer. Employees are alerted through desktop fliers and e-mail. It's interesting to note that in 2005 Ceridian fielded more resource and referral inquiries about elder care than child care, underscoring the shifting demographics.

To buttress the business case for Elder Care Management Services, Citigroup did a rudimentary cost benefit analysis—the expense of the program versus the number of workdays that would have been lost to elder care. While largely a qualitative assessment, it was compelling. "So far," says Rubino, "the program has received high marks from employees. They realize that while they may not need it now, there's a program out there that will help them deal with an older family member when the time comes. This is very comforting."[13]

TOOLKIT

Elder Care Management Services

Back in 2001, Sam Rubino, head of Citigroup's Employee Networks and Strategic Dependent Care Programs, was impressed by data showing that approximately 25 percent of the U.S. workforce was caring for an older family member—and this number would double over a five-year period.

Rubino reasoned that Citigroup employees involved in elder care would surely spend part of their working day anxious and distracted, and absenteeism rates would spike. Citigroup already offered some basic support through its employee resource and referral services. In 2003 the company decided to deepen its efforts by offering a new Elder Care Management Services program developed and managed by Ceridian Corporation to help U.S.-based employees navigate this major stressor in their lives. Ceridian was already providing Citigroup's U.S. employees with resource and referral services; the Elder Care Management Services program went a big step further. All U.S. employees were now eligible for up to six hours of free consultation each year to assist in evaluating the needs of older family members.

The Business Case

In the words of Rubino, "Companies need to understand the complex needs of today's employees as they grapple with meeting their responsibilities to older family members." The business case for meeting such needs hinges on lost productivity—absenteeism, leaving early, arriving late. And lost talent—especially high-performing professionals.

So far, a small number of employees use this program each year, but the intangible payoffs are huge. Young as well as middle-aged employees realize that they are potential stakeholders in this initiative. According to Rubino employees praise the program, and although they might not need the services today they know that they will in the future. Interestingly, elder care is now the number-one reason employees use Citigroup's resource and referral services, surpassing child care for the first time in 2005.

Getting Started

- Map the demographics of your workforce—both locally and globally—to demonstrate the need for elder-care support.
- Convince the skeptics in your organization that employees have care responsibilities that go beyond children and that these responsibilities have a bearing on engagement and productivity.
- Gather anecdotal information to find out the specifics of the elder-care challenges faced by employees.

Critical Elements

- *Demographic changes.* Citigroup's Elder Care Management Services program is built on the premise that an increasing number of employees are (and will be) caring for older family members and that these responsibilities have an impact on productivity. Companies therefore need to lighten the load for employees.
- *Established provider.* Citigroup used an existing resource and referral service as a platform from which to launch this more ambitious program.
- *Built-in options.* The company decided it would be expedient if an arm's-length vendor could provide both basic resource and referral services and an enhanced Elder Care Management Services program. Employees could not be expected to know when a care issue was serious enough to warrant a special level of assistance versus more routine help. This framework also obviates the need for Citigroup to develop these specialized services.

TIME WARNER: EMPLOYEE ASSISTANCE PROGRAM

Imagine you're a human resources vice president and you think your company offers one of the best benefits packages around—indeed, your company is often lauded in magazines and newspapers for its extensive and impressive benefits package. Yet one day your executive vice president says, "We need to revisit our benefit offerings to see how we can make them better fit the demographics of our workforce. We're not as inclusive as we could be."

Debbie Cohen was one such human resources vice president, and she revisited the issue with a vengeance. In the fall of 2005 Cohen's boss, Patricia Fili-Krushel (executive vice president for administration at Time Warner), in response to Hidden Brain Drain Task Force research on the challenges faced by minority executives, raised this issue of inclusivity at Time Warner. At a task force meeting held during that same time period and focused on the challenges faced by minorities, Fili-Krushel had listened to an African American attendee speak about having two young children of her own, but also of paying college tuition for an eighteen-year-old cousin whose mother had died of AIDS. Fili-Krushel recognized that she was being invited into a multicultural world where professionals often had responsibility for needy individuals outside the conventional bounds of the nuclear family. "I said to myself, 'Time Warner is very big on diversity but does the company cover this?' " Fili-Krushel remembers. As she suspected at the time, Time Warner only gave scholarships to direct "dependents" of employees. "A foster child or grandchild wouldn't be considered an employee's 'dependent' even though they were, for lack of a better term, a 'reliant individual' dependent on that employee for support," notes Fili-Krushel. "So I said to my team, 'Aren't we looking at our whole benefits package through a traditional lens?' "[14]

Cohen set to work brainstorming with other individuals within the corporation. "I first talked to all the affinity groups in the Time Warner family—the Asian Network, the Black Employees at Time Warner network, and so forth."[15] Cohen discovered that different minority groups had different cultural norms and the standard benefits package—no matter how comprehensive or innovative it seemed to be—didn't always cover their needs.

For instance, if a family had a teenage nephew living with them whose parents lived in Puerto Rico, under the terms of just about any corporate benefits package, this young man would not qualify as an "employee dependent." Even though his aunt and uncle fed him dinner every night, took him to the doctor when he hurt his leg playing soccer, and worried about how they would pay tuition costs when he went off to college, he would not be considered a dependent. In the United States—more than ever before—grandparents, aunts, uncles, or godparents are raising children in lieu of biological parents.

Modern communication technology has also expanded the scope and reach of extended family responsibilities. In an interview, Lily, a Time Warner executive, spoke of her recent involvement in the problems faced by a depressed, possibly suicidal, teenage nephew. Despite the fact that

Lily herself had a relatively problem-free family life (her marriage was solid, her young adult children happily launched in life), she found herself newly exhausted and distracted at work because her sister—who lived three thousand miles away—had been calling her in the early hours of the morning to share various crises in the life of her troubled son, Lily's nephew. One night he didn't come home, another night he was rushed to the hospital after swallowing a bottle of painkillers.

After weeks of sleepless nights and a hurried trip to the West Coast, Lily remembered something she'd recently read in a company memo about changes in the employee assistance program. Time Warner's Employee Assistance Program was no longer restricted to employee dependants, but included reliant individuals as well. This meant that Time Warner's Employee Assistance Program could lend a hand to Lily's sister and her troubled son. Lily gave her sister the appropriate access codes; her sister was then able to consult experts at the Employee Assistance Program who proved to be invaluable in managing the situation: finding a great therapist who would take her insurance, and—when it became necessary—identifying an in-patient treatment center appropriate for the boy.

All of this was done anonymously. Lily's manager had no idea of the unfolding drama (though she may have noticed that Lily was her highly productive self again). All the point person at the Employee Assistance Program needed to know was that Lily's sister was a reliant individual and that she had appropriate access; there was no need to divulge the nature of the relationship. But Lily's sister got the help she needed to put her son back on the road to well-being.

Cohen's vision—and her definition of family—is newly expansive. "Family is who you rely on and who relies on you," she says. Because of this new perspective, the Time Warner college scholarship program has also morphed slightly. Any Time Warner employee who pays college tuition for a financially dependent person—whether a child, a foster child, or a grand-child—is now eligible to apply to the scholarship fund.

Time Warner is now sensitized to opportunities to become inclusive—not only in its programs but in its processes. For example, a recent conversation about security passwords required for access to various benefits programs touched on the idea of changing them to be less class specific. In New York City, for instance, where many people don't own a car, it makes no sense to pose "What was the color of your first car?" as an entrée question to a series of security checks. A better question, according to Cohen, is one that people across the socioeconomic spectrum can answer, such as "What was the name of your favorite teacher?" or "Where were you born?"

Widening the tent at Time Warner—expanding the benefits package to infuse it with a greater measure of inclusivity—has had little impact on the company's benefits budget. "Basically we took what existed and did a redesign, broadening the lens in areas where it wouldn't affect cost," Cohen explains. "We also negotiated with vendors for more favorable rates."

For now, there are areas into which the company wishes it could expand but as yet simply hasn't had the opportunity. "Extending health care to 'reliant individuals' involves the same type of conversation we had when we expanded to domestic partners," says Cohen. The company intends to continue exploring ways in which it can upgrade what it offers.

TOOLKIT

Employee Assistance Program

In 2005, Patricia Fili-Krushel, Time Warner's executive vice president for administration, attended a meeting of the Hidden Brain Drain Task Force that explored the work-life challenges facing minority and multicultural employees. She discovered that many such employees were often also responsible for needy individuals outside their nuclear family. Upon her return Fili-Krushel asked human resources vice president Debbie Cohen to find out whether Time Warner's benefits package was sufficiently inclusive. Was there a need to widen the tent?

Cohen polled the company's various affinity groups and found that many minority employees did indeed reach out to support extended family and a variety of nonrelatives. So Time Warner—led by Fili-Krushel—moved to get rid of the traditional lens in its benefits package and shift the focus from employee dependents to reliant individuals—a term that includes any person an employee supports either financially or emotionally.

Today, an employee's reliant niece or grandmother can receive support through Time Warner's Employee Assistance Program. The new approach also affects the company's scholarship program. There's still a finite amount of money available, but now a Time Warner employee who is paying tuition for someone else, as long as he or she is financially dependent, even if not directly related, can apply for a scholarship. Such changes, says Cohen, are not a program but a new way of working.

The Business Case

Time Warner realizes that many of its employees reach out to support the lives of people not directly related to them. Widening the tent so that the Employee Assistance Program can include nieces, grandfathers, and housemates does not add cost to the company's bottom line; rather, it helps ensure that employees come to work free of some worrisome responsibilities.

Getting Started

- Assess the unmet needs of your employees. Time Warner, for example, reached out to its affinity groups for information and feedback.
- Make an inventory of the benefits that could be included in widening the tent and assess the cost of expansion. Time Warner, for example, negotiated with its Employee Assistance Program provider so that neither Time Warner nor its employees were hit with enhanced fees for a more inclusive program.

Critical Elements

- *An outdated traditional lens.* Time Warner moved to get rid of this lens, recognizing that minorities—especially female minorities—often have responsibilities beyond nuclear family.
- *Feedback loop.* Recognizing nontraditional family situations has allowed Time Warner to build a more inclusive work environment, which has had a positive impact on recruiting and retaining talent from a variety of cultural backgrounds.

JOHNSON & JOHNSON: TAKING CARE OF SENIORS

Two years ago Cynthia's mother started growing increasingly frail, and as the daughter who lived closest (Cynthia has two sisters), this Johnson & Johnson executive became the primary caregiver. When it came to making decisions about her mother's care, Cynthia was on the front line. She spent her time at work worrying whether her mother might suffer a fall during the day and be unable to reach a phone, or put a pot of water on to boil and accidentally set the house on fire. Realizing that her worries were impacting her ability to concentrate at work and her own mental well-being, Cynthia decided something had to be done—quickly. "Luckily I knew what my company had on offer—the information was so readily available and presented so clearly. I contacted our work-life resource—LifeWorks—and within a day a geriatric resource manager had set up appointments with a social worker and getting me the information I needed," she said.[16]

LifeWorks, which got off the ground in 1989, is one of several elder-care programs offered by Johnson & Johnson. The company also offers an Elder Caregivers Support Group; a Web site (www.strengthforcaring .com) where caregivers can get information on eldercare issues; and helps fund the Johnson & Johnson/Rosalynn Carter Institute Caregivers Program, whose mission is to support the health and quality of life of persons who act as caregivers for chronically ill, disabled, or elderly family members. All of these programs are a great fit for a company whose credo includes the words: "We must be mindful of ways to help our employees fulfill their family responsibilities." Johnson & Johnson thinks of itself as a family, and just as family members help one another out, so Johnson & Johnson attempts to continually improve the ways in which it helps employees.

LifeWorks, which is available in the United States, is part of Johnson & Johnson's Life 360 benefits package, and receives rave reviews from employees who have used its elder-care services. One employee used the program to contact social workers and elder-care facilities in Florida, where her parents live. Another employee appreciated "being understood," while many other employees commented on the speed and efficiency with which their needs were met. In the words of one especially grateful employee, "This service has been extraordinarily helpful to me . . . the case manager spent four hours with my family and provided support and options. Since that original evaluation, my dad's health has gone downhill and the social worker has continued to provide guidance and assistance. On a scale of 1 to 10, I give this service a 10+."

Marion HochbergSmith, director of the Office of Equal Opportunity and Workplace Solutions at Johnson & Johnson, explains that the company's elder-care programs are part of what she calls a "one-stop shop" on Johnson & Johnson's health and wellness benefits intranet site. "The design is robust, and we make getting help as simple and as intuitive as possible," she says. "The password is right on the portal."[17]

LifeWorks provides a case manager, who discusses the relevant issues with the employee. If appropriate, the parent is then interviewed alone, as Cynthia's mother was. "That interview was key," Cynthia says. "In its wake we were advised that my mom could no longer live alone in her home. I'm so glad that it wasn't me making this decision on my own."[18] Expert guidance eased Cynthia's burden since this input trumped one sister's opinion that their mother should be cared for at home.

Once the case manager has a clear understanding of the needs, the Life-Works staff can begin the process of providing up-to-date information on long-term-care facilities in any geographic area the family chooses. "This is invaluable for people who do not themselves have the skills to know what one should look for in a care facility," HochbergSmith says. "Experts evaluate the food and social atmosphere as well as more obvious issues such as the ratio of staff per resident and the cleanliness of rooms. They then write up reports and send them to family members, who use them to make make an informed decision." In HochbergSmith's view, "this elder-care service takes a lot off employees' plates."[19]

One powerful program was not the result of top-down management; on the contrary, it sprouted by itself at Johnson & Johnson's corporate headquarters in New Brunswick, New Jersey, taking the form of a support group for employees dealing with elder-care issues. HochbergSmith explains, "Its 'membership' is fluid depending on what's happening in employees' lives. People who attend meetings swap stories as well as information. If someone has discovered a particularly good geriatric specialist or a great long-term-care facility, he or she shares this information at the support group meeting." A third piece of Johnson & Johnson's elder-care provisions is a Web site that is known by its URL, www.strengthforcaring.com. This is not an intranet site but is open to the general public and managed by Johnson & Johnson's Consumer Products Company. The idea is to deepen the relationship of trust between Johnson & Johnson and its consumers by reaching out to the large and underserved population of family caregivers in the wider community. This Web site disseminates needed information, but also increases public awareness of the burdens borne by family caregivers. Over 50 million Americans provide an average of twenty hours a week of uncompensated care for chronically ill loved ones—mostly elders. The economic impact of this unpaid labor is enormous: a recent study estimates the value of these "free" services at $306 billion.[20] Furthermore, the caregivers' own physical and mental health often deteriorates dangerously.

The pent-up demand for such a site can be seen from the response to www.strengthforcaring.com. The site has been visited over fifteen thousand times *per month* since its launch in February 2006, and its message boards contain hundreds of notes along the lines of the one left by a woman named Flora after she read an article about cognitive impairment: "I found this article reflected my experience exactly. Not long ago my mother handled bill paying, writing Christmas cards, and preparing home-cooked meals. She's no longer able to do these things. Our roles have slowly changed—and that has been tough. Now I pay the bills, write Christmas cards (not my favorite task), and cook the meals. The last line of the article really spoke to my feelings: 'Just remember that if he or she could, the person suffering the impairment would gladly resume those tasks.'"

Along with sections that provide information on conditions such as Alzheimer's and Crohn's disease, there are instructions on providing basic daily care (bathing and so on), guidelines to help people deal with insurance issues, a checklist that helps assess housing options, and an explanation of and forms related to appointing a durable power of attorney.

Johnson & Johnson's holistic approach to elder-care issues lies at the heart of the Johnson & Johnson/Rosalynn Carter Institute Caregivers Program. Founded in 1987, the Rosalynn Carter Institute for Caregiving joined forces with Johnson & Johnson in 2001 to support community-based programs that assist those who are caring for loved ones in need. Each year Johnson & Johnson provides one-time $40,000 grants to institutions and projects directly involved in caregiver issues. This collaboration burnishes the Johnson & Johnson public image while bringing to life the section of the Johnson & Johnson credo that states that the company is "responsible to the communities in which we live and work." Currently, the institute publishes seven booklets for the general public that concern aspects of caregiving, among them "Caregiving for an Individual with Alzheimer's Disease" and "Caregiving Across the Lifespan." Like the Strength for Caring Web site described earlier, this general public–focused initiative also circles back and helps Johnson & Johnson employees who are among the one in five people nationwide—over 50 million people—who need help and guidance caring for older family members and friends.

Johnson & Johnson's senior outreach is apparent even at the company's day-care center, based at corporate headquarters New Jersey. When space is available grandchildren of current or retired employees are welcome to attend. "We're very pleased to be able to have our grandchildren in the Child Development Center at Johnson & Johnson," says one grateful grandmother. "After evaluating other child-care facilities, we chose this one because we can visit the children whenever we want and the teachers are of the highest caliber. When the children are at the Center we are not worried about them—it is like an extension of our family."

LifeWorks

Johnson & Johnson maintains several programs that target elder care. Life-Works, part of Johnson & Johnson's Life 360 overall benefits package and available in the United States, provides resources for employees caring for elderly or infirm relatives. Response time to a request for help is quick, and a case manager is assigned to each request in order to help determine the scope and type of need. Johnson & Johnson also sponsors a support group for employees dealing with elder-care issues at its corporate headquarters in New Brunswick, New Jersey. In addition, Johnson & Johnson has launched a robust Web site, Strength for Caring, for the general public that addresses elder-care issues and provides emotional support, along with valuable hands-on tools such as legal and financial forms and explanations. The company's corporate headquarters features yet another perk for its seniors: employees' grandchildren can attend Johnson & Johnson's highly rated day-care facility there.

The Business Case

Johnson & Johnson prides itself on its "family-friendly" outlook and policies. Indeed, the company thinks of itself as an extended family. Thus, LifeWorks and other elder-care programs align work-related benefits while also enhancing the Johnson & Johnson brand. Moreover, Johnson & Johnson is aware of the catastrophic effect that coping with elder care can have on a family member who is also a caregiver, and by providing services that take much of the worry and insecurity off an employee's shoulders, the company is assured that it will maintain the high-quality output of its workforce. Its Web site, Strength for Caring, supports its commitment to community well-being while burnishing the company's image and making good financial sense. People recognize Johnson & Johnson as a health-care product provider, and thus it is logical that they would approach Johnson & Johnson for help with elder-care issues. The site fills a significant need by providing excellent advice on elder-care issues, but also advertises Johnson & Johnson products and positions the company in a strongly positive light.

Getting Started

- Survey your workforce to determine whether elder-care issues are causing heartache and impacting employee performance.
- Weigh the cost of support services against the dollars lost when employees need to take time off or cannot do their jobs well because they are distracted by elder-care issues.
- Pay careful attention to the look of the intranet or Internet Web page that offers assistance/advice or acts as a portal. The design of the Johnson & Johnson sites makes them extremely easy to use.

Critical Elements

- *Alignment with credo.* Johnson & Johnson has many people-friendly policies in place, so LifeWorks wasn't too much of a stretch. The company's credo, in fact, basically calls for such a response to employee need.
- *Bottom-up momentum.* A program can develop from an ad hoc support group. One emerged at Johnson & Johnson headquarters when several employees realized they were facing similar emotional and physically draining issues. The company has seen fit to bolster the group as it fills a vital need.
- *Burnishing the brand.* Through its caregivers Web site Johnson & Johnson provides critical information to the consumer, bolstering confidence that the company understands elder-care issues. This is smart marketing because it enhances trust in the company's health-care products.

8

Claiming and Sustaining Ambition

Ambition is a problematic issue for women. Our data shows that talented women are not as ambitious as their male peers and that the gap widens as women move through their thirties and forties. In the business sector, for example, 53 percent of highly qualified women ages twenty-one to forty see themselves as "very ambitious," whereas in the forty-one to fifty-five age group that percentage drops to 37 percent.

A good part of the problem is the nonlinearity of many female careers. Off-ramps and scenic routes are difficult to recover from—it is the rare woman who emerges from a career break with her job prospects intact. DeAnne Aguirre—the senior vice president and managing partner of Booz Allen Hamilton's global organization, whom we met in chapter 6 and who off-ramped and on-ramped eight times during her sixteen-year career at this professional services firm—is highly unusual. More commonly, off-rampers are subject to a myriad of penalties. Many of them lose heart and voice and eventually reduce what they expect from themselves. Aspirations and dreams are downsized.

Another part of the problem is the glass ceiling that continues to limit and constrain the career prospects of women. Difficulties range from overt discrimination to a dearth of role models and mentors to a paucity of networks. Whatever the precise mix of reasons why women lose momentum, the result is the same: to a greater extent than their male peers (who also find the slippery slopes of upper management steep and treacherous), experienced, committed "high-potential" women are closed out of top jobs.

What to do? A key fix is employer-sponsored women's networks, which can be extremely effective in helping women claim and sustain ambition. Networks boost confidence and create traction by connecting women to peers, provide access to senior executives, serve as a showcase for leadership skills, and expand business relationships—both internally (inside the company) and externally (with clients and customers.)

The two networks featured in this chapter are state of the art. Johnson & Johnson's Women's Leadership Initiative and General Electric's Women's Network are well-established initiatives with impressive track records—they have a proven capacity to accelerate women's careers. An important defining characteristic of both programs is the emphasis on doing business better. Network events are not coffee klatches where women trade parenting tips; rather, they are substantive sessions where women hone leadership skill sets and build their business relationships.

The Women's Leadership Initiative is a little softer-edged than the Women's Network, focusing on work-life balance issues and community outreach as well as leadership skill building. General Electric's Women's Network is unapologetic in its focus on career advancement—explicitly aligning itself with the company's succession-planning processes.

Employers can also accelerate women's careers through leadership training programs that specifically target female executives—at Johnson & Johnson these programs are embedded in the Women's Leadership Initiative; at Time Warner, Breakthrough Leadership is an independent program.

The idea that companies need to offer leadership training that is customized for women is key here. Female professionals face a distinct set of challenges that revolve around a lack of role models and the absence of informal networks. But it's also true that women want different things from their work. As we discovered in chapter 2, women are motivated by a more complex series of career goals than their male peers. For female professionals, connection to colleagues, recognition from bosses, giving back to community, and flexibility all tend to trump compensation as reasons why they go to work. It therefore stands to reason that if employers want to tap into the full range of female aspirations, they need to customize leadership training for their high-potential women. Time Warner's Breakthrough Leadership program is a model on this front.

JOHNSON & JOHNSON: WOMEN'S LEADERSHIP INITIATIVE

Johnson & Johnson's Women's Leadership Initiative got off the ground in 1995. With its impressive track record and extraordinary global reach, the Women's Leadership Initiative has become an important player in women's networking—a gold standard for private-sector programs aimed at helping women claim and sustain their career ambitions.

With more than 230 operating companies and 115,000-plus employees in 57 countries around the world, Johnson & Johnson is a major force in the pharmaceutical industry, with products ranging from medical devices to baby supplies. Despite its formidable size the company has a well-deserved reputation for being woman-friendly. For twenty-one years Johnson & Johnson has appeared on *Working Mother* magazine's list of the 100 best companies to work for.

It wasn't always so. JoAnn Heffernan Heisen, chief diversity officer of Johnson & Johnson and a member of the company's executive committee, recalls that when she arrived at the company seventeen years ago she was one of just a handful of executive women. "Johnson & Johnson had a great reputation as a family-friendly company but like many other corporations at the time, there were few women in executive positions."[1] It had a comfortable—and highly entrenched—male culture. Many male employees joined the company at age twenty-two or twenty-three and spent decades working, socializing, golfing, and becoming connected with one another.

Though a supportive culture for male executives, Johnson & Johnson felt closed off to women who hadn't "grown up" at the company. Like Heisen, many of these women were midcareer hires. They didn't have strong relationships across the business units, relationships that had been cultivated by years of networking as so many men at Johnson & Johnson did. A few women had managed to achieve positions of power but they were a rarity. Heisen saw the need for creating more opportunities for women in leadership, particularly given the significant growth opportunities forecast for Johnson & Johnson in the marketplace. She knew that more and more women with credentials and ambition were entering the workforce. According to *Workforce 2000*, a 1987 study by the Hudson Institute that influenced Heisen's thinking at that time, between 1985 and 2000 only 35 percent of new workers would be men. Fully 61 percent of new entrants to the labor force would be female—42 percent of them white, 22 percent of them women of color.[2] It seemed to Heisen that Johnson & Johnson had a compelling business case for grooming more women to take leadership positions.

Heisen's personal history was also a driver. Her father had died of a brain tumor when she was nine years old leaving her mother widowed with four young children, one of them a newborn, and little in the way of earning power. Since her father had been CFO of the National Institutes of Health, the NIH reached out to the family and offered Heisen's mother a secretarial job, but it paid little and the family constantly lived on the economic edge. The adolescent Heisen became her family's intermediary with its creditors. "When the premium for our car insurance hadn't been paid or the gas bill was overdue and the bill collectors came, my mother would send me to the door to make excuses and buy us time," she says. For Heisen, it was a wake-up call. "These experiences made an indelible impression on me. I understood—deeply—the burdens and heroism of working mothers." She also understood the need for financial security. In her words, "You never knew when a husband might die or leave you."[3] Heisen vowed she would never end up in a situation where she had no other option than being a secretary.

Undoubtedly, Heisen's childhood honed her ambition and prepared her to cut a powerful path in the business world. After graduating from Syracuse University with a degree in economics, she joined Chase Manhattan Bank, where she was one of five female recruits in a pool of twenty-five new hires. While at Chase, she joined the Financial Women's Association of New York and eventually became its president. There, she says, "I saw how important it was for women to have a strong and caring network that provided support and encouragement to counter the isolation they often faced in the workplace." When Heisen was appointed treasurer of Johnson & Johnson in 1991, she became the company's top female executive and one of the highest-ranked women in the corporate world—but she hung onto her keen awareness of the need for female solidarity across management levels.

The Birth of the Women's Leadership Initiative

In her new position Heisen got to know many senior-level women in the various Johnson & Johnson operating companies, and she reached out to each of them. Simultaneously she was developing solid working relationships with the company's top male executives and began talking to them about an initiative that could accelerate the progress of women at Johnson & Johnson. "They were totally supportive of the idea of a women's network," she says, "just not savvy about how to make that happen."

Beginning in 1990 Heisen and thirty other top-tier women at Johnson & Johnson—vice president level and above—began meeting for regular dinners to discuss their business concerns. The executive committee of the company, which was then all male, would join the group for cocktails. They understood the importance of meeting these high-achieving women—most of whom they only knew on paper through HR reviews. Then, Heisen says, "We would send the men packing and we would get down to business." The group grew over time, and, realizing what an impact this small network was having on their own professional development, began to feel a responsibility to the wider pool of women at Johnson & Johnson. The next step: they decided to hold a conference to explore the changing landscape of women's leadership at Johnson & Johnson and in the business world in general. In March 1995 over three hundred Johnson & Johnson women, director level and above, gathered at the company's New Brunswick, New Jersey, headquarters, and the Women's Leadership Initiative was born.

Chaired by Heisen, the Women's Leadership Initiative determined that its mission was "to challenge the Johnson & Johnson family of operating companies to define and enhance policies that will attract, develop and retain talented women."[4] The stakes are big. The data shows that almost 80 percent of graduate degrees in the health sciences now go to women; if Johnson & Johnson can effectively tap into this rich talent pool, the payoff for the company will be huge.

As its framework evolved the Women's Leadership Initiative became a powerful yet decentralized network that united women around common interests and activities across Johnson & Johnson's 230 operating companies. It is governed by a steering committee comprising many of the company's most senior women who represent all the major business lines. Within each operating company, the Women's Leadership Initiative is led by business unit chairs—like Amy Jumbelic, an operations leader for the Johnson & Johnson Consumer Products Company. Jumbelic took over as chair of the Women's Leadership Initiative at her operating company in 2004.

Business unit chairs such as Jumbelic provide their respective operating companies with leadership to support the Women's Leadership Initiative mission. They also plan activities for women in their division. At the Johnson & Johnson Consumer Products Company Jumbelic and her team sponsor more than a dozen meetings each year and, through their communications liaison, contribute news and feature articles to the Women's Leadership Initiative Web site, which is accessible to employees worldwide.

In addition, subcommittees appointed by Jumbelic and her Women's Leadership Steering team have reached out and offered help to female employees with mentoring, networking, and professional development.[5]

Scope and Reach

The Women's Leadership Initiative's impact is both broad and deep. Take executive education. On this front the Women's Leadership Initiative has introduced three kinds of training opportunities for women. First was a decision to join the Smith College Consortium, a collaboration between six major corporations to provide management and leadership training for high-potential women—Jumbelic was a participant in 1999. Second, the Women's Leadership Initiative worked with Smith College and Dartmouth's Tuck School of Business to create a program that provides management training for women with international responsibilities. Each year Johnson & Johnson sends a contingent of high-potential women to the Smith-Tuck program for global women leaders. And third, the Women's Leadership Initiative approached Smith to customize a leadership training program for manager-level women. This program is held annually and is open exclusively to Johnson & Johnson women.

The Women's Leadership Initiative has expanded far beyond its original purpose. "Initially it was simply, 'Let's get together and talk about how we survive as women,'" says Ellen Griffith, speaking on a promotional DVD created to showcase the Women's Leadership Initiative.[6] Today Women's Leadership Initiative activities range from the training and education programs described above to promoting work-life balance to girl power and community outreach. For Jumbelic work-life issues are a priority. "'Work-life effectiveness is one of our key issues," she says. "This can mean anything from helping a single mother secure a flexible work arrangement to making sure women across the board know about the benefits and programs on offer at our companies. We find that many women don't know what's available—and are afraid to ask."[7]

Attendance at Women's Leadership Initiative events has also grown exponentially since that inaugural conference in 1995. At the five-year mark (2000), the number of conference attendees—women at the director level and above—had grown to eight hundred. At the ten-year mark (2005), well over two thousand senior-level women attended eight conferences and celebrations around the world.

The impact of the Women's Leadership Initiative is unambiguous—the network has been a powerful force in accelerating women's progress at Johnson & Johnson. Between 1995 and 2005 the percentage of women at the vice president level or above rose from 14 percent to 30 percent. While Johnson & Johnson had no women on the executive committee in 1995 and only one in 2000, by 2005 four out of the eleven members were women. Today, women have reached the company's top rungs—Christine Poon, vice chairman of the board and worldwide chairman of Medicines & Nutritionals, and Colleen Goggins, chairman of the Consumer and Personal Care Group, lead two of the company's three main business units.

Still, the work of the Women's Leadership Initiative is far from over. While over half of Johnson & Johnson's employees are women, only a third of the top earners at the company are female. Jami Miller, regional account director for Johnson & Johnson Health Care Systems, notes that, like herself, women with children continue to face barriers and hurdles as they try to move up within the company. For example, to advance her career at Johnson & Johnson, Miller has been required to relocate four times. As Miller points out, she was lucky—her husband was supportive of the many moves. Often women with families don't have this luxury.

Miller is clear on one score: the Women's Leadership Initiative has been a huge door opener. "When you're involved in the Women's Leadership Initiative you see how things have changed, how women are getting promoted across the company. When I joined the company fifteen years ago I went through a management training program that had sixteen people in it, fifteen guys and me. I was one woman in a sea of men. That kind of ratio is a thing of the past."[8]

What accounts for the Women's Leadership Initiative's success? One factor, according to Heisen, is that its focus has always been on doing business better. "Those early dinner meetings always focused on honing skill sets and enhancing business relationships—they weren't just social gatherings. Conversation centered on issues such as market share, market trends, and growth prospects. We were developing a relationship network with our business peers, just like the men who had 'grown up' together at Johnson & Johnson," Heisen says.[9]

Thanks to both its longevity and its conspicuous success, the Women's Leadership Initiative now serves as the prototype for a greatly expanded roster of affinity groups at Johnson & Johnson—the African American Leadership Council (AALC), the Community of Asian Association at Johnson & Johnson (CAAJJ), the Gay & Lesbian Organization for Business and Leadership (GLOBAL), the Hispanic Organization for Leadership and Achievement (HOLA), among others. Despite this explosion of affinity group activity, the Women's Leadership Initiative remains the largest network and the only one that has expanded worldwide.

Going Global

The Women's Leadership Initiative has expanded overseas to support women in Johnson & Johnson operating companies around the world. The challenges vary according to region. For example, with regard to equality, European women lag behind women in the United States but are making progress. Heisen believes that—in terms of how women are doing—some Asian countries have leapfrogged over Europe. China is particularly impressive, at least in part because of its recent history. "Chairman Mao said that 'women hold up half the sky,' and during the decades of communist rule Chinese women were fifty-fifty partners in the workplace," notes Heisen. But while China has surged ahead, other Asian countries have lagged behind.

According to Sakiki Kon, who works for the Johnson & Johnson Medical Company in Tokyo, the Women's Leadership Initiative has been particularly important in Japan. Kon is head of the Women's Health Business Unit, which is responsible for a variety of medical devices including those used in breast cancer surgery and minimally invasive surgery. In her country, Kon says, there are not nearly enough women at the top, and there's a dearth of female role models. "The programs of the Women's Leadership Initiative are therefore extremely helpful in establishing a culture that is more receptive to women in senior positions," she says.[10]

Kon is convinced that the main obstacle to women's advancement in Japan is the local culture—which prefers to see women as wives and mothers rather than as powerful professionals. This is a more significant obstacle than the absence of support programs and policies. On the work-life front, flexibility is at the top of women's wish lists, but the Johnson & Johnson Medical Company in Tokyo already does well on this front, offering flexible and extensive maternity leave and providing a $1,500 bonus per year to working mothers to help defray child-care expenses. These programs dovetail with recent government policies designed to combat low birth rates by encouraging working women to have children.

Kon, who has a bachelor's degree in anthropology from the University of Arizona, was asked to head a Women's Leadership Initiative program soon after she joined the Johnson & Johnson Medical Company in Tokyo in 2002. She plunged right in, organizing a team of six women to help her identify the most pressing problems and develop a vision that would guide the new program. The team then came up with an agenda that focused on two things: ambition and acceleration. The company was pushed to promote more women, and women were encouraged to set their sights high. For a first move, Kon's team met with over one hundred senior executives at the company to discuss their objectives and propose a target—25 percent of executive ranks should be female within five years. This target was accepted and three years later a great deal of progress has been made. The number of female managers rose from 9 percent in 2002 to 19 percent in 2005.

According to Kon, the increased visibility of women has prompted a noticeable change of attitude among senior male managers, who now seem more willing to consider young, high-potential women for promotion. Women are also beginning to help themselves. Kon sees women at the company taking advantage of leadership training and networking opportunities provided by the Women's Leadership Initiative and becoming more proactive. One hundred thirty women attended the tenth anniversary Women's Leadership Initiative celebrations in Tokyo in June 2005—along with thirty senior male executives.

In 2005, Johnson & Johnson received an equal rights award from the Japanese government for the role the company has played in promoting women's rights through the Women's Leadership Initiative. That same year, fifty private-sector companies including Johnson & Johnson, IBM, Pfizer, and Panasonic, joined to form the Japan Women's Innovation Network (JWIN) to promote the idea that accelerating women's progress is good for companies and good for the Japanese economy. "We've helped create a private-sector movement that is driving a new message and a new reality: women have talent and credentials and *deserve* to be in leadership positions" says Kon. "What's more, women are no longer alone in their struggle to achieve this—their companies are right behind them."

Heisen has every reason to be proud of the Women's Leadership Initiative's impact in Japan—and elsewhere. She considers her job to be one of the best in the world. "I get to go around the globe spreading the good news— that a diverse and inclusive organization such as Johnson & Johnson has a competitive advantage. We have every intention of running with this issue," she says. "We will brand it, own it, and deliver it."[11]

TOOLKIT
Women's Leadership Initiative

Johnson & Johnson produces everything from shampoo to medical devices used in breast cancer surgery. With more than 230 operating companies and 115,000 employees in 57 countries, Johnson & Johnson has long been known as a family-friendly company that supports women. In 1995 JoAnn Heffernan Heisen, then treasurer of Johnson & Johnson, founded the Women's Leadership Initiative to accelerate the progress of women at the company. Over the next decade the

Women's Leadership Initiative grew and flourished. At its tenth anniversary in 2005 over two thousand senior-level women attended eight conferences and celebrations around the world.

The Women's Leadership Initiative unites women around common interests and activities across the Johnson & Johnson operating companies. It's headed by a steering committee that includes many of the company's senior women representing all the major business lines. Within Johnson & Johnson's decentralized structure, the Women's Leadership Initiative is governed by business-unit chairs who provide localized leadership and planning support. Subcommittees take responsibility for particular activities, such as organizing networking and mentoring events, or maintaining and enriching the Women's Leadership Initiative's Web site.

·The Women's Leadership Initiative has undoubtedly helped drive change at Johnson & Johnson. Between 1995 and 2005 the percentage of women holding positions at the vice president level or above rose from 14 percent to 30 percent. The Women's Leadership Initiative has also gone global. In Europe, Asia, and Latin America, Johnson & Johnson operating companies have established Women's Leadership Initiative programs that have had a powerful impact—accelerating female progress worldwide.

The Business Case

Women are particularly well positioned to do well in the pharmaceutical field. Current estimates suggest that nearly 80 percent of graduate degrees in the health sciences now go to women. Johnson & Johnson has already learned to tap into this talent pool—60 percent of its college hires in the United States are now female.[12] The mission of the Women's Leadership Initiative is to help this rich pool of women fully realize their potential at Johnson & Johnson. If the Women's Leadership Initiative can pull this off—and retention and advancement figures are beginning to look very good—the payoff for the company will be huge. Attrition rates will go down, engagement rates will go up, and a huge pool of new talent will be more fully utilized.

Getting Started

- Identify your organization's top champion for women and ask her to spearhead a woman's network. JoAnn Heisen was essential to the Women's Leadership Initiative's success within Johnson & Johnson. Her prominence and dedication enabled the program to take off.
- Start with a small group of committed, high-level women who span different business units or divisions. Once this group is up and running, it can grow into a network that will evolve over time, creating a distinct structure that will mirror the characteristics of the organization within which it operates.

Critical Elements

- *Focus on business.* The emphasis of the Women's Leadership Initiative has always been on doing business better.
- *Link to mission and brand.* Johnson & Johnson's senior leadership decided to make the realization of female talent part of the company's mission—to own it, brand it, and deliver on it.
- *Emphasis on substance.* Rather than enrolling members, the Women's Leadership Initiative organizes women around common interests and activities taking place across Johnson & Johnson's 230 operating companies.
- *Shared responsibility.* The Women's Leadership Initiative is built on a model of shared responsibility. It acknowledges that women are partners in their own advancement and this positions them well in the next generation of leadership.

TIME WARNER: BREAKTHROUGH LEADERSHIP

Time Warner, the world's largest media company, boasts several innovative programs that nurture the ambitions of female employees. One of the most successful is Breakthrough Leadership, a program developed in partnership with the Simmons School of Management in Boston.

This program was the brainchild of Patricia Fili-Krushel, executive vice president for administration at Time Warner. Inspired by the "camaraderie and bonding" she experienced while participating in a women's leadership event at ABC, the television network, Fili-Krushel decided to host an event for Time Warner women—a screening of a "chick flick" produced by the company, followed by a cocktail hour. Richard Parsons, chairman and CEO of Time Warner, was an invited guest, but when he walked into the room none of the other attendees paid him any attention. The women were too busy talking among themselves. Another CEO may have been put out, but Parsons got excited. "He said to me, 'What is this? Something huge is going on," remembers Fili-Krushel.[13]

At the end of the evening it dawned on Fili-Krushel that the event actually underscored a negative at Time Warner. Women executives at the company had no community within which to bond, no place to come together and make connections. This created a situation where the few women in senior positions felt extremely isolated.

Fili-Krushel's fix took a lot of thought and planning. She approached the Simmons School of Management and explored the possibility of designing a customized women's leadership program. Then her team, along with representatives from each of the company's divisions, spent a year working with the school to design it. They interviewed leaders around the company in an effort to understand what women really needed to succeed at Time Warner, and incorporated modules on developing those specific skills into the final program.

The Breakthrough Leadership program was launched in October 2003. It was hosted by the Simmons School of Management and took place at the school's Boston campus. As thirty Time Warner women gathered for that first five-day program Fili-Krushel assumed she would offer some introductory remarks and then fly back to New York, returning on the last day of the program to give a "what we learned and now goodbye" type of closing speech. To her great surprise she ended up staying the entire week, drawn by the power of the workshops, the presentations, and the participants themselves. "This was simply the most energizing and rewarding experience of my career," says Fili-Krushel. "When I left Boston, I felt I had birthed a third child." (Fili-Krushel has two children.)

Companywide the repercussions were immediate. "I had managers calling me and saying, 'What did you do up at that management meeting? I've had two women in my office today asking for raises!'" recalls Fili-Krushel.

That first Breakthrough Leadership program had a powerful effect on attendees. This inaugural class refer to themselves as the "tiara" class because of the way one participant described her work mode before the program—head down, incredibly busy and focused, she somehow expected a tiara to fall from the sky and crown her. A significant insight for this group came from realizing that rather than expecting automatic rewards for industriousness, women need to pick up their heads and strategically manage their own careers. The tiara metaphor was so resonant that one member of the inaugural class handed out tiaras at the final dinner. Some of these tiaras—rather tarnished at this point—can still be found hanging proudly on corner office walls.

What are the "ingredients" of Breakthrough Leadership? What makes it so special? To begin with, away from their desks and everyday responsibilities, participants become immersed in a fourteen-hour-a-day symposium. The sessions cover five basic areas:

1. *Personal leadership.* In this module attendees, all of whom are female, middle- and upper-level executives, delve into what Time Warner perceives as "good leadership"—what behaviors participants need to cultivate in order to progress at Time Warner.

2. *Skill building.* Over the course of the program, participants focus on developing leadership presence—and the ability to inspire others. They also learn to negotiate for the components of leadership success—specifically resources and support for their next career move. (A guiding prompt for this aspect of the program—studies reveal that while women tend to get promoted on performance, men tend to get promoted on potential.) In addition, women analyze their networks and discuss how well they are positioned for leadership success.

3. *Peer mentoring.* Throughout the program participants work with "peer" mentors with whom they discuss leadership and career and business issues. Vera Vitels, vice president for People Development at Time Warner and one of the designers of the Breakthrough Leadership program, says that many participants stay in touch with their mentors long after they're back at their Time Warner jobs.[14]

4. *Exposure to role models.* Several highly placed female executives from across the Time Warner divisions take time out from their work and fly up to Boston to join a series of panels focused on leadership and career. They talk about how they achieved their positions and other "secrets" to climbing the corporate ladder at Time Warner. These panels put a face on success and provide the participants with an opportunity to learn from both the achievements and the mistakes of women who have made it.

5. *Interaction with senior leaders.* A final element in the program is the presence of the top brass. Richard Parsons, Time Warner's President and CEO, attends each year to meet participants and share his views on leadership, Time Warner's businesses, and the importance of advancing women within the company. Ann Moore, President and CEO of Time, Inc., also spends an afternoon with participants, discussing leadership and sharing lessons from her own career.

How are women selected for the Breakthrough Leadership program? Vitels, the program's principle designer, reaches out to divisional HR heads within Time Warner and asks them to recommend women who are deemed high potential (in terms of their performance ratings) and see themselves as potential leaders. Most years there are more nominations than there are places in the program. Getting into Breakthrough Leadership is increasingly competitive.

One member of the inaugural class, Maja Thomas, vice president for Digital Content Strategy at the Time Warner Book Group, remembers that she didn't know anything about the program when she was tapped to go. "But I was excited because it sounded like going back to college— without final exams," she says. Thomas had been at Time Warner for thirteen years and compares her Breakthrough Leadership experience to a couple in a good marriage who end up "going into therapy" to make their relationship even better.

Thomas had never had any formal leadership training nor had she taken presentation or speech classes. "I felt I was filling in a gap, and now I tend to think of my career as 'before Breakthrough' and 'after Breakthrough.'"[15]

Rhonda Joy McLean, associate general counsel at Time, Inc., and another member of the inaugural class, seconds the positive feedback. "It was a gift of time away from the everyday concerns of my job where I could focus on personal development," she says. McLean notes that she and other participants feel that the Breakthrough Leadership program "brought a new richness to the quality" of their work experience. "I felt really valued," she adds.[16]

Thomas particularly appreciated practicing negotiating skills. "I've never liked negotiating on my own behalf," she says. But the program taught her how to walk in and tell her boss about things she could do to take a broader role in the company. "Since Breakthrough Leadership, I've had three promotions," says Thomas.[17]

Another valuable tool is the 360-degree feedback participants receive from classmates. Thomas talks about her feedback as being both flattering and critical but always revelatory. In her words: "I don't consider myself a natural leader but the 360 really helped show me the way."

Although participants are stimulated by the panels, inspired by the workshops, and motivated by their 360s, in the end they all say that the most powerful aspect of Breakthrough Leadership is connection to other women executives. "For me, it was all about the people," says Tina Sharkey, senior vice president for Network and Community Programming at America Online and a graduate of the third Breakthrough Leadership class. "To have the opportunity of meeting so many women from other divisions of Time Warner was invaluable," she says.[18]

As of October 2006 there have been nine Breakthrough Leadership programs, involving 229 attendees. One additional session is scheduled for 2007.[19] According to Fili-Krushel women who go through this program are more likely to get promoted than women who don't. Besides promotions, women who attended the program are more likely to move into different jobs with increased responsibility.

The program has been tweaked a bit over time: Vitels and her colleagues survey attendees to find out what worked well and what didn't. More substantively, Time Warner ensures that Breakthrough Leadership alumnae keep their skills honed and their network fresh by organizing annual "reunions." Graduates of the program gather in an off-site meeting space—generally a hotel—and participate in a day and a half of refresher sessions. Because the reunion group is larger than any one class, women have yet more opportunities to network.

Today, Breakthrough Leadership has a huge underground reputation and has become an extremely sought-after program. Vitels is constantly receiving calls—from women who want to attend the program and from senior managers wanting to nominate an outstanding woman in their division.

TOOLKIT

Breakthrough Leadership

Inspired by the camaraderie and bonding she experienced while participating in a women's leadership event for women executives at ABC, Patricia Fili-Krushel, executive vice president for administration was moved to organize a women's networking event at Time Warner. Her event featured a chick flick and an appearance by Richard Parsons, chairman and CEO of Time Warner. However, when he walked into the room, none of the women paid much attention. They were too busy talking to each other.

Fili-Krushel theorized that senior women within the company were starved for community, a place to come together and make connections. Thus, she joined with the Simmons School of Management to custom-design a leadership program for Time Warner women called Breakthrough Leadership.

The Business Case

The Breakthrough Leadership program is a powerful acceleration tool. Women who attend this program are more likely to get promoted than women who don't. The fact that Time Warner is now doing a better job of seeking out and training its own women reduces the need for expensive talent searches—the company can now look right in its own backyard. Breakthrough Leadership has also helped on the recruitment front: women at Time Warner believe that this leadership program has advanced the company to the top of the list for women looking for positions in the entertainment industry—and they tell their friends.

Getting Started

- Give priority—and allocate resources—to women's leadership training. These programs, whether run by Simmons or Smith, are not inexpensive but the payoffs are real.
- Devise a method for quantifying results. Time Warner has metrics proving that women who take part in Breakthrough Leadership are more likely to be promoted.

Critical Elements

- *A powerful leader.* The impact of this program owes much to the clout and commitment of Pat Fili-Krushel.
- *Highly customized leadership training.* This is at the heart of the Breakthrough Leadership program.
- *Business plus.* The program centers on business opportunities—but also includes a bit of fun. After all, entertainment is part of what one is selling at Time Warner.
- *Networking and relationships.* While women who have gone through the program value the skills they have gained, most emphasize that "it's all about the people."

GENERAL ELECTRIC: WOMEN'S NETWORK

The General Electric Company is an industrial colossus, producing engines, plastics, refrigerators, and power plants in over one hundred countries around the world. The company has three hundred thousand employees, and in 2005, revenues topped $150 billion. *Fortune* magazine's list of "Most Admired Companies" ranks General Electric number one.

If the company is known for its industrial might, it is also known for its uncompromising macho culture. But times are a-changing. In recent years General Electric has made huge efforts to be woman-friendly. Indeed, in 2004 the company won the prestigious Catalyst Award—given to a company that has made significant strides in advancing women—and for the last four years General Electric has been on *Working Mother* magazine's "100 Best Companies" list.

A great deal of credit goes to chairman and CEO Jeffrey Immelt who has pushed General Electric to "look more like the world" that buys its products. That world contains a great many women. Immelt also stresses the competitive strength inherent in expanding the talent pool. As Deborah Elam, General Electric's vice president and chief diversity officer, points out, to maximize growth opportunities, General Electric must have "global brains." According to Elam, "GE needs to be inclusive if it is to access a broad range of talent across the world."[20]

General Electric's diversity efforts began with the development of affinity networks. The first of these, the African American Forum (AAF), which was founded in 1993, has become a powerful tool in the company's drive for more diversity and an aid in identifying individuals with leadership potential.

In 1996, at the fourth annual AAF symposium, former CEO Jack Welch was struck by how helpful and effective the affinity group was for its members, and decided that a women's organization along the same lines had real potential and would be a boon for the company. So he met with senior women at General Electric's various businesses and discussed how to create such an entity. The end result: the General Electric Women's

Network, which was launched in 1997. The top 120 women at General Electric were invited to the kickoff event at the company's Crotonville, New York, campus. There they were encouraged to consult with their units and figure out what a women's network could do for them—and what they could do for other women at the company.

The Women's Network rapidly expanded. Although the Network was inspired by the AAF, the founding members didn't position the new network as an affinity group. Rather, they chose to position their mission as helping women compete in the no-holds-barred meritocracy that exists at General Electric.

This mission infuses everything the Network does. For example, Network members do not ask for special treatment, nor do they focus particularly on flexible working hours or work-family issues. Instead, to help women navigate the intensely competitive General Electric playing field, the Women's Network teaches members how to develop their leadership skills and provides career-broadening opportunities as well as tools for advancement. In addition, it offers a "safe haven"—a place where women can talk honestly and openly about their career challenges without fear of reprisal.

One of the Women's Network's main initiatives is recruiting talented women in technology and engineering—fields that are still predominately male. "Our recent track record is impressive," says Jeanne Rosario, vice president and general manager of General Electric and a founding member of the Women's Network. "In terms of the percentage of women in entry-level engineering jobs, we're hitting upward of 28 percent. Considering women comprise only 20 percent of graduates at engineering schools around the country, the Women's Network is doing a pretty good job," she adds.[21]

The Women's Network has other, yet more ambitious objectives, which are intertwined with General Electric's succession planning. When leadership slots open up the Women's Network attempts to find well-qualified, in-house female candidates. To facilitate this objective, the Network has aligned itself with the company's leadership development and performance management system known as Session C—which uses an annual review process to pinpoint and promote leaders. These initiatives have put more women into the pipeline of potential General Electric leaders. As Susan Peters, vice president for Executive Development and a founding member of the Women's Network, says: "The Network is about creating a forum for women. It's about focusing the company's resources on developing leaders who also happen to be women."[22]

Because the Women's Network is run like a business, being female does not automatically open the door to a potential leadership role. Network leaders aren't volunteers, rather, they are identified through Session C's list of high potentials—the idea being that the Women's Network provides high-potential women with the experience they need to give their careers a lift. Once appointed, Network leaders select officers, create an operating plan, and establish annual goals.

While leadership roles are tightly controlled by the company, Network events are open to all employees—women and men—and cover a broad range of topics: performance, networking, customer service, and work-life issues. Sometimes forums include speakers; other times the Network may offer workshops or networking dinners.

Like many new business ventures under the General Electric umbrella, the Women's Network was created in the United States and then expanded overseas. Currently the Network has four U.S. and nine international regions. There are 130 "hubs," or chapters, of the Women's Network worldwide and over forty thousand members. The Network's impact on the retention and advancement of women at General Electric has been dramatic. Thirteen percent of General Electric's top officers are now women—up from 5 percent ten years ago. In 1996 female attrition levels were high—General Electric was losing 14 percent of its senior women every year. But by 2002 this rate had fallen to 7 percent—a major improvement. At the same time the pipeline has strengthened significantly. The number of women in the first band of management at General Electric—which represents "bench strength" for the future—has gone up 79 percent over the last decade.[23]

The Women's Network has a high profile on other fronts. Since "customer centricity" is a core principle at General Electric—everything the company does must offer value to customers—the network hosts an annual "Leading & Learning" event that provides the opportunity for General Electric women to interact with female customers and build business relationships. The Network also hosts an annual "mega-event" that brings together hundreds of General Electric women from around the world who have been identified as potential leaders in the Session C evaluation process.

Visibility is a huge issue for General Electric women—in a company of over three hundred thousand employees it's difficult to get the attention of senior management. In interviews many women stressed that an important function of the Women's Network is to create opportunities for members to get connected, meet others, stand out, and shine. Elam elaborates, "We see the power of the Network in providing opportunities for mentors and role models for younger women. This is such a huge company, so spread out, so acquisitive, that the Women's Network creates important glue for women. It's easy for isolation to set in, especially among women scientists and engineers. It's possible to be working in a division without another senior woman around."[24]

Worldwide Influence

General Electric's Women's Network has become an important presence around the world. Heather Wang, the Network's leader for Asia and China, points out that women face particularly difficult challenges in Japan and Korea where cultural barriers are high. But the Women's Network is helping change that reality, creating opportunity and access. Over the past three years approximately 370 women have been promoted to executive or senior professional "bands" in General Electric's Asian operations.

Wang brought the Women's Network to China in 2002. "Within months we had launched hubs in Shanghai and Beijing," she remembers. Immelt was visiting Japan, and Wang invited him to speak to her fledgling network—a group of two hundred General Electric women. "They were so impressed that despite a killer schedule the CEO found time to visit with them—the Network was that important to the company," says Wang. Currently, approximately three thousand of General Electric's eleven thousand female employees in Asia attend Network events. "It's helped a lot," Wang says. "Many of us feel newly appreciated in the company."[25] The Network has allowed Wang to improve her leadership skills and has given her the opportunity to understand the needs of a range of people— an important skill set for an HR leader.

Elam is extremely pleased with the measurable success of the Women's Network but knows there's work ahead. For example, she wants to involve more senior women—to have them act as role models for new members just joining the Network. According to Elam, in the early years senior women were skeptical of the Women's Network. Their feeling was, "I've gotten where I am on my own, so why should younger women need help?" However, Elam is finding that senior-level colleagues are beginning to see the benefits of the Network.

While General Electric's Women's Network is still a work in progress, it has already become an admired program within the business world and has helped propel the company to the forefront of change. Elam describes the Women's Network as a "crown jewel" at General Electric.

TOOLKIT

Women's Network

An industrial juggernaut with revenues of nearly $150 billion in 2005, General Electric employs more than three hundred thousand employees in more than one hundred countries. Despite its reputation as a bastion of tradition-bound males, General Electric has become much more woman-friendly. In 2004, General Electric won the prestigious Catalyst Award for its efforts to advance women, and for the last four years, the company has made *Working Mother* magazine's "100 Best Companies" list.

General Electric's Women's Network has helped propel this transformation. Founded in 1997, the Network does not emphasize soft-focus issues such as flextime or child care. Rather, it helps General Electric women advance in a fiercely meritocratic environment. The Women's Network is intertwined with General Electric's succession planning and aligns with Session C—General Electric's leadership development and performance management system.

Today the Women's Network has 130 hubs worldwide and over forty thousand members—including two-thirds of General Electric's senior women, some of whom were initially skeptics. The impact of the Women's Network has been huge. Thirteen percent of General Electric's top officers are now women, up from a meager 5 percent ten years ago. The number of women in the first tier of management increased 79 percent over the same time period.

The Business Case

An essential value of the Women's Network is customer centricity. To that end, the organization hosts an annual "Leading & Learning" event, providing General Electric women with opportunities to interact with customers, build relationships, and participate in a strategic General Electric initiative.

CEO Jeffrey Immelt wants the senior ranks at General Electric to "look more like the world" that makes and buys General Electric products. A lot of that world is female. As Immelt notes, ten years from now General Electric will be a company that has 60 percent to 70 percent of its employees working outside the United States.

Getting Started

- Consider your customer or client base—how well do your senior executives mirror this reality? Create a business case for a woman's network.
- How can a network contribute to staffing requirements in support of strategic objectives? General Electric's answer was that to take advantage of growth opportunities, the company needed "global brains"—a diverse employee base around the world.

- In addition to standout women leaders (Deb Elam comes to mind) are there senior male leaders who can champion a women's network? At General Electric that role was played by Jack Welch (former CEO) and Dennis Dammerman (former vice chairman) and is now played by Jeff Immelt (CEO) and Mike O'Neal (vice chairman and CEO of Commercial Finance).

Critical Elements

- *Walking the talk at the top.* The Women's Network has had strong support from General Electric's most senior executives.
- *Alignment with succession planning.* The Network is linked to Session C and explicitly designed to help high-potential employees compete successfully for promotion.
- *An open door policy.* Any employee (male or female) can participate in events that focus on building leadership skills and enhancing performance.
- *Global expansion.* Consistent with General Electric's global strategy, the Network has expanded overseas. About seven thousand female employees attend Women's Network events in Asia.

Tapping into Altruism

Women are very clear about the reasons they go to work and most say it's not just about the money. The data presented in chapters 2 and 3 demonstrates that the aspirations of talented women are multidimensional. Compensation is certainly important to women, but it's not nearly as powerful a motivator as it is for men. While men list money as either the first or second priority on their wish list, women tend to rank this goal much further down on their list of career drivers. For example, among women with extreme jobs, only 28 percent say money is a prime motivator, while among men, this figure rises to 43 percent. For women career goals such as working with "high-quality colleagues," deriving "meaning and purpose" from work, and "giving back to society" are more powerful drivers than money. Fully 56 percent of highly qualified women say giving back to the community is enormously important to them.

This data offers a window of opportunity for companies. The fact is firms that create real outlets for altruism—especially those that go beyond donning a company T-shirt and participating in a Saturday-morning walkathon—have a better chance of attracting and retaining female talent.

The case studies showcased in this chapter demonstrate how companies are developing a rich range of programs in volunteer and community outreach space that share two characteristics. To begin with, they are organically linked to each company's credo. Whether one is talking about a tradition of public service at Goldman Sachs, connection to corporate "Blue Box Values" at American Express, or alignment with a start-up culture at Cisco, these programs are grounded in a company's core belief system. In addition, these initiatives are deliberately positioned as potent recruitment and retention tools. At Goldman Sachs, American Express, and Cisco, senior executives understand that sabbaticals and public service programs are attractive lures.

Irrespective of the potential on the strategic-positioning front, however, opportunities for volunteer activity provide professionals with much-valued "food for the soul." In focus groups and interviews, women (and, more rarely, men) talked poignantly about how "giving back" lifted them up and replenished their store of spiritual and emotional energy. No matter how stretched they were at work (and some were amazingly overloaded), there was something restorative and deeply refreshing about helping heal the wounds of the world. An employer that recognizes and supports volunteer activity wins accolades, buoys spirits, and, perhaps most significantly, generates ongoing loyalty.

GOLDMAN SACHS: AFTER-HOURS LEADERS

In 1995 when she was a junior analyst at Goldman Sachs, Aynesh Johnson wrote a memo about a company-sponsored social outreach program she was involved with. The memo stands out in her memory because of the name of its intended recipient: Jon Corzine, then chairman and chief executive officer of Goldman Sachs, later to be elected United States senator and governor of New Jersey. Someone at Johnson's level writing a memo to someone at the CEO's level wasn't exactly standard practice at Goldman Sachs, but because public service work is something that the company both recognizes and celebrates, Johnson felt comfortable contacting a fellow volunteer, albeit someone many levels above her. She also knew Corzine would be receptive because public service was a subject close to Corzine's heart.

In addition to working sixty-to-eighty-hour weeks at Goldman Sachs—an investment banking firm of twenty-two thousand employees with revenues of $24.7 billion, serving corporations, financial institutions, governments, and high–net worth individuals in more than twenty-three countries—Johnson was on the board of Street Project, a volunteer organization founded in 1987 by Goldman Sachs. Over a ten-year period, the organization had grown from a loosely knit collective of volunteers to a highly focused network of young professionals from over three hundred companies. In the memo she wrote to Corzine, Johnson described Street Project's evolution under Goldman Sachs's leadership. The firm provided more volunteers than any other participating company: eleven Goldman analysts had served as directors of the organization since its founding and Goldman Sachs employees had taken on key leadership roles in recruiting coordinators and organizing volunteers.

Corzine's response was honest and sincere: "Dear Aynesh," he wrote. "Because I know very well that the demands you face daily in your career and home-life are sufficient challenges to manage, I admire all the more, the talent and compassion you invest in serving the communities in which we live and work."[1]

Johnson's energy and talents are indeed impressive but they are not rare in her peer group. Goldman Sachs understands this and knows that such energies need to be engaged beyond the world of work. A graduate of Duke University and the Harvard Business School, Johnson is a natural leader. As a student she held top positions in almost every student extracurricular effort she became involved in: class council, student orientation, and a scholarship association. Duke University chose her as a student ambassador and a member of the gift committee. Not surprisingly, Johnson came to Goldman Sachs because the firm offered a range of programs designed to facilitate employees' altruistic endeavors—endeavors that played an important role in Johnson's personal life. These programs are separate from the philanthropic work of the Goldman Sachs Foundation, which boasts a $200 million endowment of its own.

Like Johnson, "today's college and business school graduates—particularly female graduates—want something more than money," says Edith Hunt, Goldman Sachs's managing director of human capital management. They want self-actualization and a workplace that helps them reach it. "That's why," says Hunt, "the material Goldman Sachs prepares for its recruiters features information on the firm's many public service offerings." These include Community TeamWorks, which encourages employees to take a day a year for volunteer activity; a mentoring program for inner-city kids; the chance to serve on nonprofit boards; not-for-profit leadership training; and matching gifts for charities of the employee's choice. "When we talk to potential recruits about Community TeamWorks or our mentoring program, we see their eyes light up," Hunt says.[2] She emphasizes that Goldman has had a long-standing commitment to public service. "Governor Corzine isn't the first Goldman executive to tread the path toward government or nonprofit leadership," Johnson says, noting that many leaders at the firm have "two lives," one within Goldman Sachs and one as an activist or a public servant outside the company.[3] Hank Paulson, who left the top job at Goldman in July 2006 to become secretary of the treasury, is the most recent example of this pattern.

Most Goldman Sachs employees do some kind of public service work. Mentoring is the most important year-round volunteering activity, and mentoring opportunities are available for Goldman Sachs employees in New York, London, Atlanta, Chicago, and San Francisco, among other cities. Over 85 percent of the Goldman workforce participates in Community TeamWorks. The firm makes it easy for employees to take part: they simply log on to the company's internal Web site to sign up for a Community TeamWorks project. The company provides transportation, meals, even T-shirts for participants. Though the company helps facilitate participation, management is well aware that employees wouldn't get involved if they felt they might be penalized for taking a Community TeamWorks day.

Goldman's urgent and ever-present need to attract, retain, and fully engage top talent is the main reason behind its emphasis on public service. In focus groups the firm conducts with prospective recruits, the desire to get involved with public service comes up repeatedly. The fact that Goldman supports community service helps differentiate the firm from other potential employers and gives it an edge in the labor market. Moreover, volunteer initiatives build leadership capability and burnish the company's image in the communities within which it does business. Not only do employees sharpen their skill sets when they engage in volunteer activities, but they reinforce the activities of the Goldman Sachs Foundation by contributing human capital (as board members, organizers, or problem solvers) to investments Goldman Sachs is already making in a variety of nonprofit organizations.

The company's attitude toward employees' volunteer efforts is straightforward: as long as employees get their work done, no eyebrows are raised in reaction to absences for a worthy cause. The firm helps foster this positive attitude by naming "champions" of public service from among its employees and charging them with the mission of transmitting the value of giving back. Champions have a variety of roles including maintaining relationships with local nonprofits, increasing business unit participation in community activities, and training volunteers to ensure a high standard of service delivery.

Stepping out of the office to volunteer in the wider community can have a positive effect on a Goldman career, providing junior employees with easier, more natural access to senior managers who may well be participants in the same volunteer program. Witness Johnson's ease in writing to then-CEO Jon Corzine. Johnson and Hunt agree that while a lack of interest in community service will not slow the progress of a top producer—he or she will still progress up the Goldman Sachs corporate ladder—commitment to public service can give an employee a leg up. "Service gets you connected," Hunt says.[4]

Johnson's devotion to public service has remained steady even as she's risen through the firm's ranks, from analyst to associate, to three different vice president roles in both investment banking and human capital management (Goldman's human resources department). Johnson attributes some of her success to her work in the community, which, she says, has nourished transferable skill sets that benefit the firm—particularly in the area of leadership. From her work outside Goldman's doors, Johnson has gleaned valuable lessons. "Community service work has taught me how to deal with a wide range of individuals," she says.[5] As the board vice president for the Lincoln Square Neighborhood Center, a nonprofit situated in New York City's Upper West Side that services low-income elderly clients and at-risk youth, Johnson figures out how to help families who earn less than $20,000 a year yet live in a zip code that is also home to some of the wealthiest people in the world. "They're surrounded by all this wealth, but their reality is a low-income housing project," Johnson says. "How are these families supposed to get by when it takes so much money to live in this part of New York City?" Johnson views developing funding for this center as a marketing challenge so problematic that it could be a business school case study.

"It's a very rich and wonderful opportunity," Johnson says, carefully. "But it's not glamorous." Most of the children served by the Lincoln Square Neighborhood Center are not potential prodigies who would score in the top 10 percent on standardized tests if only they had access to better schools. Rather, they are regular kids struggling with some of society's most difficult problems: poverty, illness, unstable home environments, drugs, and crime.

Precisely because the population served by the center is so challenging, its goals are modest and incremental at times—not the type of mission that inspires donors to whip out their checkbooks. "We're starting out at a very basic level," Johnson says. "For instance, how do we get these kids lunch and dinner and then how do we get them to go to school? That's not a mission that's easy to fund. One thing this work has taught me is how to listen gracefully when a prospective donor says *no*, and how not to take *no* for an answer—again gracefully." These particular skills are the ones that Johnson can easily take back to Goldman Sachs—raising money, being persistent and persuasive, and not taking no for an answer are, after all, at the heart of investment banking.

TOOLKIT
After-Hours Leaders

Aynesh Johnson, a vice president at Goldman Sachs, is strongly committed to her community. As board vice president of the Lincoln Square Neighborhood Center, a New York nonprofit that supports public-housing residents who happen to share a zip code with some of the wealthiest people in the world, Johnson raises significant amounts of money for families in need.

"It's a very rich opportunity," Johnson says, "but it's not glamorous or easy." Nevertheless she thinks of it as central to her career. "It has taught me how to raise money, how to be persistent and persuasive, and how to work with a wide range of individuals," she says.

While lack of interest in community service will not slow anyone's progress up Goldman's ladder, a commitment to public service can give careers a boost. In 2005, more than 13,500 of Goldman's 22,000 employees participated in mentoring or some other community activity.

The Business Case

Public service is embedded in the Goldman Sachs culture. Chief among the business reasons for that commitment is the firm's battle to attract and retain the best talent in the financial services industry. Its own research suggests that this is a pool with a strong predilection for community involvement.

Moreover, the leadership skills that someone such as Johnson gains from volunteer commitments spills over into professional life. It therefore makes business sense for senior management to endorse this kind of extracurricular activity. Public service at Goldman Sachs is seen as both a leadership development tool and a tool for retention of key talent. For these reasons, employees are urged to wear their volunteer commitments as a badge of honor.

Getting Started

- Develop a business case for volunteerism. Highlight how it will raise the profile of the company, create client-building opportunities, and enhance leadership development.

- Review the contributions your company currently makes through its foundation or charitable giving department, and leverage existing relationships with nonprofits.
- Encourage high-profile individuals within your company to participate in a community service project. Highlight their work in a newsletter or on the company Web site.
- Create an infrastructure within your firm that allows employees to access critical information about volunteer opportunities. A Web-enabled system is optimal, but simple listings can be a first step.

Critical Elements

- *Alignment with core values.* Programs like Community TeamWorks draw on a long-standing commitment to public service within the Goldman Sachs culture. This linkage to core values makes these programs sustainable.
- *Easy access.* Goldman encourages public service participation by making it easy. Community TeamWorks, for instance, lets employees simply log on to the company's internal Web site and sign up for an event.
- *Recognition and celebration.* Community outreach is recognized, supported, and celebrated. Goldman's employees are encouraged to undertake volunteer roles as long as job performance is unaffected.

CISCO SYSTEMS: LEADERSHIP FELLOWS PROGRAM

In the summer of 2004 Molly Tschang did something unusual for her vacation: she volunteered to join a Save the Children delegation to Ethiopia and Uganda and participated in projects that empowered local women and girls—helping build a girl's school and improving the clean water supply. Tschang, who had spent the previous ten years in mergers and acquisitions (M&A) at Cisco Systems—the supplier of networking technology for the Internet, with sales in 2006 of $28.5 billion and more than forty-seven thousand employees worldwide—found the experience transformative. Upon returning to work she sought an opportunity that would keep her connected to this broader world of need.

Tschang discovered the outlet she needed at her workplace in the form of Cisco's Leadership Fellows Program—an initiative that allows high-potential executives such as Tschang to work for a nonprofit organization full-time for up to one year, at no cost to the nonprofit, because the employee continues on Cisco's payroll.

This fellowship program has multiple stakeholders and beneficiaries. Cisco employees benefit because the program allows them to develop their managerial and technical skills while investing in a cause that's important to them. Nonprofits such as NetHope and CompuMentor benefit because Cisco fellows bring leadership skills and technological savvy. These borrowed assets allow the nonprofit organizations to build capacity and better achieve their goals and purposes. And Cisco benefits because the fellowship program permits the company to align corporate philanthropy with employee volunteerism, and in so doing, create additional value by enhancing employee engagement and loyalty.

The Leadership Fellows Program is open to "top talent"—high-performing vice presidents and directors who are committed to their own professional development. Employees are selected for the program after interviewing both at Cisco and at participating nonprofit organizations. The fellows are typically diverse in background and come from all areas of the firm—engineering, marketing, and administration.

There appears to be substantial community need for this program. Barbara Jones, director of the Leadership Fellows Program, explains that in the nonprofit world demand for Cisco fellows is high. She notes that it's easy to find nonprofit "slots" for employees who are approved by management and interested in the program. Participating organizations are often entities that Cisco has funded or partnered with on other initiatives. Generally, these nonprofits focus on issues such as education, health care, and basic human needs—and can use all the help they can get because they sorely need the skills that Cisco employees bring to bear. Cisco fellows often serve as strategic planners or project managers during their year of service—roles similar to that of management consultants in the private sector.[6]

As mentioned earlier fellows continue to be Cisco employees with full salary and benefits. Jones stresses that fellowship work is included in performance reviews, underscoring the fact that Cisco genuinely values this nonprofit work and views it as developing transferable skill sets.

For her year of public service Tschang selected NetHope, a nonprofit consortium of leading international nongovernment organizations (NGOs) dedicated to using technology to improve the ability of participating NGOs to deliver services to clients around the world. In 2004 NetHope needed a new executive director, and Tschang decided she would like to fill that role for one year while the organization searched for a permanent leader.

Tschang brought a considerable array of skills to her role as NetHope's acting executive director. She was able to help bridge the digital divide on two fronts: facilitating connectivity within participating NGOs so that field operations could communicate more effectively with each other and with headquarters, and building connectivity and strengthening relationships between the seventeen NGO agencies that make up the NetHope consortium—each of which had a different mission and a different organizational structure. Tschang's technical and managerial know-how were invaluable. Among other projects, she oversaw the installation of new communications technology, devised training programs, and developed strategic partnerships. Upon completing her fellowship, Tschang transferred significant new skills back to Cisco.

A world leader in the development of Internet-based networking technologies, Cisco is also a leader in the world of employee altruism. More than fourteen thousand Cisco employees now participate in volunteer programs, and the company has been recognized by the Points of Light Foundation and the Committee to Encourage Corporate Philanthropy.

According to Noni Allwood, senior director of Worldwide Diversity and Inclusion, the company has always believed it should be an active and caring member of the community.[7] While Cisco was still a start-up in East Menlo Park, California, it was not unusual for employees to walk next door to volunteer at the neighborhood school. Cisco employees later adopted the school and many became mentors and tutors, devoting large chunks of time to needy students. This was a first step in what became a companywide strategy for addressing social needs through strategic partnerships. For example, Cisco partnered with the World Economic Forum to create the Jordan Education Initiative, which is reforming education at the K–12 level in the Hashemite kingdom of Jordan. In a similar vein, Cisco has partnered with Community Voice Mail to provide voice mail access to the homeless—an initiative that enables homeless individuals sustain a job search, contact outreach services, and stay in touch with family and relatives. Cisco provides the technology for this partnership.

Cisco has also created the 21st Century Schools Initiative, a program aimed at reconstructing schools in New Orleans and other Gulf Coast areas that were most affected by Hurricane Katrina. The company is investing $40 million in this effort as well as volunteer energy through its Leadership Fellows Program. Several fellows have moved to the Gulf region to help rebuild area schools.

Cisco employees are deeply committed to community service. In May 2004, to mark the company's twentieth anniversary year, Cisco president and CEO John Chambers instituted the 20 Years of Community Service Campaign. Chambers asked that employees collectively attempt to devote 175,200 hours—or twenty years—of time to volunteer work. If the challenge was met within a year, Cisco would donate $3 million to an array of nonprofit organizations. Cisco employees easily met—and surpassed—Chambers's challenge. Indeed, at the seven-month mark, employees had already volunteered 200,000 hours.

Cisco's Leadership Fellows Program is not easy—for the company or the employee. Implementing and managing such a program is challenging. Fellows are sent to countries all over the world, and their fellowships last for varying lengths of time. In addition, as Tschang points out, not many companies are visionary enough to pull employees out of their jobs for several months at a time and continue to pay them.

The Leadership Fellows Program can also be problematic for employees. Tschang realized there was a risk to taking herself off the job for such an extended period of time. But for Tschang the experience yielded triple rewards: she did something that satisfied her desire to give back; she provided real help where it was needed; and she brought back skills she could not have learned within the company. Cisco says it thrives on employees like Tschang, and she is immensely grateful to be working for a company that offers such an unusual opportunity.

TOOLKIT

Leadership Fellows Program

In 2004 Molly Tschang spent her vacation volunteering on a Save the Children delegation to Ethiopia and Uganda. The experience was transformative, and upon her return, Tschang, who works in M&A at Cisco Systems, knew she needed to find an outlet for her newfound passion for community service. She found it through Cisco's Leadership Fellows Program.

This program enables employees to work with a nonprofit for one year and then return to the company reenergized and carrying new skills. Participants are typically high-potential, high-performing managers who want to lend their talents to a cause they believe in. Fellows continue to be Cisco employees during their time away, receiving full salary and benefits. The work they complete during their fellowship tenure is included in performance reviews—underscoring the value Cisco places on the experience as a wellspring of transferable skills. At the same time, Cisco stresses that the fellow must "leave something behind" at the nonprofit—that is, each fellow is expected to accomplish something tangible.

Tschang, for example, took on the role of acting executive director at Net-Hope, a consortium of global NGOs. While the organization conducted its search for a full-time director, Tschang went to work helping bridge the digital divide for NetHope. She oversaw the installation of new communications technology, devised training programs, and built connectivity between the seventeen NGOs that make up the NetHope consortium. One day the connections she developed as a Leadership Fellow may well generate new business for Cisco!

The Business Case

Cisco believes that the Leadership Fellows Program enhances the capacity of employees so that when they return to their jobs they bring leadership skills they could not have learned within the company. Before employees begin their fellowship Cisco defines the goals and terms of success. After the fellowship is completed, Cisco looks at before-and-after statistics within the nonprofit to measure impact and success. These measures are then fed into a formal performance review.

Giving back to the community has always been a core value at Cisco—the company believes that when a community benefits, so do businesses based in that community. Cisco sums up the business case for its fellows program with the acronym G3: grow the business; grow our team; grow yourself.

Getting Started

- Look for important strengths/competencies in your organization that could be of value to nonprofit groups.
- In the fellowship screening process look for "high-potentials" and evaluate how selected employees perform during their fellowship year. This enhances the likelihood of leadership development.
- Choose the most dedicated employees. Wherever the fellows work they will be ambassadors for your company.
- Link these fellowships to your organization's philanthropic platform. The nonprofits and NGOs that participate in Cisco's Leadership Fellows Program are often partners in other initiatives.
- Acknowledge the challenges posed by this type of program. Cisco's fellows, for instance, are taken out of their jobs for months at a time without headcount replacement. This places a considerable burden on coworkers.

Critical Elements

- *Alignment with core competencies.* The fellows program taps Cisco's core strengths with its focus on helping nonprofits utilize modern communication technology.
- *Performance and promotion.* Measures of success in the fellowship program are included in performance reviews. Fellowships are viewed as a form of leadership "action learning" and are often able to give careers a "lift."
- *Outlets for altruism.* Through this fellowship program Cisco is able to provide key talent powerful outlets for altruism. This both enhances engagement and improves retention.

AMERICAN EXPRESS: PAID SABBATICAL PROGRAM

Here's the dilemma: you've always done community service. It's an integral part of your life and has been since you were young. You volunteer at a neighborhood soup kitchen, you help paint benches in a school playground, and you're on the board of a nonprofit that provides meals on wheels for elderly shut-ins. And you'd like to take these good works further still—but, well, you have a day job.

If you work for American Express you might be in luck. One feature of the company's employment benefits package—introduced in 1991—is a Paid Sabbatical Program. Any employee who has worked for the company for ten years (and has achieved certain performance ratings) can apply to take a leave of absence for up to six months in order to work at a nonprofit of his or her choice. Employees remain on the Amex payroll with paid benefits.

The Paid Sabbatical Program—which is marketed to all employees in the United States and Canada annually through e-mail and other electronic communications—features an application with six open-ended questions and a request for a detailed project plan describing what the employee will do during their time out. Prior experience with the employee's nonprofit of choice—although not required—will help bolster a person's application and chances of approval. An acceptance letter from the non-profit is also required.

Applications are evaluated by a rotating sabbatical committee made up of American Express employees from a variety of divisions. Because the selection process is designed to be both rigorous and inclusive, elements such as the quality of the write-up, the caliber of the organization the applicant wants to work for, and the geographic location of the organization are taken into account. On average twelve employees are awarded sabbaticals every year. Sabbatical leaves are taken for a range of activities that include counseling hospice patients, teaching at an inner-city school, and working at a homeless shelter. Since the program's inception Amex has "loaned" more than 190 employees to nonprofits across the United States and Canada—which translates into a donation of thousands of hours of high-impact volunteer labor. A separate, similar program also operates in the United Kingdom.

American Express, which today has 65,800 employees in 130 countries and revenues that exceed $24 billion, aligns its sabbatical program with a set of beliefs referred to within Amex as Blue Box Values.[8] These values inform the way employees are treated and define what's expected of them. Steve Richardson, senior vice president and chief talent officer at American Express, stresses that "it is not enough for American Express employees to be good performers at work; we also encourage them to be 'good human beings' who give back to their communities."[9]

Francine Darragh, a thirteen-year veteran with American Express, agrees. The sabbatical program caught her attention when she joined the company and she kept it at the back of her mind ever since. "I always thought it would be great using my corporate skills at a nonprofit," said Darragh, now a senior manager in American Express's publishing division.[10] As she built her long-range development plan, a sabbatical leave was something she targeted as one of her professional goals, believing it would enhance her skills in a nontraditional way.

As she began framing her application, Darragh's big question was what to do and where to do it. She'd always been interested in art history—so much so that she went back to school to get a second degree in the subject. When, during her research into nonprofit organizations, she discovered the World Monuments Fund (WMF), an organization that Amex had a well-established relationship with, Darragh knew she'd found the right nonprofit for her sabbatical.

The World Monuments Fund, which was founded in 1965, is the foremost nonprofit organization dedicated to the preservation of historic art and architecture worldwide. Through extensive fieldwork the organization identifies sites in disrepair and then educates and trains people to both assess the damage and oversee reconstruction and preservation. In 1995 American Express became a founding sponsor of the fund's World Monuments Watch, committing $10 million over a ten-year period. This global initiative was created to spur and catalyze worldwide efforts to protect and preserve monuments in peril. Every other year, the Watch releases a *List of 100 Most Endangered Sites* to help raise the funds needed for their rescue. Among the well-known sites saved from ruin is Preah Khan in Cambodia.

American Express' commitment to the World Monuments Watch created a "leverage factor" that helped draw additional funding from a variety of government and private sources. Darragh figured the best thing she could do for the fund was to use her sabbatical leave to develop a strategic plan for the organization so that it could secure a steady stream of corporate largesse.

Before Darragh began the application process she met with senior staff at the World Monuments Fund "to brainstorm about my skill set and their needs. They were thrilled when it became clear I had the ability to craft a corporate giving program for the organization," she remembers.

Then began the Amex application process, which Darragh describes as rigorous. "I had to present an action plan along with a letter from WMF explaining why they really needed me. I then reviewed everything with my manager, and she shared it with her VP. Only eleven sabbaticals were granted that year, and mine was among them, so I felt really pleased," says Darragh.

Before she embarked on her sabbatical Darragh and her coworkers figured out how her duties would be distributed in her absence. Because

American Express touts the value of this program as part of its Blue Box Values everyone was willing to chip in. "All my clients knew what I was doing; in fact, they were impressed that the company was supporting me in this way," Darragh says. Although she was nervous about leaving her portfolio and her clients, Darragh felt it was important to "walk away" and trust her group to work out how to get everything done while she was gone. "I needed to focus on the World Monuments Fund. For three months that was my job," she explains.

Just as American Express prepared for Darragh's absence, the World Monuments Fund got ready for her presence. She began by brainstorming with its vice president of external affairs, looking to understand the strengths and weaknesses of previous fund solicitation efforts. Then she took the information and went to work.

"I looked at the WMF's mission and developed a plan to achieve the stated goals. I then broke this down into steps so we could get up and running. All of this strategic thinking was turned into a write-up that could be taken to the organization's board for approval."

Tangible success didn't occur until Darragh was back at American Express—the fund-raiser she designed and mapped out raised over $200,000 for the World Monuments Fund. "When you work on a project it's nice to see it through to completion. But I was happy with this result even though I wasn't there at the end. After all, they had pursued and implemented *my* idea. I knew how much I had helped," Darragh remembers.

Though she gave a lot Darragh received a significant amount in return. "I didn't come back a different worker," she notes, "but I had a new level of confidence. One thing my sabbatical experience did for me was make me understand how much I had learned during my years at American Express. The realization gave me a new focus. I had built successful strategic relationships at the WMF and I was able to parlay that into a new role in publishing.

Interestingly, over the last few years the great majority of sabbatical leaves at Amex have gone to women. Indeed, in the three-year period 2003–2005, only one out of thirty-six leaves awarded went to a man.

Very few men, it appears, are applying. This fact underscores the heft of the data presented in chapter 2—professional women do seem to attach enormous importance to altruism and giving back. Darragh, for one, latched onto the sabbatical program at Amex when she was hired, and the self-development opportunities she accessed through the program increased her capacity—and made her an extremely proud and loyal employee. In the words of Richardson, "There's a celebratory response when our sabbatical participants return to work. What a wonderful thing it is to go out into the community and do something like this. These people are great ambassadors for American Express."[11]

TOOLKIT

Sabbatical Program

In 1991 American Express rolled out a Paid Sabbatical Program as an ongoing commitment to employees and to the wider community. Through this program Amex employees can take time off (up to six months) to work for a nonprofit organization of their choice—and remain on the American Express payroll.

The program is marketed to all employees through e-mail and other electronic communications. The target audience is the veteran employee with at least ten years on the job and a satisfactory performance record for the three most recent years. The application has six open-ended questions and requires a detailed project plan. Prior experience with the nonprofit bolsters the chance of approval.

Application forms are put before a rotating sabbatical committee made up of Amex executives. A range of criteria, from the quality of the write-up to the type of organization, to the geographic location, are taken into account. Approximately twelve employees are awarded sabbatical leaves every year. Activities include counseling at a hospice, teaching at an inner-city school, and working at a homeless shelter.

Francine Darragh was approaching her ten-year anniversary at Amex when she applied for—and won—a sabbatical leave. She ended up working at the World Monuments Fund, a nonprofit organization devoted to the preservation of endangered historical sites. Darragh used her business skills to revamp the fund's corporate giving program, an effort that was enormously successful—an event she planned raised $200,000 for the WMF. "It's such a creative form of professional development," Darragh says.[12] After three months at the World Monuments Fund she came back to Amex with a new level of confidence and subsequently moved into a more senior position in the Amex publishing division.

The Business Case

Senior executives see this program as an important recruitment, retention, and acceleration tool. Sabbaticals can be used to reward a motivated long-timer or accelerate the development of a high-potential employee—building skills and stretching talents. Operating without these talented people while they're on sabbatical is, however, challenging for managers and coworkers alike, but Amex is convinced that in the long run everyone benefits. Those who take a sabbatical nearly always return to Amex with transferable skill sets, and everyone involved is touched by the Blue Box Values embedded in the program.

Richard Schack, a director of human resources at Amex, was awarded a sabbatical leave to spend six months building a database for hotline counselors at the Gay Men's Health Crisis. Schack talked about how his leave cemented his loyalty to the company. "My time on sabbatical allowed me to fulfill both a personal and corporate mission to give back to the community. While I was always loyal to American Express, this helped seal the deal."[13]

Getting Started

- Market the program broadly so that sabbaticals become a recruitment and retention tool.
- Involve senior management in talking up the value set that surround these sabbaticals. This will encourage work teams to pitch in when colleagues take time out for a paid sabbatical.

- Encourage applicants to seek out nonprofits with a "track record" with your company.
- Recognize the challenges involved in operating with colleagues who are out on sabbatical. There should be a plan for distributing critical parts of a person's job while he or she is away.

Critical Elements

- *Alignment with core values.* This paid sabbatical program aligns with the corporate culture, reinforcing the Blue Box Values that are so important to American Express.
- *Megaphone effect.* Employees returning from sabbaticals are spotlighted by Amex in its internal communications. This recognition further reinforces underlying corporate values.
- *Performance plus longevity.* Serious contenders for the program have a solid performance record and longevity at the company.
- *Matched skill sets.* Creating a match between employee and selected nonprofit organization ensures that the employee will be able to use existing skill sets while on sabbatical, and leverage new ones learned at the nonprofit once back at Amex.

10

Combating Stigma
and Stereotypes

Corporate cultures are rife with stig-
ma and stereotypes. Despite the fact that these barriers exist in the realm
of the "intangible" and are hard to tease out and identify, they can have
an extremely pernicious effect—forcing women off-ramp and stalling
progress for many of those who stay in their careers.

Stigma—defined as a mark of shame, stain, or reproach—often leads
to marginalization in the contemporary workplace.[1] This term perfectly
describes the invisible and unspoken, yet palpably negative, aura that
attaches to nonstandard work arrangements—particularly flexible work
arrangements.

Where does stigma come from? It is inextricably linked to stereotypes—
in this case, gender stereotypes that reflect a narrow, oversimplified, and
often heavily prejudiced view of the innate differences between men and
women.[2]

One result of stigma is that in many corporate environments flexible
work arrangements and other "accommodations" to women's work and
personal lives become so heavily laced with disapproval and illegitimacy
that they ultimately become "off limits" to ambitious, talented individuals.

Indeed, some corporate cultures have even managed to stigmatize something as basic as vacation. The not-so-subtle message: if you want to be a player on the A team, you'd better learn to do without time off. The end result: all too often ambitious women learn to avoid flexible work arrangements—and steer clear of women's network events—because they don't want to contaminate their professional reputations. In the words of one focus group participant, "I've spent twenty years honing a hard-edged reputation—quite frankly I don't want to jeopardize this by getting involved with women's initiatives."

Reducing stigma is perhaps the most challenging of the elements in the core package laid out in part II of this book. As any HR executive will tell you, it's relatively easy to create a rich set of programs and policies to help employees better manage their work and personal lives, but extremely difficult to create a corporate culture where these initiatives are actually used. As we saw in our survey data (see chapter 2), 35 percent of female respondents feel that part-time work is heavily stigmatized—so loaded with penalties that women are hesitant to even ask for it. And fully 39 percent of female respondents feel that telecommuting is a pipe dream. Although it is theoretically "on the books," in reality, one dare not take up this option.

The good news in this chapter is that companies are beginning to tackle stigma head-on. Lehman Brothers has had the good sense to embed flexibility in a mainstream strategic initiative that has rolled out sophisticated remote-access technology as a response to a possible bird flu pandemic and other potential disasters. This has greatly reduced the stigma attached to flexible work arrangements at Lehman. By dealing vigorously with microinequities, Cisco has been able to weaken—if not eliminate—the power of both stigma and stereotype to undermine a career. And Ernst & Young has orchestrated a pincer movement—through programs as varied as the Women's Leadership Conference, Career Watch, and People Point, this professional services company has tackled stigma from various directions and become much more vigilant and effective at keeping negative influences at bay.

LEHMAN BROTHERS: VIRTUAL WORKPLACE

Since September 11, 2001, two words increasingly crop up when business leaders discuss continuity. "What if?" they ask. What if there's a mass transit strike and no one can get to work? What if there's a huge blizzard and the streets are impassable? What if a major pandemic hits the region and people are advised not to enter a quarantined area that includes their business headquarters? And what if, just what if, terrorists attack again?

Lehman Brothers confronted these grim scenarios head-on in the wake of the 9/11 attacks, when the firm was forced to evacuate its headquarters in lower Manhattan near the World Trade Center. Since then, imagining disaster scenarios and designing solution sets that would keep businesses up and running has become a strategic imperative for this investment banking firm. Part of the solution is obvious: if, under crisis conditions, workers can't get to their office, the thing to do is to provide sophisticated communication technology that extends the boundaries of the firm to alternate locations including employees' homes.

Lehman's business was significantly affected by the World Trade Center attacks. The company's technology center was in the North Tower—the first building hit. Debbie Cohen, vice president and director of HR for IT, was in her fortieth-floor office at the time. "We didn't know what had hit. There was confusion all around us—should we leave or not?" Cohen remembers. She says she has no recollection of any official announcement and her group made their own decision. "One person was a volunteer fireman in his town, and he suggested we take a look at the stairwells," she recounts.[3] Outside the windows, they could see debris flying, so when they opened the stairwell doors and saw people making their way downstairs, their question was, "Is it smokier where you came from or is it smokier as you go down?" After receiving the answer that it was less smoky the closer they got to the ground floor, Cohen collected her people and started down the stairs.

When they reached ground level, police, firefighters, and other first responders were everywhere, and it quickly became apparent there was very little the Lehman group could do to help. Besides, Cohen adds, her group had been working at the company's World Trade Center offices for only a month, having just moved from offices in New Jersey, the state in which they all also lived; so it seemed natural for them to head back over to their old Jersey City offices. "We had ferry tickets on us," Cohen remembers. By the time the first tower fell, they were "long gone, sitting in a diner in Jersey City trying to sort things out."

The next several weeks were chaotic at Lehman. Along with the old Jersey City offices Lehman took over two Sheraton hotels. "But we still had space for only three thousand people," says Bridget O'Connor, Lehman's chief information officer.[4] Eventually, employees were placed in more than twenty locations. Even so, they were often sitting four people to a desk, Cohen says, and junior people—administrative assistants and the like—were asked not to come in at all. Cohen's HR staff was on a "round-robin" schedule, working in the office two days a week and from home the rest of the time. In the office everyone was elbow-to-elbow.

Coincidentally, at this same time, the IT department was working to provide secure access to all firmwide applications over the Internet. Citrix MetaFrame Presentation Server for Windows was used internally within the firm, but could not be deployed across the Internet due to a lack of advanced security. Lehman was developing a proprietary software solution called Tocket that utilized advanced security facilities such as 128-bit encryption to allow secure Internet access from locations outside the office—replicating office technology in noncompany spaces. Six weeks after 9/11, forty-five hundred users were connected and eighty-one applications were rolled out.

The deficit of office space after 9/11 also provided the impetus for the company to roll out Cisco IP phones. "We had been piloting them but didn't think we were ready for a complete rollout across the firm," says O'Connor. Today, through additional innovation, Lehman has expanded the functionality of these phones to enable Lehman employees to speak to clients and customers from anywhere as though they are calling from their offices. The phone's technology also enables call forwarding so that it rings in the office, on a cell phone, and at a home number at the same time, or forwards to whatever other number the user designates.

This new computer and telephone technology potentially touches every division within Lehman. Even traders—who need elaborate technology to do their jobs—can benefit. O'Conner says her "challenge" now is to give traders the option of transacting business from alternate locations so business can go on even if some major catastrophe were to affect employees' ability to get to the office.

Although Lehman Brothers eventually moved back to Manhattan and settled into new space, senior management continued to focus on disaster recovery. By 2004, the firm had clearly survived 9/11; indeed, it had grown rapidly. Then, in mid-2005, avian flu suddenly became a concern, and Lehman looked to its out-of-the-office technology as a way to keep employees working through a range of new potential disasters that might threaten the firm. It seemed the right time to pilot a program to see what would happen when a large number of employees actually worked from home.

Work-from-Home Pilot Project

Conversations began about how to carry out this pilot. At one meeting, O'Connor, Anne Erni—the firm's chief diversity officer—and their teams had a eureka moment. They realized that all this impressive new technology was as much about providing workplace flexibility as about disaster preparedness. As O'Connor says, "Without realizing it, we'd found a new way to support and position flexibility—one that conferred a great deal of legitimacy on the effort."[5]

Some of the employees who participated in the pilot project were people who worked from home already. Joanne Petrossian, a senior vice president in Fixed Income, had started working from home eight years earlier when her daughter was born. "I was prepared to leave the firm completely," Petrossian remembers. Instead, her boss told her she could work on special projects three days a week from home for a six-month trial period. "Since then we've gone through many flexible variations. Now I'm in the office two days a week, but those days are not fixed, it depends on business needs. The key to the whole arrangement is flexibility on both sides," Petrossian explains. "I'll come in four days if necessary. But on the other hand, if it's, say, the week my son is starting kindergarten, I may work remotely the whole week."[6]

At the time Petrossian began working from home she thought her arrangement was "completely set up." She had a phone line, a dial-up Internet connection, and a computer. When the firm ramped up its remote technology capability after 9/11, Petrossian benefited from the new equipment that became available. Now she has Tocket PC, access to Bloomberg data services, and a Cisco IP phone. "In the beginning people didn't quite accept that what I was doing at home was working. They would call and say, 'Sorry to bother you at home, but . . .' Now they don't know whether I'm in the office or at home."

According to Petrossian, over the last few years as more people have taken advantage of Lehman's sophisticated remote technology, there has been an increased acceptance of flexible work arrangements within the company culture. Her manager has been extremely supportive, and their twelve-year relationship has been built around high levels of trust. He knows she won't abuse her remote-working situation, and she's up front about stepping away from her desk, whether it's at the office or at her home.

Petrossian believes that telecommuting actually enables her to work more than she would if she were in the office full-time. What she's eliminated is a long commute, which frees up energy and time—some of which can be spent on "life business." Remote working allows Petrossian to see her children and have dinner with them. It means that she can have a sane family life and live in the suburbs in exactly the type of home she wants. "If I had to work in the office full-time and wanted to see my family at all I would have to live in the city—which I prefer not to do," she says. "I'm in the office full-time, but I'm not 'physically' there," Petrossian says to sum up.

Another early user of Virtual Workplace technology was Alan Pace, a managing director and global head of Business Advisory. After 9/11, instead of driving into New York City from his Connecticut home, Pace found himself driving from Connecticut to Jersey City—a commute that could take as long as three hours each way. In order to make life bearable, he found himself staying overnight in New Jersey two or three times a week. When IT asked for volunteers for the pilot Pace jokingly says he raised his hand and shouted, "Me, me, me!" As a manager, Pace was responsible for figuring out who should work remotely and who needed precious office space. "Most people wanted to be in the office because of the camaraderie—especially at that time," he remembers. And interestingly, most people who were then working from home said they didn't like it. Since Pace's group wasn't deemed "critical," his boss was delighted that Pace himself volunteered for a home setup. "I wanted to be able to see my kids before they went to bed; I didn't want to live away from my family several days a week," Pace says.[7]

For most of his team remote working was relatively short-lived. Pace, however, has had his technology upgraded so that working from home is possible whenever he wants, although these days he mostly works in the office. Still, ongoing opportunities for flexibility are incredibly important to Pace. "It's not just e-mail—that you can get on your BlackBerry. Lehman technology gives me access to documents on our shared server. With my Virtual Workplace setup, I can spend time with my children, then go back to work when they're in bed," Pace says.

Pace believes that Lehman employees are more open to working from home than they were pre-9/11. "There's less stigma attached to it because we all know that flexibility helped us survive as a firm; besides which, new technology makes working from home seamless and efficient."

Still, Pace points out, some stigma lingers. Certain people still think that working from home means working less. But after a few weeks working remotely with Tocket, Pace points out, these people come to understand that it's the work that counts, not the location. If the work has to get done, it does get done. Pace frequently puts in twelve hours on weekends, and his total workweek exceeds sixty hours whether he's "at home" or in the office.

Because the technology works so well for him Pace has become a champion of flexibility within Lehman, proactively reaching out to help make flexibility work for at least a dozen people. For example, one colleague was struggling—his wife had relocated to Florida for her job. Pace got him set up with Tocket and this employee was able to keep both his marriage and his job at Lehman. He now works from Florida part of each week.

Another great advocate for flexibility is Rick Rieder, a managing director and head of Global Principal Strategies. "For the past three years I've had people working partially from home—people who have commitments that require more flexibility," he says. "There's no question that Virtual Workplace technology is a necessity in a world that must plan for disaster scenarios, but just as important is the fact that it gives people more control over their lives."[8]

For Rieder personally, the Virtual Workplace has been a boon—even though he does not have a formal flexible work arrangement. "In the old days, I would get phone calls in the middle of the night when something important was happening in the overseas markets. I couldn't do much because I didn't have enough information. Now I can get up and check everything on the computer. Tocket gives you an extraordinary ability to provide informed feedback 24/7," he says.

Does home access to all this technology mean that Rieder works more than he might otherwise? "Sure," he says, and he shrugs. But, he adds, "I love my job and I feel more at ease knowing what's going on with global markets. It's a big stressor dealing with unknowns until I get to the office. As long as I know things are stable I can settle back and live my life. Having Tocket at home makes my workload less stressful and allows me to be a more relaxed person when I'm at home," he says.

As the Virtual Workplace project has spread throughout the firm, Lehman has looked closely at feedback about the productivity of participants. Those with at-home setups report increased flexibility in their daily schedule, along with such attendant rewards as more time spent with family and less time spent commuting. The most frequently cited problems were minor challenges with the setup and use of hardware.

Good news abounds for productivity: 62 percent of respondents reported an increase in productivity, and 82 percent also reported that managers, coworkers, and clients were pleased with the change. Communication was barely affected—95 percent of respondents reported no impact; they had merely substituted in-person meetings with "virtual" meetings. Fully 95 percent of managers said they would be willing to let their staff participate in this program.

Lehman has published a brochure that serves as an introduction to flexible work arrangements that now include: a reduced workweek, a compressed workweek, flextime, telecommuting, and job sharing. Before applying for a flexible work arrangement employees are asked to read the "Guide to Flexible Work Arrangements," available on LehmanLive (the company's intranet). An application prompt encourages users to answer questions that help them assess the feasibility of their request. Lehman recognizes that not all positions lend themselves to being done flexibly, and stresses that each case will be reviewed on its own merits. In other words, the fact that one employee has a flexible work arrangement does not automatically guarantee that another person in the same area will be granted one as well. However, applicants need not provide a reason for requesting flexibility—all applications are evaluated on how business needs will be met and how work will get done.

TOOLKIT

Virtual Workplace

When, during the winter of 2005–2006, business leaders became concerned about the effects of a possible bird-flu epidemic on the ability of companies to function, Lehman Brothers, remembering the impact 9/11 had on the firm and the business community, put development of remote technology into high gear. Many employees had been working from home on and off since 9/11, and much of the new technology was already in the works. With the bird-flu concern, telecommuting became mainstream: if a major catastrophe meant employees couldn't get to the office, the firm would provide the technology to turn their homes into remote work sites. A not-altogether-unintended consequence of this disaster planning has been to make the concept of working flexibly newly acceptable and legitimate at Lehman. As Lehman's diversity team points out, at the heart of any disaster scenario are flexible work arrangements.

The Business Case

The original case for Lehman's pursuit of mobility and flexibility centered on disaster preparedness. But then the firm's diversity and life-balance champions seized the opportunity to use a gender-neutral business imperative to make flex options more generally acceptable, which helped lessen the stigma that often attaches to employees (especially female employees) who avail themselves of these options. Lehman is also beginning to establish the connection between employee productivity and successful flex options. Recent surveys indicate that employees working from home are as productive, or more productive, than those working in office settings.

Getting Started

- Ask the question, "Is it possible for your employees to work from home—if so, which jobs lend themselves to flexibility? In the wake of 9/11 when space was at a premium, many Lehman employees worked flexibility from home— and did so successfully.
- Take stock of employee needs on the technology front and understand that people working in different functions/divisions have different needs. Lehman had a lot to work with here since many employees were already using remote technology.
- Develop a system to chart the success of the program. A key metric is productivity.

Critical Elements

- *Heroic antecedents.* Right out of the starting gate Lehman's virtual workplace had an advantage—it was linked to 9/11 and the firm's heroic struggle to survive.
- *A gender-neutral business imperative.* The rationale for Lehman's remote-work initiative is rooted in disaster preparedness—a strategic imperative. In addition, the opportunity to apply for a flexible schedule is open to both women and men. Both of these facts confer legitimacy.
- *Measuring and tracking.* The champions of flexibility at Lehman are focused on demonstrating its ROI—putting a premium on establishing ways to track performance and measure success.
- *Double-edged metrics.* Lehman had metrics early on. Establishing productivity gains is enormously important. But metrics that demonstrate increased job satisfaction are also critical because these figures are at the heart of the retention challenge.

CISCO: MICROINEQUITIES WORKSHOPS

The woman—a senior manager—had spent hours preparing for this meeting. She arrived bearing a stack of printed documents, which she handed to George O'Meara, senior vice president at Cisco Services for the United States and Canada and the chair of the meeting. At the end of the session he took the pile of papers and tossed them into the recycling bin. No slight was intended. But the woman looked at the discarded papers and then at O'Meara—a man older than herself and more highly placed in the organization and said, "Do you know how that makes me feel when you discard my work like that?" Five years previously, perhaps even two years earlier, she would probably have simply left the room, gone to her desk or the ladies' room, and nursed her hurt feelings. But this was the new Cisco, a Cisco that had rolled out microinequities workshops across the company.[9]

The Microinequities initiative focuses on eradicating the ways in which people within the company may make each other feel "small." O'Meara is a devoted champion of this program and was therefore startled by his colleague's reaction to his getting rid of her papers. The last thing he had intended was to devalue this member of his team. But he was pleased and proud that she'd had the courage to confront him so directly. This was tangible evidence that the Cisco culture had absorbed the concept of microinequities to the point that one of his direct reports felt able to confront him.

Microinequities is a term that was coined in 1973 by Mary Rowe of the Massachusetts Institute of Technology to describe the subtle put-downs, snubs, dismissive gestures, and sarcastic tones that people sometimes use— mostly unconsciously—when communicating with colleagues, particularly colleagues who are "different" in some way. When they are pervasive, microinequities can poison a working environment.

In any encounter people can send hundreds of messages by their behavior—without needing to spell out the message in spoken words. The key is to identify these behaviors and messages—and change the stereotypes that transmit them.

Imagine that a female executive (and it's likely that there are only one or two) spearheads an innovative product. It's now presentation time and her boss—the account manager—passes her over and instead asks a male colleague to describe the new product to a prospective client, who bites. The product is a huge success but the role of the female innovator is lost in the mists of time, while credit rubs off on her male colleague. Now this account manager wouldn't say—and probably doesn't consciously believe— that women aren't innovative or can't do great work. But his behavior reveals an ingrained prejudice.

Microinequities are costly—they depress productivity and drive up attrition rates among women and minorities. After all, it must be extremely difficult for a woman to collaborate with a man who gets recognition for her ideas. Microinequities are legion and show up in all shapes and guises: a colleague (male) who jabs at his BlackBerry while you go through a painstakingly prepared PowerPoint presentation; a colleague (female) who pivots around when a senior executive shows up, leaving you with your mouth open midway through a sentence; a colleague (male) who assumes that because you're a mother with a young child you would not be interested in a sought-after posting to Singapore and does not even ask; a colleague (male) who addresses your team as if no women were present—"Remember how in your college fraternity . . ."; a colleague (female) who dumps all the scut work on your shoulders because you happen to be working a flex schedule. The list goes on. There are innumerable ways of making people feel badly used and small.

In 2001 Cisco decided to fight the negative consequences of micro-inequities with a truly big initiative. "We really wanted to strengthen the culture of inclusion," says Laura Quintana, a former director of World-wide Diversity.[10] "The business case," adds Peggy Wolf, communications program manager, "was pretty evident." Senior management at Cisco is primarily white and predominantly male. "But that's not what our partners and customers look like, and if we can't immediately look more like them, we at least need to know how to talk to them," she says. "A lot of the small businesses we deal with are women-owned. If the only thing they ever hear is 'guy talk,' how are we going to relate to them?" asks Wolf.[11]

So Cisco approached Stephen Young, founder and senior partner of Insight Education Systems. Young put together a three-hour training seminar directed at helping people recognize microinequities—those they experience and those they perpetrate.

This kind of training is also part of Cisco's commitment to a diverse workforce: "If you want to attract talent, you have to make sure a broad range of people feel comfortable," Wolf says. According to Naomi Chavez, executive communications manager, "Over the last two years, the number of female hires has increased significantly."[12]

At first glance microinequities training appears not to be expensive: per person it costs $280 for a three-hour training seminar. However, as Chavez points out, when you multiply this figure by forty-seven thousand (the number of employees at Cisco), it becomes a significant expense. Currently, Cisco has no way of measuring return on this investment. If female retention rates improve, there's no way of correlating this trend with the microinequities program. Nevertheless, "it feels right," says Chavez, using words that are repeated throughout the company.[13] People viscerally know this type of training is making a difference in retention, and in the way Cisco does business.

The microinequities program was launched three years ago within the sales group—a place where Cisco programs often start—and was then rolled out to the rest of the company. As mentioned earlier, Insight Education Systems customized the program for Cisco. A key feature of the Cisco version is a cameo role for a senior executive at the beginning of each session. Typically a vice president will speak first, giving an overview of diversity at Cisco. He or she will then outline the importance of the microinequities seminar and introduce the facilitator from Insight Education. "This format conveys an important message because the senior executive not only talks about the program but shows [his or her] commitment by being an integral part of the seminar," Quintana says.[14]

The goal: over time, every Cisco employee will receive microinequities training and, to use Wolf's words, learn "a common language that, in a non-threatening way, will help them identify unconscious turns of phrase or mannerisms that devalue other people."[15] Given the scale of the company, this is a monumental task—however, it is one that sparks deep commitment. For the next stage Cisco is looking at marrying the microinequities initiative with executive education—which has the potential of taking training to a deeper level. "We also want to somehow pay attention to microinequities in performance reviews—but how does one measure something like this? It's hard to do but we're trying to figure it out," says Wolf.

Wolf recalls the first time she heard Stephen Young repeat, six times, the sentence "I didn't say she stole the book." Each time he emphasized a different word within the sentence. The effect was dramatic. "Where you put the stress changes the meaning entirely," says Wolf. Her reaction, she remembers, was, "Wow, such a little thing has such a tremendous effect on how people hear you and what they take away."

The microinequities training seminar puts a lot of weight on what people "hear" or "observe." According to Young and his colleagues, in many conversations there are actually three participants: the speaker, the listener, and the observer. Exercises in microinequities training demonstrate how much power the observer has. "That person is far enough away from the actual dialogue to identify small lapses in speech that might lead to a misunderstanding—or to someone feeling devalued," explains Chavez. "If we want Cisco to be a kinder, gentler environment where people feel comfortable, we need to find ways to encourage observers to speak up."[16]

This was exactly George O'Meara's rationale when he initiated the Courageous Observer Award. "You want to catch people doing it right. That's what the award is about," he says. Once a quarter, on the Cisco intranet, O'Meara presents the award to an employee who has had the courage to stand up to—or point out—a microinequity.

O'Meara is a staunch and vocal supporter of the program, and the basic concepts continue to excite him, leading him to ponder what "right behavior" looks like in certain situations. For example, when O'Meara tossed those documents, which belonged to a female colleague, into a recycling bin at the end of that meeting, he was following what he thought was good business practice—he was merely showing that an agenda item was finished with, that it was off the table. When this woman told him of her hurt feelings, O'Meara was taken aback—the micromessage he had sent was exactly the opposite of what he had intended. "You might say this was a moment of personal growth," O'Meara admits.[17]

For many Cisco employees, the microinequities workshop has been a life-altering program, since it has prompted individuals to reexamine the way they relate to others both within the company and outside. "If you had asked me before the class, I would have said, 'Me discriminate?' I'm a fifty-year-old woman and an immigrant. What could I possibly learn?" asks Monica Cojocneanu, manager of the Worldwide General Certification Program.[18]

But at the end of the program, Cojocneanu went back to her office and rearranged her furniture. "I had it configured so that my back was to the door. It gave the micromessage that I didn't really want to be bothered by the people who came in to speak with me," she explains. "Once I understood that, I moved the furniture. I didn't want it to appear that I thought I was too important to turn around." Other behavior changed as well. Cojocneanu always thought multitasking was a good thing, but the microinequities program caused her to realize that using her BlackBerry at a meeting or writing e-mails while on a conference call was extraordinarily disrespectful—her colleagues deserved her full attention.

One of the more interesting effects of the microinequities program is that employees are noticing how negative micromessages affect their personal lives as well. "I realized how much I discriminated against my husband. I often didn't give him my full attention—I'd be checking my voice mail or working on the computer while he was trying to speak with me—he had a right to be upset," says Cojocneanu. Mimish L'Esperance, channel marketing manager at Cisco, says that her experience with microinequities means that she's more cautious about what she says in front of her seven-year-old daughter. "Sometimes, with family, you take things for granted, but if my daughter hears me using negative micromessages in my speech, she's going to learn something from me I don't want her to learn."[19]

The microinequities program hits a nerve at least in part because it resonates with everyone's experience. "We've all been there, done that. We've all been at both ends and now we are learning that it doesn't have to be that way," says Wolf.[20] Neither she nor the program's leaders believe that the effects of the training are as profound over the long run as they are immediately upon completion. Still, she and others trust that a substantial part of the learnings remain "in their blood," so to speak. "Maybe I won't remember it all, but it has had a definite impact on my behavior," Cojocneanu says.[21]

TOOLKIT

Microinequities Workshops

Coined in 1973 by Mary Rowe of the Massachusetts Institute of Technology, the term *microinequities* describes the subtle put-downs, snubs, dismissive gestures, and sarcastic tones that people sometimes use when communicating with colleagues. As Laura Quintana, director of Worldwide Diversity, explained, Cisco wanted to strengthen the culture of inclusion and retain valuable female and minority talent. To help achieve this goal Cisco signed on with Steve Young, founder of Insight Education Systems, to customize a series of interactive seminars on microinequities. The idea was for employees to learn to recognize and deal with microinequities in the workplace.

The Business Case

Senior management at Cisco is primarily white and predominantly male. However that's not what the company's partners and customers look like. Cisco was concerned that if the culture didn't change, employees would not know how to "talk to" customers and business would fall off. For example, many small businesses are women-owned and salespeople need to know how to avoid "guy talk." Cisco also feels that to attract and keep top talent the company needs to foster inclusivity.

Getting Started

- Ask the question, "Are the behaviors and subliminal messages that dominate your workplace respectful and supportive of clients/customers/partners?"
- Ask the question, "Are high rates of turnover among women and minorities linked to subtle bias/microinequities in the workplace?"
- Investigate whether your HR team can develop a program suited to your needs or whether it would be more efficient to hire an outside consultant.
- Rally senior management. Any program that seeks to change key elements in the corporate culture needs visible and vocal support from leaders.

Critical Elements

- *Acceptance at the watercooler.* Cisco has made microinequities part of watercooler conversation and "regular" vocabulary. These ideas are now familiar to most employees and have infiltrated the company culture.

- *Personal transformation.* For many employees the microinequities workshop has been "life altering." People have taken the lessons to heart and applied them in their personal lives as well as making adjustments in workplace behavior.
- *Reliance on intangibles.* So far Cisco has been unable to prove that the microinequities workshops pay off in financial terms—although the company believes that this training improves morale and retention.
- *An open-ended commitment.* Cisco realizes that new hires will need to be trained and refresher courses for all employees are likely to be necessary.

ERNST & YOUNG: ACHIEVING GENDER EQUITY

Ask Ernst & Young's senior executives about the firm's efforts to achieve gender equity and you're likely to hear something like this: "It's not a destination but a journey. We've come a long way and I'm proud we've come that distance but powerful barriers still stand in the way."

Among these barriers are stigma and stereotypes. These issues are particularly stubborn because they're rooted in deep-seated beliefs—albeit narrow and prejudicial—and long-established ways of working. It therefore stands to reason that undoing stigma requires a thorough transformation of a corporate culture. And this kind of transformation doesn't happen overnight.

If any company has begun this journey of transformation it's Ernst & Young. The distance the company has already come is impressive. Consider the following facts: between 1996 and 2005, the percentage of women in Ernst & Young's top executive management tier increased from zero to approximately 15 percent, and in 2005 14 percent of Ernst & Young partners were women, compared with just 5 percent in 1996. This acceleration of female careers is intimately linked to the availability of flexible work arrangements. As we discovered in chapter 5, 10 percent of female partners or principles at Ernst & Young work on a flexible work arrangement, as do nearly 30 percent of the women right below the partner or principal level.

How has Ernst & Young managed to remove at least part of the stigma surrounding flexible work arrangements? There's no one magic bullet. Rather, a multitude of initiatives tackle the problem from all sides. Programs range from the Women's Leadership Conference at the national level to Professional Women's Networks at the local level to "career watching" and People Point. These initiatives are beginning to change the culture, allowing Ernst & Young women to take advantage of the imaginative flexible work arrangements described earlier in this book.

Women's Leadership Conference

In 1996, with the creation of the Women's Leadership Conference, Ernst & Young's women began to take the gender equity imperative into their own hands. At the time of the first conference, there was already a strong national focus on gender equity within the company, championed by the firm's then chairman, Phil Laskawy (for more details on this, see chapter 5). Despite Laskawy's successes, however, Ernst & Young's women were still not satisfied. They felt something was missing.

In the fall of 1996 sixty female partners from across the firm came together for a day. They met in the basement of an airport hotel in Chicago. Over time, this meeting evolved into the Women's Leadership Conference, which is now held every eighteen months and is attended by five hundred women partners, principals, executive directors, and directors from the Americas and other Ernst & Young locations abroad. The conference focuses on all aspects of women's leadership. Attendees include the entire executive board and a select group of male partners. For the men in attendance, to be in the minority for three days in an environment dominated by high-octane women is an eye-opener and really helps bring home the female point of view. Male attendees leave the conference "getting it."

The Women's Leadership Conference empowers women—and men— to go back to work and drive change in the corporate culture as it relates to women's experience at the firm. The goal is to create an environment that celebrates women's unique gifts rather than stigmatizing women for having a life outside of work.

Since the Women's Leadership Conference's inception, forty-one Professional Women's Networks have sprung up at Ernst & Young offices across the country. These networks operate at the grassroots level and focus on building the skills, confidence, and internal and external networks necessary for the firm's women to be successful. The most advanced of these Professional Women's Networks have their own budget and have taken control of key initiatives in training, mentoring, community outreach, philanthropic giving, and business development. The Professional Women's Networks at Ernst & Young are fast becoming the new "old girls'" network in the company. The results are impressive: 45 percent of the new crop of partners at Ernst & Young are women—most of them active participants in the Professional Women's Networks.

Career Watch

The experience and testimony of the women active in the Women's Leadership Conference informed the creation of Career Watch—a mentoring program led by a group of male and female partners who keep a close eye on the caliber of the projects and clients assigned to Ernst & Young women. The idea here is that a young professional cannot shine if she is constantly being given low-visibility accounts or clients.[22] Through Career Watch the quality of work assigned to high-performing/high-potential female managers is closely monitored. In this program there's a focus on treating women on flexible work arrangements exactly the same as everyone else. Career Watch is a way of making sure that talented women have the wherewithal to master the right skills, are recognized for that mastery, and are given every reason to believe that they can achieve ambitious goals. It's all about landing the right assignments and being mentored by the right people.

Designated "career watchers" meet periodically to discuss the progress of all high-potential women irrespective of whether they are working on a flexible work arrangement. As the watchers consider each high-potential woman they ask such questions as: (1) Is this woman acquiring the right skills to get promoted? (2) Is she working with the right mix of clients? (3) Is she being exposed to a wide enough group of partners? (4) And is she involved in a Professional Women's Network? Career watchers have the authority to make whatever changes are necessary to enhance the development of these talented, ambitious women.

At bottom, Career Watch ensures that stereotypes about a woman's commitment to work aren't allowed to impact work assignments negatively and therefore hamper the attainment of visibility, which is so essential to career progression. Carolyn Buck Luce, Ernst & Young's global pharmaceutical sector leader, notes,

> Career Watch is about making sure that top talent is deployed on the top jobs regardless of whether these individuals can devote 100 percent of their time to Ernst & Young, 80 percent of their time to Ernst & Young, or 50 percent of their time to Ernst & Young. Particularly for women who are on a reduced-schedule flexible work arrangement, Career Watch helps ensure they are eligible for promotion, remain on a partner or principal track, and are in line to be assigned to top clients. In essence, it neutralizes any gender bias that might creep into formal or informal evaluations. Career Watch is about how Ernst & Young matches work to the talent.[23]

People Point

Created in 2001, People Point is a Web-based survey that provides quick, individualized feedback on people management skill sets—men and women at all levels are given a voice through which they can rate their managers. People Point is a simple, one-question survey taken online. On a scale of one to ten, employees are asked to rate how successfully their various managers are in creating an environment that allows them to flourish. Respondent feedback is anonymous but the data is collected and becomes an important part of the performance evaluation process. Thus, through

People Point, partners, principals, and senior managers are measured and held accountable for how they treat their staff. This initiative has the ability to drive changes in behavior and ultimately corporate culture. During the program's first three years, 116,246 People Point surveys were submitted at Ernst & Young. In the words of Maryella Gockel, Ernst & Young's flexibility strategy leader, "We believe People Point has been a powerful tool in making Ernst & Young a better place for women to work."[24]

Measuring Progress

Ernst & Young has established a series of metrics to keep track of women's progress within the firm. The fact that everyone is aware of these figures creates a pressure of its own. For instance, Ernst & Young monitors the percentage of women versus men serving top accounts area by area and then tracks the relationship of that number to the percentage of women in client service. This sets the stage for "adjustments." To play out an example: if women make up 40 percent of the client service staff but only 20 percent of those serving top accounts, it's clear that changes need to be made. Indeed, a big part of making sure that stereotypes and stigma are eradicated companywide is generating these types of critical measurements so that leadership can be held accountable.

With these metrics in place local leadership is encouraged to focus on where they stand on the list of things the company tracks to keep women fully engaged. If an area's numbers are off, local management must answer the following questions:

- Do you have a Professional Women's Network in your area?

- Does that Professional Women's Network focus externally on building business relationships?

- What percentage of women are working on top accounts versus the total percentage of women in client service?

- How strong is your pipeline of women coming up to partnership?

- What percentage of your partners or principals are women?

- What type of commitment are your leaders (partners and principals) making to ensure the development and advancement of women in your area?

It's important to point out that this kind of scrutiny has "teeth." When an area doesn't score well, compensation is reduced—the amount of money made available for year-end compensation of partners and principals goes down. Billie Williamson, partner and Americas' director of flexibility and gender equity strategy, notes, "That's another way of saying that our ability to eliminate stereotypes and stigma and fully engage women has become a strategic imperative. Measuring and creating accountability—these are important ways of figuring out how to win."[25]

TOOLKIT

Achieving Gender Equity

Ernst & Young boasts several programs that combat stigma and help women gain traction at the firm. Among them are the Women's Leadership Conference, which is held every eighteen months and focuses on all aspects of women's leadership; Career Watch, a mentoring program staffed by both male and female partners that closely monitors high-potential women and sets them on a road to promotion and leadership; and People Point, a Web-based survey that provides a quick, individualized assessment of leadership skills and creates accountability.

The Business Case

These policies and programs have accelerated progress for women at Ernst & Young. Between 1996 and 2005, the percentage of women in top executive management roles increased from zero to approximately 15 percent, while 14 percent of partners are women, up from 5 percent in 1996. While women have advanced, so has the bottom line. Among other achievements, Ernst & Young has stanched the outflow of female talent, saving the company $10 million in 2005.

Getting Started

- Encourage your women's network to stage a leadership conference. Spearheading initiatives and forging alliances with senior men should be integral parts of such an event.
- Institute some type of career watch for high-potential women and pay particular attention to those on flexible work arrangements. Involve senior men as well as senior women as career watchers.
- Collect measures that matter—through programs such as People Point—to lay the groundwork for accountability.

Critical Elements

- *Multifaceted change.* Ernst & Young recognizes that undoing stigma requires a thoroughgoing transformation of the corporate culture. There's no one silver bullet. Hence the multipronged approach.
- *High-caliber projects.* No matter how talented, a young professional cannot shine if she is constantly being given low visibility accounts or clients. Through Career Watch Ernst & Young monitors the quality of work assigned to high potentials.
- *Accountability is key.* Ernst & Young scrutinizes a variety of metrics that measure how well women are doing. The firm then creates "teeth"—reducing annual compensation when senior executives (partners and principles) don't score well.

11

Canaries in the Coal Mine

Throughout these pages, we've heard the voices of disenchanted women, tangled with the reasons behind the disenchantment, and showcased a variety of forward-looking companies that have started to make inroads into reinventing the way work is done—giving women (and men) who need alternative work models new opportunities to succeed at work without failing themselves or their families. But the biggest question still remains: what are the prospects for messing with the male competitive model in the larger labor market—over the long haul?

I think they are reasonably good, provided we come to grips with one additional—and hugely important—challenge: how do we scale the core package of career-altering options described in chapters 5 through 10?

How do we accelerate and expand the scope of the policies and practices described in the second half of this book so that they'll reach a much larger group of people? How do we ensure that Goldman Sachs's New Directions success stories number two hundred rather than twenty, and that Cisco's Leadership Fellows program affects five hundred talented women rather than fifty? This second generation of policy needs to reach a critical mass if it is to transform corporate cultures.

CEOs such as Niall FitzGerald can get us a good part of the way there. When it comes to accelerating change, FitzGerald, chairman of Reuters and former co-chairman of Unilever, has all the right moves. Not only does he talk the talk—and no business leader is as eloquent about the need to "reimagine inclusion" and "transform the workplace"—he also walks the talk. With rare courage and a good deal of fanfare, FitzGerald lives his vision, and lets everyone know that he telecommutes on Fridays and has a standing daily breakfast date with his five-year-old daughter. In a September 2006 interview, he told me,

> Flaunting my flexible work arrangement is one of the most important things I can do. It starts to change the culture. Suddenly, many of my junior colleagues are saying, 'If the boss is doing this, maybe it's possible for me to do something similar.' If you want a flexibility strategy to succeed, there's no substitute for actually seeing the CEO act out some of these policies and practices in his or her daily life. Otherwise, smart, ambitious employees are simply not convinced that these programs are for real. It's not sufficient to say the right thing. You need to do the right thing.[1]

FitzGerald was at pains to point out that none of this is easy, that walking the talk is a difficult thing to do. In his words, "There's so much pressure out there to look tough, to act tough. It's hard to go against the grain. These days our alpha culture is very strong."

Until recently, FitzGerald himself was part of this alpha culture. As he describes it:

> I would often finish a business trip on a Thursday evening, flying into Heathrow early Friday morning. I would then go straight from the airport to my office, plunging into a regular twelve- to fourteen-hour day. Sunday would find me at Heathrow again, heading off for a Monday-morning breakfast meeting in Jakarta— or Tokyo.
>
> Looking back on this behavior I am now appalled. It detracted from performance, was damaging to my health, and sent out all

kinds of wrong signals to my team. With the boss intent on being a "road warrior," everyone else felt constrained to fall into line.

My youngest child was born in 2001—a late-in-life, particularly precious child. That sparked a transformation. Keenly aware of how much I had missed of my older children's early years, I began placing boundaries around my work. I made it clear to everyone I worked with that there were to be no early-morning meetings—I planned to have breakfast with my daughter. I also started avoiding flying on Sunday. I was willing to catch a flight early Monday morning—but not Sunday afternoon.

Was I being selfish? Maybe. But the impact of my change of heart was powerful. I became this high-profile role model. And I also became a devotee of flexible work arrangements, newly convinced that these options enhance a company's ability to retain key talent. I was at Unilever at the time, and in collaboration with Rhodora Palomar-Fresnedi—who headed up the diversity team—crafted an expansive vision of flexibility which took as a starting point that there was no job that could not be done flexibly.

Over a several-year period we went some distance towards institutionalizing flexibility at Unilever—which is part of the reason the company became much better at accelerating women's careers. Over the last decade the percentage of women in top management at Unilever has more than doubled.

TONE AT THE TOP

FitzGerald's attitudes and actions are the missing link—the alchemy that has the potential of converting the core package of policies and practices presented in chapters 5 through 10 from an experiment conducted at a handful of companies into a widely used reality affecting the entire high-echelon workforce.

The magic operates on two levels. To begin with, walking the talk at the top is immensely powerful. As we discovered in chapter 5, over the last few years, corporations as dissimilar as Citigroup and Cisco have rolled out flexible work arrangements companywide. But making these options available does not necessarily mean they are taken advantage of. As we've already seen, stigma is distressingly prevalent.

Which is where senior executives such as Niall FitzGerald enter the picture. When FitzGerald telecommutes—and wears it on his sleeve—he gives permission to high-flying more-junior employees to avail themselves of work-life policies currently on offer without worrying that their careers will be derailed. Flex schedules and public service sabbaticals cannot be hidden away and treated as something shameful if they are to acquire credibility in our workplaces. Rather, they must be made conspicuous and honorable. *Powerful fifty-year-old executives—women as well as men—need to strut this stuff if vulnerable midcareer thirty-five-year-olds are to use them.*

It's impossible to overemphasize the importance of this point. Time and time again, in interviews and focus groups, senior women admitted to working flexible schedules or heading philanthropic ventures—but doing so secretly so that colleagues and managers wouldn't view them as less than fully dedicated to their jobs. Glenda is a case in point.

I met Glenda in Phoenix, Arizona. I had been invited to speak to a group of prominent lawyers about "Redesigning Career Paths" and Glenda was part of the welcome committee. One of the few female partners at a well-respected local law firm, she was eager to tell me about her successful flex schedule that had allowed her to stay on track at her firm. A reduced client load and a telecommuting arrangement on Thursdays had made "all the difference" to Glenda, permitting her to both do top-notch work and spend real time with her seven-year-old son. I was impressed. Just before giving my speech I checked with Glenda. Could I share her story? The young women in the audience would be so appreciative. Glenda was horrified. "Don't say anything," she implored. "I don't want to go public. All these years, I've kept my flex arrangement under wraps. No one except the managing partner knows about it, and his advice has always been to not let the cat out of the bag. He's afraid of negative feedback.

The thing is, no one need know. It's easy for me to be effective from home—I'm all set up on the technology front—I have broadband, a BlackBerry, a fax, and so on. My clients and colleagues simply don't know where I am working from."[2]

I tried to persuade Glenda that it would be good idea if her colleagues did know—particularly young, female colleagues who might feel empowered by her flextime schedule and imagine that they might fashion such a schedule for themselves someday. But she was not to be persuaded. Convinced that the flextime tag would get her in trouble with her boss and tarnish her professional image, Glenda stuck to her guns, and I was not able to showcase her story.

Like Niall FitzGerald, Patricia Fili-Krushel (executive vice president at Time Warner), Barbara Byrne (vice chair at Lehman Brothers), and Jeanne Rosario (vice president and general manager for Aviation at GE) share a rare willingness to stand up and be counted.

Fili-Krushel, who spearheaded Breakthrough Leadership at Time Warner (see chapter 7), is thoroughly transparent about her personal commitments. She doesn't do business dinners: it's an ironclad rule. She'll do anything else—crack-of-dawn meetings, late-evening conference calls, early breakfasts, lengthy lunches, whatever it takes—but at 7:30 p.m., she's at home cooking dinner for her husband and two teenage children. Not only does she make this a firm rule, but she makes sure that the entire universe knows about it—which does much to enhance the legitimacy of family responsibilities at Time Warner.

Byrne has a tougher nut to crack. One of the most senior women on Wall Street and the only female vice chairman at Lehman Brothers, Byrne operates in a sector that has more than its fair share of extreme jobs. What does Byrne do that's so powerful? Like Fili-Krushel, she's created an ironclad rule—every July she takes a two-week vacation with her husband and children. Not only does she stick firmly to this plan—no matter what—she makes sure the entire world knows about it.[3]

It's not easy to take this kind of time off. In the upper reaches of the investment banking world, planning a two-week vacation and then actually taking it is practically unheard of. Byrne moves mountains to make sure she doesn't drop any balls and is well covered—preparing clients, assembling a trusted backup team to deal with contingencies and emergencies—but it's still a big deal.

Rosario sees herself as an of-the-moment role model for any woman interested in a successful engineering career at General Electric. "I must tell my story at dozens of Women's Network events every year," she says. "I've had the ultimate nonstandard, flex career—and young women need to know about it."[4] As she explains:

> After my first child was born twenty-one years ago, I actually quit work (GE had no flex policies at that time), but two years later I was invited back. I told the company that I would love to return but needed reduced hours. I was offered a twenty-hour week. Subsequently I had a second child and again took a break, then came back on a reduced-hour schedule. If you add it up, I worked part-time for ten years. But here's the miracle. After a decade of reduced hours, I was able to ramp up, get promoted (four or five times), and eventually become a vice president in the aviation division.
>
> How did I do it? Eventually I put in the necessary hours. In the years that followed my part-time stint I worked my tail off—sometimes clocking up to eighty hours a week. I was also strategic, always making sure that I stretched myself—taking up new challenges every two years or so even when I was part-time. Obviously, this was contingent upon being given the opportunity to do so, and I'm deeply grateful to my bosses at GE who trusted my abilities and gave me a second shot at ambition.
>
> So I take my story and leverage it all across GE. I'm happy to report that the number of women in executive bands is growing. The pool of women five to eight years into their careers at GE and just below the executive band is looking particularly awesome.
>
> One of my proudest moments: in 2005, my daughter graduated from Vanderbilt University with a degree in civil engineer-

ing. She's just landed her first job—at GE. There's a ton of father-son pairs at the company, but we're one of the first-ever mother-daughter engineering pairs. It's about time.

Clearly, seeing highly placed executives "strutting their stuff" is hugely powerful—and potentially transformative. It's equally important to involve men—another way in which Niall FitzGerald has shown the way.

MEN AS DEVOTED ALLIES

Although the Hidden Brain Drain Task Force is driven by female leaders (eight out of ten co-chairs are women), its work is marked by a vigorous effort to involve men both as allies and as stakeholders. Indeed, when the task force held its first summit in June 2006, one-third of the participants were men. This commitment to male involvement is both strategic and substantive.

On the strategic and symbolic front the logic is simple: 98 percent of the leadership at *Fortune* 500 companies is male. It stands to reason, then, that men must be involved—as passionate advocates as well as passive supporters—if we are to scale action and ensure that the programs described in the second half of this book expand and proliferate. Carolyn Buck Luce—chair of the Hidden Brain Drain Task Force—makes the distinction between business leaders who are "committed" to policies that fully realize female talent, and leaders who are "devoted" to those policies. When male CEOs are devoted they can create serious momentum since at most companies men are still the ones in charge. FitzGerald fits this bill, as does Phil Laskawy, who, when he was CEO of Ernst & Young in the late 1990s, made the bold decision to create a culture of flexibility at his firm. His actions were intended to demonstrate to business unit leaders and employees alike that creating the conditions that promote women's advancement was not just a fad but central to Ernst & Young's continued business success.

On the substantive front the arguments for male involvement are even more compelling. The fact is, certain groups of men have a vested interest in "messing with the model" because of changes in their own career needs. Gen Y men and retiring baby boomers are particularly likely candidates. These groups have the potential of becoming coconspirators in the struggle to establish a second generation of policy.

Let's start with Gen Y—otherwise known as the "millennials." The research shows that this younger generation values work-life balance more than financial success. According to interviews conducted by Universum, a company that helps companies attract top-flight talent, Gen Y men (as well as women) are more interested in social responsibility, high ethical standards, and time for family than they are in salary. According to Claudia Tattanelli, founder and CEO of Universum, there's been a real shift over the years. In the past, top male talent prioritized competitive compensation.[5] Today, quality-of-life factors dominate.

All of which jibes with the data presented in chapters 2 and 3. Gen Y men face a much-changed world. They are working longer hours and dealing with more onerous performance pressures than their fathers did. They are also less likely to have an at-home spouse and therefore cannot rely on a wife to look after the home and raise the children—at least not single-handedly. No wonder priorities have shifted. Young men have every reason to be keenly interested in the core package presented in chapters 5 through 10.

Aging baby boomers are also in a discovery mode when it comes to figuring out the value of the policies and practices described in chapters 5 through 10. The year 2006 was a watershed moment—the year leading-edge baby boomers (Bill Clinton among them) turned sixty. Over the next twenty years, some 78 million baby boomers will grapple with the question of how not to retire—how to ramp down without ramping off. Studies show that more than 70 percent of the professionals in this huge generation would prefer not to give up work. Rather, they would like to "chunk it out" in different ways. Flexible work arrangements and reduced-hour schedules are particularly appealing, as is employer-supported philanthropic activity. All of which sounds strangely familiar. The goals and objectives of fifty-five-year-old men (and women) are newly—and power-fully—in synch with those of thirty-five-year-old working mothers.

Remember Jeremy Isaacs? In his capacity as CEO of Lehman Brothers, Europe and Asia, Isaacs helped launch Encore in Europe. His voice was featured in chapter 1. In a June 2006 interview Isaacs speculated on where to find the catalytic energy that would really "move the dial on diversity." Halfway through our conversation he offered a key insight: "The way to break the back of change is to utilize the clout of the baby boom generation. This huge group has always been filled with pioneers. Ever since the 1960s they've moved the culture—politically, musically, you name it. As they enter their fifties and sixties, they may well succeed in restructuring work. They do, after all, hold a great many leadership positions, which means they have power on their side. If fifty-five-year-old men succeed in this goal, it will feed right into the needs of talented younger women."[6]

Isaacs may have hit the nail on the head. Despite the urgency of the problem women continue to have a hard time breaking the mold. The male competitive model remains remarkably resilient. Although recently women seem to have the wind behind them, heavyweight help is always appreciated—and may finally be on the way.

For the last three years the phrase "canaries in the coal mine" has reverberated through task force discussions, popping up in brainstorming sessions on both sides of the Atlantic. Talented women are indeed the proverbial canaries in the mine: harbingers of a better world who expire before their time, poignant victims whose tragic fates point to malfunctions and dysfunctions in the system. But here's a new way of seeing the situation: these ill-fated canaries are no longer alone. Following close behind them, partially obscured in the gloom of the coal mine, are two other impressively large and populous groups: men in their twenties, married to career women and seriously seeking a better work-life balance; and men in their fifties, determined to leave seventy-hour workweeks behind and refashion their careers so they can lead rich, multidimensional lives in their maturity. Thanks to the strength of these auxiliary groups, particularly the seasoned warriors who are used to walking the corridors of power, there may indeed be light at the end of the tunnel.

I, for one, am convinced that we're at a turning point. If the Hidden Brain Drain Task Force is a measure—and I believe it is—the private sector is ready to take radical action and make the workplace an environment where rich, complex lives can flower and flourish. And this action comes just in time. With jobs and careers becoming more extreme by the minute, messing with the model has huge potential—to burnish our competitive edge and restore hope and greater productivity to women's lives.

A PERSONAL PERSPECTIVE

A final note: as I close out this book, I want to reflect on my own on-ramping experiences. Nonfiction authors should not be opaque figures, floating above the fray. Rather, they should share at least some of the life experiences that shape their value set and vantage point.

Over the thirty-five-year span of my career, like so many women, I have grappled with a variety of off-ramps and scenic routes. One of my off-ramps was voluntary; the others were forced on me by the rigidities of career ladders and the realities of a highly competitive marketplace.

In the early 1980s I lost twins in the seventh month of pregnancy. This heart-wrenching personal loss triggered a protracted struggle on the childbearing front—subsequent attempts to carry a child to term proved to be extremely difficult—and created a huge window of vulnerability in my career. The presenting challenge was a tenure battle. I was at the seven-year mark in my career as a college professor and was in the midst of a tenure review. Despite unanimous recommendations by the Barnard College Economics Department I was eventually turned down by the Ad Hoc Committee at Columbia University. My chairman told me that I was seen as not sufficiently committed. In the words of one committee member, I had "allowed childbearing to dilute my focus."

As I packed up my office at the end of that academic year—having lost both my job and my babies—I pondered the significance of the predicament I found myself in. It struck me that the peak demand of many careers, not just mine, hit women in their midthirties, clashing and colliding in the worst way with the urgent demands of the biological clock. So many of us were trying to have children before it was too late—and running into all kinds of punishments and penalties.

One particular irony for me was that Barnard College had no family-friendly policies in the 1980s. This flagship of feminism simply didn't see the need for them. Indeed, my earlier attempts to organize a committee to press for more flexibility in the academic career ladder were beaten back; such initiatives smacked of special privilege in an era when newly liberated professional women were sporting pin-striped suits and bow ties. Cloning the male competitive model was the objective of the day.

Notwithstanding the pain and humiliation wrapped up in losing my job in academe, finding an on-ramp wasn't difficult this first time around. I was a thirty-four-year-old economist with an impressive publication record. Within three weeks I landed a great job—as executive director of the Economic Policy Council, a labor management group with an important presence in Washington, D.C. I spent six exhilarating, productive years at the council, managing a debate across the political divide, crafting position papers, and testifying on the Hill on issues that ranged from immigration reform to international debt.

Then, in 1987, I hit a wall. The mounting pressures of my high-profile job were beginning to crowd out the legitimate demands of my then-small children. I was becoming a burned-out, tuned-out wife and mother. How could I help my five-year-old deal with separation anxiety when I needed to catch the 7:30 a.m. shuttle to Washington two out of his first three days in kindergarten? I was spread too thin. Something had to go. I tried to negotiate some light and space (a four-day week, a lighter travel schedule!). When this failed, I reluctantly quit my job. One day I just walked in and resigned this glamorous plum of a job. At the time, I tried to focus on the positives. I did, after all, have options. I had a hugely supportive husband who earned a good living, so I did not have to maximize my earnings. Besides which, I was fortunate enough to have a viable scenic route. I could build on the success of my last book and write from home—a career much more compatible with small children. Still, there was a painful undertow of regret.

I resigned the week of my birthday and as I moved out of my corner office on East Forty-second Street, I knew that I was shooting myself in the foot, that this was the end of my "male" competitive career. Even if I managed to become a successful freelance writer I would never again be seen as an up-and-coming hotshot, a contender for the big bucks or the impressive title. But I knew what I had to do. I went home, regrouped, and started a new career as an author and activist. I worked odd hours, traveled only rarely, and saw a great deal of my kids.

My scenic route was moderately successful. In the 1990s, I wrote a series of books about women, work, and public policy—*When the Bough Breaks, Child Neglect in Rich Nations, The War Against Parents*—that both earned me a modest living and gave me a voice in the national debate about how to better support American families.

Then, in the early 2000s, I veered off course for the third time. My career was in trouble again, and this time it had nothing to do with recalcitrant employers or needy children. It was a market thing. My books were not selling. Part of the problem was that they were infused with a liberal public policy perspective that was increasingly unfashionable in a George W. America. The repercussions in my life were distressing, to say the least. I will always remember a meeting I had in September 2002 with my literary agent—a wonderful woman known for her business acumen and brutal honesty. Molly didn't mince words. "You're washed up," she told me, looking me straight in the eye. "It's time to find a day job—relying on books to provide a serious presence or a serious income is not something I can recommend."

It took me a while to absorb my bitter disappointment. My most recent book, *Creating a Life,* had been a *Time* magazine cover story and had been named by *BusinessWeek* as one of the ten best books of 2002—it was hard to accept that my freelance writing career was over.

For a few weeks I felt sorry for myself. Then I hit the ground running. Over the next twelve months, I landed myself two teaching positions (one at Princeton, the other at Columbia) to burnish my reputation and raise my profile. I then took on corporate America—taking my knowledge base, skill set, and passionate commitment to women's advancement—and putting them to work in the private sector. Eighteen months later I founded the Hidden Brain Drain Task Force and while the rest is not quite history—with thirty-four global corporations involved in this effort—it might become so.

Where did this most recent burst of on-ramping energy come from? In an immediate sense I was highly motivated. Four children—two of whom were still dependent—and a husband newly working in the non-profit sector served to focus my mind. I had a huge sense of urgency. As a woman on the "north" side of fifty, I knew that time was not on my side. Whatever shot I had at a late-in-life career was now—not later.

More profoundly, I was tremendously energized by the notion that this time around I really could make a difference. I was convinced that the tectonic structural shifts described in this book—the demographic and competitive pressures—meant that employers were newly receptive to my message and my solutions. How glorious it would be to really create some alternative career paths. For me, this would be the ultimate legacy—to make a difference in the concrete options facing my daughters and an entire new generation of young women.

Last but not least, I had an extraordinary role model. In 2002 and 2003, whenever I felt faint of heart, I just remembered my mother's courage. After all, at an identical point in her life—we were both in our midfifties when we attempted particularly audacious on-ramps—she had gone to the ends of the earth to fashion a whole new identity, and in so doing saved her life. The least I could do was to take my track record and figure how to drive some real change.

Isak Dinesen was right—there is something fierce and unfathomable about the resolve we older women can put together.

NOTES

Foreword

1. E-mail communication, June 22, 2006.

2. Interview, July 17, 2006.

3. Carol Hymowitz, "Women Swell Ranks as Middle Managers, but Are Scarce at Top," *Wall Street Journal,* July 24, 2006.

4. Remarks made at House of Commons, London, February 24, 2005.

Part 1

1. Adrian Wooldridge, "The Battle for Brainpower," special report "A Survey of Talent," *The Economist,* October 7, 2006, 3.

Chapter 1

1. Jeremy Isaacs, Lehman Brothers Encore launch event, London, February 9, 2006.

2. Catalyst, "Rates of Women's Advancement to Top Corporate Officer Positions Slow, New Catalyst Tenth Anniversary Report Reveals," news release, July 26, 2006.

3. Ibid.

4. Women are also thinly represented on boards. A mere 16 percent of board positions at *Fortune* 100 companies are held by women. See Peninah Thomson and Jacey Graham, *A Woman's Place Is in the Boardroom* (London: Palgrave Macmillan, 2005), 13.

5. American Bar Association Commission on Women in the Profession, "A Current Glance at Women in the Law," 3, http://www.abanet.org/women/Current

GlanceStatistics2006.pdf; Catalyst, "Quick Takes: Women MBAs," http://www
.catalyst.org/files/quicktakes/Quick%20Takes%20-%20Women%20MBAs.pdf.

6. See Sheila Wellington et al., "What's Holding Women Back?" *Harvard
Business Review,* June 2003.

7. Some names and affiliations have been changed. When only first names
are used, they are pseudonyms. Interviews, December 8, 2003, and December 12,
2005.

8. For an early discussion of this issue, see Terri Apter, *Working Women
Don't Have Wives: Professional Success in the 1990s* (New York: St. Martin's Press,
1993), 1–23.

9. See Dawn S. Carlson, et al., "What Men Think They Know About Executive Women," *Harvard Business Review,* September 2006.

10. It's paradoxical that in some ways flexible work options are a gender-
neutral version of Felice Schwartz's infamous "mommy track"—a term she
never actually used, talking instead about "career primary women" and "career
and family women." See Felice N. Schwartz, "Management Women and the New
Facts of Life," *Harvard Business Review,* January–February 1989, 65–76. For a
discussion of the contemporary reaction to her proposal from feminists, trade
unionists, and other progressives, appalled at an idea that they saw as "trying to
shunt female employees off on a slow road to nowhere," see Ann Crittenden, *The
Price of Motherhood* (New York: Henry Holt, 2001), 21.

11. Interview, May 25, 2006.

12. Interview, July 8, 2004.

13. See Beth Anne Shelton, "The Division of Household Labor," *Annual
Review of Sociology* (August 1996): 299–322.

14. See Carol Gilligan, *In a Different Voice: Psychological Theory and Women's
Development* (Cambridge, MA: Harvard University Press, 1982), 149. Gilligan
makes the point that women give a much higher priority to relationships and
family than do men.

15. National Center for Education Statistics, *Digest of Education Statistics
Tables and Figures 2005*, table 246, "Degrees conferred by degree-granting institutions, by level of degree and sex of student: Selected years, 1869–70 through
2013–14," http://nces.ed.gov/programs/digest/d05/tables/dt05_246.asp. Data is
for academic year 2004–2005.

16. National Center for Education Statistics, *Projections of Education Statistics to 2012*. Data projection to 2012. Calculations by the Center for Work-Life
Policy.

17. The Conference Board 2006 Annual Diversity Conference, New York,
May 11, 2006.

18. Peggy McIntosh, "White Privilege: Unpacking the Invisible Knapsack,"
Independent School 49 (Winter 1990): 31–36. Lester Thurow makes a similar

point. Looking at privilege through the eyes of an economist, he advances the theory that discrimination against women and minorities will disappear only when the losses incurred from restricting the operation of free markets outweighs the gains enjoyed by a privileged white, male elite. See *Poverty and Discrimination* (Washington, DC: Brookings Institution, 1969), 111–138.

19. See Adrian Wooldridge, "The Battle for Brainpower," special report "A Survey of Talent," *The Economist*, October 7, 2006, 3–5.

20. Nonfarm payroll employment increased over the previous months: 337,000 in October 2004, 96,000 in September 2004, 144,000 in August 2004, and 32,000 in July 2004, according to the Bureau of Labor Statistics.

21. "More Demand for MBAs," *Management Issues News*, September 5, 2006.

22. According to the Graduate Management Admission Council, the starting annual base salary in 2006 ($92,360) is up 17 percent from 2004 ($78,608). Sixty-five percent will receive a signing bonus that averages $17,603. Graduate Management Admission Council, *Global MBA Graduate Survey, 2006* (McLean, VA: Graduate Management Admission Council, 2006), 15.

23. Ibid.

24. "Good Times Roll for Headhunters; Industry Posts 21 Percent Gain," *Executive Search Review* 18, no. 3 (March 2006): 1, http://www.leadersunlimited .co.za/html/PressRoom/ESRMarch06rankings.pdf.

25. "Labor Force," *Occupational Outlook Quarterly* (Winter 2003–2004): 44, www.bls.gov/opub/ooq.

26. Xenia Montenegro, Linda Fisher, and Shereen Remez, *Staying Ahead of the Curve: The AARP Work and Career Study,* executive summary (Washington, DC: AARP, 2002), 4–5.

27. Saritha Rai, "Indians Find They Can Go Home Again," *New York Times,* December 26, 2005.

28. National Center for Education Statistics, *Digest of Education Statistics Tables and Figures 2005.*

29. Remarks by Chairman Ben S. Bernanke before the National Italian American Foundation, New York, November 28, 2006.

30. Interview, New York City, September 18, 2005.

31. Remarks at Hidden Brain Drain Task Force meeting, New York, October 28, 2005.

32. Qualified respondents had earned a graduate degree or a college degree with honors. Women and men were interviewed online using a self-administered questionnaire. Interviews averaged twenty-two minutes in length and were conducted between June 23 and July 15, 2004. See chapter 2, note 2.

33. The surveys comprised a U.S. representative sample of 1,564 high-income employees age twenty-five to sixty and a survey of 975 managers at global

companies. Participants were interviewed online using a self-administered questionnaire. Interviews averaged eighteen minutes in length and were conducted
from November 2005 through April 2006. See chapter 3, note 4.

Chapter 2

1. Interviews, December 8, 2003, and October 26, 2004; e-mail communications, 2006.

2. The survey targeted a nationally representative sample of 2,443 women
and 653 men in the United States age twenty-eight to fifty-five who have a college degree with honors or a graduate degree. Quotas were set for women by
employment status and type of graduate degree. Graduate degrees were classi-
fied into five categories: business, law, medicine, doctorate, and other graduate
degree. Data was weighted to reflect the national population of women and men
in this segment. The survey was conducted online by Harris Interactive in June–
July 2004.

3. Journalist Susan Chira points out that women often see work as a form
of power, mainly because it confers on them a precious degree of independence.
Susan Chira, *A Mother's Place: Choosing Work and Family without Guilt or Blame*
(New York: HarperCollins, 1998), 151.

4. For this question, multiple responses were allowed. Scenic routes often
result in lower pay and help explain the family wage gap. Jane Waldfogel finds
that mothers earn less than other women even when data is controlled for mari-
tal status, experience, and education. One child produces a wage "penalty" of 6
percent of earnings, while two children produce a wage penalty of 13 percent.
Jane Waldfogel, "The Effects of Children on Women's Wages," *American Sociology Review* 62 (1997): 209–217.

5. Interview, August 4, 2006.

6. Off-Ramps and On-Ramps study, unpublished data.

7. AARP, "Providing Care for Another Adult a Second Job for Many,
National Alliance for Caregiving/AARP Study Shows," news release, April 6, 2004.

8. Jane Gross, "As Parents Age, Baby Boomers and Business Struggle to
Cope," *New York Times*, March 25, 2006.

9. Sylvia Ann Hewlett, Carolyn Buck Luce et al., *Invisible Lives: Celebrating
and Leveraging Diversity in the Executive Suite* (New York: Center for Work-Life
Policy, 2005), 20–27.

10. Ibid., 23.

11. Scott Coltrane, "Research on Household Labor: Modeling and Measuring the Social Embeddedness of Routine Family Work," *Journal of Marriage and
the Family* 62 (November 2000): 1208–1233.

12. Office of Federal Housing Enterprise Oversight (OFHEO), "House Price
Appreciate Slows from Record-Setting Pace, but Remains Strong," news release,

December 1, 2005; State Farm, citing data from the College Board, "College Tuition Costs," Paying for College, http://partners.financenter.com/statefarm /learn/guides/collegesav/csprice.tcs; and Milt Freudenheim, "Health Care Costs Rise Twice as Much as Inflation," *New York Times*, September 27, 2006.

13. E-mail received March 18, 2005.

14. Jane Waldfogel, interview by author, July 17, 2001. See also Susan Harkness and Jane Waldfogel, "The Family Gap in Pay: Evidence from Seven Industrialised Countries Centre for Analysis of Social Exclusion," London School of Economics, November 1999, table 3.

15. Lester C. Thurow, "63 Cents to the Dollar: The Earnings Gap Doesn't Go Away," *Working Mother*, October 1984, 42.

16. Anna Fels, *Necessary Dreams: Ambition in Women's Changing Lives* (New York: Pantheon Books, 2004).

17. Ellen Galinsky, et al., *Leaders in a Global Economy: A Study of Executive Women and Men*, study conducted by the Families and Work Institute, Catalyst, and the Center for Work & Family at Boston College, 2003, 30.

18. Ibid., 31.

19. ISR, "Motivating Men and Women at Work: Relationships vs. Rewards," news release, August 3, 2004.

20. Legal scholar Cynthia Estlund emphasizes the importance of connection and friendship in contemporary workplaces. See *Working Together: How Workplace Bonds Strengthen a Diverse Democracy* (New York: Oxford University Press, 2003), 23–105.

21. Interview, February 14, 2006.

22. Interview, June 20, 2005.

23. Sylvia Ann Hewlett et al., "The Hidden Brain Drain: Off-Ramps and On-Ramps in Women's Careers," *Harvard Business Review*, March 2005.

24. Sylvia Ann Hewlett, "Executive Women and the Myth of Having It All," *Harvard Business Review*, April 2002.

Chapter 3

1. Interview, June 16, 2005.

2. Kanter identified this trend as far back as 1989. See *When Giants Learn to Dance* (New York: Touchstone, 1989), 267, 269.

3. Interview, December 5, 2000.

4. The underlying research consists of two surveys—U.S. and global— fourteen focus groups, and thirty-five one-on-one interviews. The U.S. survey targeted the top 6 percent of earners in the United States and comprised 1,564 highly qualified full-time employees ages twenty-five to sixty (844 men, 720 women). Data was weighted to reflect the national population of women and men in this segment. The survey of managers at global companies comprised

652 men and 323 women at director level or above; 54 percent were from the United States or Canada, and 46 percent were from Europe, the Middle East, or Africa. The data for the global survey was not weighted. The data cited refers to the U.S. survey unless specifically attributed to the global survey. The surveys were conducted online by Harris Interactive from November 1, 2005, through April 6, 2006.

5. Madeleine Bunting notes that in the United Kingdom, where European Union Working Time Regulations limit the working week to forty-eight hours, one-fifth of the labor force has signed a waiver that allows them to work the amount of hours their employer asks. *Willing Slaves* (London: HarperCollins, 2004), 5.

6. The data here jibe with current literature on the phenomenon of "burn-out." See Christina Maslach, author of the seminal study *Burnout: The Cost of Caring* (Cambridge, MA: Malor Books, 2003), 59–91.

7. Interview, July 24, 2006.

8. Interview, January 30, 2006.

9. Interview, January 27, 2006.

10. Katherine Rosman's *Wall Street Journal* article "BlackBerry Orphans" (December 8, 2006) detailed the unexpected impact handheld e-mail devices are having on family dynamics as children feel angered by not being able to garner the full attention of parents consumed by their e-mail.

11. According to James Gleick, having everything at our fingertips has affected the way we perceive time and, by extension, work and leisure. We have the technological ability to do things more quickly, and thus we feel that we're always working, always busy. Doctors and sociologists have dubbed this sensation of continually being harried as "hurry sickness." See *Faster: The Acceleration of Just About Everything* (New York: Vintage, 2000), 9, 16–21.

12. This question asked how important various aspects of your work are to being successful at your job.

13. Interview, May 20, 2006.

14. Anna Fels, *Necessary Dreams: Ambition in Women's Changing Lives* (New York: Pantheon Books, 2004).

15. Michael Noer, "Point: Don't Marry a Career Woman," *Forbes,* August 22, 2006, http://www.forbes.com/home/2006/08/23/Marriage-Careers-Divorce_cx _mn_land.html.

16. Interviews, May 31, 2006, and August 9, 2006.

17. Lack of sleep has been tied to a variety of serious health problems including obesity, hypertension, and memory loss. See, for instance, "Medical Matters: Sleep Deprivation Can Put on Pounds," *Consumer Reports on Health,* April 2005, 7; Ven Griva, "Sleep Deprivation Can Lead to Serious Health Prob-

lems," Copley News Service, May 15, 2005; Nicholas Bakalar, "Research Ties Lack of Sleep to Risk for Hypertension," *New York Times,* April 18, 2006.

18. Interview, October 21, 2005.

19. See Ellen Galinsky, *Ask the Children: What America's Children Really Think About Working Parents* (New York: William Morrow, 1999).

20. Interview, January 30, 2006.

21. Interview, January 30, 2006.

22. Arlie Hochschild, *The Time Bind: When Work Becomes Home and Home Becomes Work* (New York: Henry Holt & Co., 1997).

23. Interview, October 21, 2005.

24. Interview, February 9, 2006.

25. Interview, November 21, 2005.

26. Interview, July 27, 2006.

27. See Thomas L. Friedman, *The World is Flat: A Brief History of the Twenty-First Century* (New York: Farrar, Strauss and Giroux, 2005). Friedman argues that the new global economy has erased time zones and made it possible for business to operate virtually anytime, anywhere.

28. See Juliet B. Schor, "Time Crunch Among American Parents," in Sylvia Ann Hewlett, Nancy Rankin, and Cornel West, eds. *Taking Parenting Public: The Case for a New Social Movement* (Lanham, MD: Rowman and Littlefield, 2002).

29. There is considerable evidence on this point. See Mahlon Apgar IV, "The Alternative Workplace: Changing Where and How People Work," in *Harvard Business Review on Work and Life Balance* (Boston: Harvard Business School Press, 2000), 157–158. Apgar lists the benefits of a flexible workplace.

30. Peter Kuhn and Fernando Lozano, "The Expanding Workweek? Understanding Trends in Long Work Hours Among U.S. Men, 1979–2004" (Bonn, Germany: Institute for the Study of Labor, January 2006); see also Juliet B. Schor, *The Overworked American: The Unexpected Decline of Leisure* (New York: Basic Books, 1992).

31. Nora Ephron provides a brilliant description of ways we perpetuate male hegemony: the husband agrees to clear the table, does so once, and hopes never to do it again. "They hoped the whole thing would go away. And mostly it did." In *Heartburn* (New York: Pocket Books, 1983), 104. Though less universal now than in the twentieth century, wives, even women with extreme jobs, often bear the lion's share of household responsibilities.

Chapter 4

1. Interview, September 9, 2006.

2. Joan Williams, "Work Life Issues Among Attorneys," paper prepared for the Hidden Brain Drain Task Force meeting, February 20, 2004.

3. Interview, January 27, 2006.

4. American Bar Association Commission on Women in the Profession, *Balanced Lives: Changing the Culture of Legal Practice*, http://womenlaw.stanford.edu/balanced.lives.pdf.

5. "Why Small Business Is Big," Knowledge@W. P. Carey, July 19, 2006, http://knowledge.wpcarey.asu.edu.

6. Sylvia Ann Hewlett, *Creating a Life: Professional Women and the Quest for Children* (New York: Hyperion, 2002), 274.

7. Bliss & Associates, Inc., "Cost of Turnover," www.blissassociates.com/html/articles/cost_of_turnover15.html.

8. Hewlett, *Creating a Life*, 305–306.

9. "EEOC and Morgan Stanley Announce Settlement of Sex Discrimination Lawsuit," news release, July 12, 2004, www.eeoc.gov/press/7-12-04.html; Dan Ackman, "EOC Takes Up Morgan Stanley Case," *Forbes.com*, September 11, 2001, www.forbes.com/2001/09/11/0911topnews_print.html.

10. *Beck v. Boeing Company, McDonnell Douglas Corporation, and Boeing North American, Inc.,* case summary, WAGE, http://www.wageproject.org/sexdiscDB/sexdiscDB.php?mode=full&id=151; "Boeing to Pay $72.5 million for Gender Discrimination," *Business and Legal Reports,* November 14, 2005, http://hrbeta.blr.com/news.aspx?id=17018.

11. "Merrill Lynch to Pay $2.2 Million to Plaintiff who Claimed Systematic Gender Discrimination," Institute for Global Ethics, *Ethics Newsline*, April 26, 2004; "EEOC Announces $47 Million Agreement in Principle to Settle Claims of Class-Wide Sex Bias Against Rent-A-Center," news release, March 8, 2002.

12. Elizabeth G. Chambers et al., "The War for Talent," *McKinsey Quarterly* 1998, 45–57.

13. Ibid.

14. For a definitive treatment, see Ken Dychtwald et al., *Workforce Crisis: How to Beat the Coming Shortage of Skills and Talent.* (Boston: Harvard Business School Press, 2006), 3–12.

15. Graduate Management Admission Council, *Global MBA Graduate Survey, 2006* (McLean, VA: Graduate Management Admission Council, 2006), 13, 17.

16. Roddy Boyd, "Street Fights—Investment Banks Battle to Steal Rivals' Top Talent," *New York Post*, September 24, 2005.

17. Simon Constable, "Labor Market Beginning to Tighten as Generational Shift Gets Under Way," *New York Sun*, July 14, 2005.

18. National Association of Colleges and Employers, *Salary Survey*, Summer 2006, http://www.naceweb.org.

19. Ibid.

20. Hunt-Scanlon, "Top 10 U.S. Search Firms," *Executive Search Review* 18, no. 3 (2005): 1.

21. Ibid.

22. Ibid., 3.

23. Tommy Fernandez, "Workers Job-Hop as Economy Pops," *Crain's New York Business*, December 6, 2004, 1.

24. "Labor Force," *Occupational Outlook Quarterly* (Winter 2003–04): 44, www.bls.gov/opub/ooq.

25. Shaila Dewan, "Cities Compete in Hipness to Attract Young," *New York Times*, November 25, 2006.

26. Xenia Montenegro, Linda Fisher, and Shereen Remez, *Staying Ahead of the Curve: The AARP Work and Career Study Executive Summary* (Washington, DC: AARP, 2002), 5.

27. Ibid., 8.

28. Ibid., 5.

29. Loretta Chao, "For Gen Xers, It's Work to Live," *Wall Street Journal*, November 29, 2005.

30. Devesh Kapur and John McHale, "Are We Losing the Global Race for Talent?" *Wall Street Journal*, November 21, 2005.

31. Council of Graduate Schools, "Council of Graduate Schools Finds Decline in International Graduate Students for the Second Consecutive Year," news release, March 9, 2005; and Council of Graduate Schools, "Graduate Schools Admit 12% More International Applicants Than Last Year," news release, August 9, 2006.

32. Valerie Strauss, "Competition Worries Graduate Programs," *Washington Post*, April 18, 2006.

33. Gary S. Becker, "Give Us Your Skilled Masses," *Wall Street Journal*, November 30, 2005.

34. Khozem Merchant, "Economic Revival Could Lead to 'A Reverse Brain Drain,'" *Financial Times*, December 9, 2003; Saritha Rai, "Indians Find They Can Go Home Again," *New York Times*, December 26, 2005.

35. Interview, June 6, 2006.

36. Kyodo News Service, "Australia to Combat 'Brain Drain' with Global Search for Workers," August 16, 2005.

37. Sarah Laitner, "EU Could Offer Citizenship to Top Students from Overseas," *Financial Times*, November 14, 2005.

38. U.S. Census Bureau, "IDB Population Pyramids, Population Division, International Programs Center," http://www.census.gov/ipc/www/idbpyr.html.

39. Andrew Balls, "Greying Baby Boomers Pose Demographic Conundrum," *Financial Times*, August 30, 2004.

40. Organisation for Economic Co-operation and Development (OECD), *Education at a Glance 2006*, http://www.oecd.org/document/52/0,2340,en_2649 _34515_37328564_1_1_1_1,00.html; see also UNESCO Institute for Statistics, *Global Education Digest 2006: Comparing Education Statistics Across the World*

(Montreal: UNESCO Institute for Statistics, 2006), http://www.uis.unesco.org /TEMPLATE/pdf/ged/2006/GED2006.pdf.

41. National Center for Education Statistics, *Digest of Education Statistics Tables and Figures 2005*, table 246, "Degrees conferred by degree-granting institutions, by level of degree and sex of student: Selected years, 1869–70 through 2013–14," http://nces.ed.gov/programs/digest/d05/tables/dt_246.asp/.

42. Project for Attorney Retention, "Balanced Hours Are Key to Law Firms' Viability," news release, June 1, 2001; Ibid.; and U.S. Department of Education, National Center for Education Statistics, *The Condition of Education 2006: NCES 2006-071* (Washington, DC: U.S. Government Printing Office, 2006), 176, Table 30-2, http://nces.ed.gov/programs/coe/2006/pdf/30_2006.pdf.

43. Sylvia Ann Hewlett and Carolyn Buck Luce, "Off-Ramps and On-Ramps: Keeping Talented Women on the Road to Success," *Harvard Business Review*, March 1, 2005, 43–54.

44. James Surowiecki, *The Wisdom of Crowds* (New York: Anchor Books, 2005), xx–xxi.

45. Ibid., 23–39.

46. This theme has been developed by Cornel West. See *Race Matters* (New York: Vintage Books, 2001), 93–101.

47. Billy Dexter, *The Case for Diversity: Attaining Global Competitive Advantage* (New York: Hudson Highland Group, 2004).

48. Tom Peters, *Re-imagine! Business Excellence in a Disruptive Age* (London: Dorling Kindersley, 2004).

49. Peninah Thomson and Jacey Graham, *A Woman's Place Is in the Boardroom* (London: Palgrave Macmillan, 2005), 6–19.

50. Interview, November 14, 2006.

51. Thomson and Graham, *A Woman's Place Is in the Boardroom*, 8.

52. George S. Day, *The Market Driven Organization: Understanding, Attracting, and Keeping Valuable Customers* (New York: The Free Press, 1999).

53. Catalyst, *The Bottom Line: Connecting Corporate Performance and Gender Diversity* (New York: Catalyst, 2004), 3.

54. Catalyst controlled for interindustry differences, such as the robust financial performance of pharmaceutical companies during the period covered.

55. Catalyst, *The Bottom Line*, 7.

56. Roy Adler, *Women in the Executive Suite Correlate to High Profits*, Glass Ceiling Research Center, 2001, 5.

57. Graduate School of Management, University of California–Davis, *UC Davis Study of California Women Business Leaders: A Census of Women Directors and Executive Officers*, 2005 (February 2006), 15, http://www.gsm.ucdavis.edu/census.

58. Tommy Fernandez, "Firms Told: No Lip Service," *Crain's New York Business*, September 19, 2005.

59. Anthony Lin, "City Bar, NYCLA Set Initiatives for Diversity," *New York Law Journal*, December 15, 2003.

60. Fernandez, "Firms Told: No Lip Service."

61. Karen Donovan, "Pushed by Clients, Law Firms Step Up Diversity Efforts," *New York Times*, July 21, 2006.

62. Ibid.

63. Meredith Hobbs, "Wal-Mart Demands Diversity at Outside Law Firms," *New York Lawyer*, July 6, 2005.

64. U.S. Census Bureau, "Cash and Security Holdings of Major Public Employee—Retirement Systems: Quarter Ending June 30, 2005 and Prior Periods," http://ftp2.census.gov/govs/qpr/table1.txt.

65. Richard A. Johnson and Daniel W. Greening, "The Effects of Corporate Governance and Institutional Ownership Types on Corporate Social Performance," *Academy of Management Journal* 42, no. 5 (1999): 564–576.

66. Marc Gunther, "Corporate Governance: Forecasting the Next Big Blowup," *Fortune*, November 14, 2005, 46–48.

67. Johnson and Greening. "The Effects of Corporate Governance."

68. Gilbert Chan, "CalPERS Steps Up Push for Diversity," *Sacramento Bee*, November 15, 2005.

69. CalPERS, "CalPERS Names Richard Aldama Diversity Outreach Program Manager," news release, September 17, 2004.

70. Niall FitzGerald, interview, September 12, 2006.

Part II

1. "The Best vs. the Rest," *Working Mother*, October 2006, 74.

Chapter 5

1. Interview, October 26, 2004.

2. E-mail communication, October 30, 2006.

3. Stewart D. Friedman et al., "Proving Leo Durocher Wrong: Driving Work/Life Change at Ernst & Young," case study, September 2000, 3, http://wfnetwork.bc.edu/activities_entry.php?id=804&area=All

4. Pamela Kruger, "Jobs for Life," *Fast Company*, May 2000, http://pf.fastcompany.com/magazine/34/ernst.html.

5. Friedman et al., "Proving Leo Durocher Wrong," 2.

6. Interview, February 6, 2006.

7. Interview, November 4, 2005.

8. Interview, April 20, 2006.

9. Interview, April 20, 2006.

10. Most recent data as of December 8, 2006, e-mail communication.

Chapter 6

1. Interview, October 28, 2004.
2. Interview, September 22, 2005.
3. Interview, October 7, 2004.
4. Interview, September 22, 2005.
5. Interview, February 23, 2006.
6. Lehman Brothers Encore launch event, New York, November 8, 2006.
7. Hidden Brain Drain Co-chairs meeting, September 13, 2005. Hanson founded 85 Broads, a networking organization, in 1999.
8. Lehman Brothers, Encore launch event, London, February 9, 2006.
9. Interview, December 8, 2005.
10. Lehman Brothers, Encore launch event, New York, November 1, 2005.
11. Interview, December 8, 2006.
12. Interview, December 8, 2006.
13. Lehman Brothers, Encore launch event, New York, November 1, 2005.
14. Lehman Brothers, Encore launch event, London, February 9, 2006.
15. Interview, July 25, 2006.
16. Interview, July 20, 2006.
17. Interview, July 17, 2006.
18. Interview, July 25, 2006.

Chapter 7

1. Center for Work-Life Policy, Off-Ramps and On-Ramps study, unpublished data.
2. Ibid.
3. Ibid.
4. Ibid.; Sylvia Ann Hewlett et al., *Invisible Lives: Celebrating and Leveraging Diversity in the Executive Suite* (New York: Center for Work-Life Policy, November 2005), 20.
5. Jane Gross, "As Parents Age, Baby Boomers and Business Struggle to Cope," *New York Times*, March 25, 2006.
6. Jane Gross, "The Daughter Track: Caring for the Parents," *International Herald Tribune*, November 24, 2005.
7. Hewlett et al., *Invisible Lives*, 20, 24; See also Sylvia Hewlett, Carolyn Buck Luce, and Cornel West, "Leadership in Your Midst: Tapping the Hidden Strengths of Minority Executives," *Harvard Business Review*, November 2005.
8. Eliza K. Pavalko and Julie E. Artis, "Women's Caregiving and Paid Work: Causal Relationships in Late Midlife," *Journal of Gerontology* 52B, no. 4 (1997): S170–S179.
9. Ceridian communication, November 17, 2006.
10. Interview, April 10, 2006.

11. MetLife Mature Market Institute and National Alliance for Caregiving, *The MetLife Caregiving Cost Study: Productivity Losses to U.S. Business*, July 2006. They calculate that the cost to employers is, on average, $2,110 per employee for all full-time, employed caregivers and $2,441 for those with intense caregiving responsibilities.

12. Interview, April 10, 2006.

13. Interview, April 10, 2006.

14. Hidden Brain Drain Task Force Advisory Group meeting, London, February 24, 2005.

15. Interview February 17, 2006.

16. Interview, October 31, 2006.

17. Interview, October 31, 2006.

18. Interview, October 31, 2006.

19. Interview, October 31, 2006.

20. Family Caregiving in America: Facts at a Glance," Strength for Caring, http://www.strengthforcaring.com/util/press/facts/facts-at-a-glance.html; see also National Family Caregivers Association, "Caregiving Statistics," www.thefamily caregiver.org/who/stats.cfm

Chapter 8

1. Interview, December 19, 2005.

2. William B. Johnson and Arnold H. Packer, *Workforce 2000: Work and Workers for the Twenty-first Century* (Indianapolis: Hudson Institute, June 1987), 85, 95.

3. Interview, December 19, 2005.

4. Ibid.

5. Interview, December 22, 2005.

6. Shown at the Women's Leadership Initiative 10th Anniversary Conference, New Brunswick, New Jersey, April 6, 2005.

7. Interview, December 22, 2005.

8. Interview, January 10, 2006.

9. Interview, December 19, 2005.

10. Interview, December 23, 2005.

11. Interview, December 19, 2005.

12. U.S. Department of Education, National Center for Education Statistics. (2006) *The Condition of Education 2006:* NCES 2006-071 (Washington, DC: U.S. Government Printing Office), 176, Table 30–2, http://nces.ed.gov/programs/coe/2006/pdf/30_2006.pdf; e-mail communication, March 8, 2006.

13. Interview, January 23, 2006.

14. Interview, December 14, 2005.

15. Interview, December 17, 2005,

16. Interviews, December 30, 2005, and January 11, 2006.

17. Interview, December 17, 2005.

18. Interview, December 27, 2005.

19. E-mail communication, Vera Vitels, vice president for people development, Time Warner, December 12, 2006.

20. Interview, March 17, 2006.

21. Interview, January 27, 2006.

22. Interview, February 3, 2006.

23. Catalyst, "Developing Women Leaders: Synergistic Forces Driving Change: General Electric Company," www.catalyst.org/award/files/winners/2004 General%20Electric.pdf; e-mail communication, Linda Boff, manager, organizational communications, May 31, 2006.

24. Interview, March 17, 2006.

25. Interview, February 2, 2006.

Chapter 9

1. Interview, December 7, 2004.

2. Interview, December 5, 2005.

3. Interview, October 3, 2005.

4. Interview, December 5, 2005.

5. Interview, October 3, 2005.

6. Interview, November 10, 2005.

7. Interview, February 14, 2005.

8. "Blue Box Values" are guiding principles that have become linked with the company's brand, products, services, and people. The core principles address customer commitment, quality, integrity, teamwork, respect for people, good citizenship, a will to win, and personal accountability.

9. Interview, October 27, 2006.

10. Interview, April 5, 2006.

11. Interview, October 27, 2006.

12. Interview, April 5, 2006.

13. Interview, March 29, 2006.

Chapter 10

1. See the discussion in Joan Williams, *Unbending Gender: Why Family and Work Conflict and What to Do About It* (New York: Oxford University Press, 1999).

2. See the discussion in Catalyst, *Women "Take Care," Men "Take Charge": Stereotyping of U.S. Business Leaders Exposed* (New York: Catalyst, 2005).

3. Interview, August 10, 2006.

4. Interview, July 25, 2006.

5. Interview, July 25, 2006.

6. Interview, August 3, 2006.

7. Interview, August 3, 2006.

8. Interview, August 3, 2006.

9. Interview, July 26, 2006.

10. Interview, February 27, 2006.

11. Interview, July 14, 2006.

12. Interview, July 19, 2006.

13. Interview, July 19, 2006.

14. Interview, February 27, 2006.

15. Interview, July 14, 2006.

16. Interview, July 19, 2006.

17. Interview, July 26, 2006.

18. Interview, July 29, 2006.

19. Interview, July 28, 2006.

20. Interview, July 14, 2006.

21. Interview, July 29, 2006.

22. See discussion in Deborah L. Rhode, ed., *The Difference "Difference" Makes: Women and Leadership* (Stanford, CA: Stanford University Press, 2003), 13.

23. Interview, December 13, 2005.

24. Interview, March 9, 2006

25. Interview, December 17, 2006.

Chapter 11

1. Interview, September 12, 2006.

2. Interview, March 28, 2006

3. Interview, July 24, 2006.

4. Interview, January 27, 2006.

5. Jenny Anderson, "The Fork in the Road," *New York Times,* August 6, 2006.

6. Interview, June 8, 2006.

INDEX

Note: Page numbers in *italics* indicate figures (graphics).

ABOUT THE AUTHOR

Sylvia Ann Hewlett is an economist and the founding president of the Center for Work-Life Policy, a nonprofit think tank seeking to fully realize female and minority talent over the career life span. She is also the director of the Gender and Policy Program at the School of International and Public Affairs, Columbia University. In the 1980s she became the first woman to head up the Economic Policy Council, a think tank composed of 125 business and labor leaders. Hewlett is well known for her expertise on gender and workplace issues. She is the author of five critically acclaimed nonfiction books, including *When the Bough Breaks, Creating a Life,* and *The War Against Parents* (coauthored with Cornel West). Most recently she is also the coauthor of *Harvard Business Review* articles, "Off-Ramps and On-Ramps: Keeping Talented Women on the Road to Success," "Leadership in Your Midst: Tapping the Hidden Strengths of Minority Executives," and "Extreme Jobs: The Dangerous Allure of the 70-Hour Workweek."